ADVANCE PRAISE FOR

Awakenings to the Calling of Nonviolence in Curriculum Studies

"'Starlight is everywhere', Hongyu Wang exclaims—That starlight is nonviolence, lighting the way in dark times; but we must awaken to it, as the call of this moment, and as a call that is educational. Advancing nonviolence as an everyday practice of education, rooted in a sense of our interconnectedness, she proposes a positive force for the cultivation of flourishing personhood and planet, a promising response to the challenges of division and difference, and a transformational path for creatively restoring and sustaining human happiness and community. She invites us, as well, to imbue our understandings of curriculum as lived with such energy and intention, by which violence and its normalization may not only be denounced, and systems of domination and dualism deconstructed, but also dynamic, nonviolent relationality nurtured within and among us respecting self, others, and the world.

A truly beautiful and phenomenal achievement, this seminal and systematic treatment of nonviolence in education and curriculum studies is at once: intellectually productive—illumining the limitations of as well as lines of affiliation with current literature in the field advancing democracy, equity and social justice; theoretically sophisticated—deftly integrating international/indigenous wisdom traditions, nonviolence and peace studies & movements, as well as diverse theoretical perspectives (e.g., critical, poststructural, psychoanalytic, feminist); and emotionally stirring—infused with the experiential insight and autobiographical heart of this foremost scholar on the subject. If King reminds us that the arc of the moral universe bends toward justice, Hongyu Wang convinces us that it bends toward nonviolence too."

—Molly Quinn, PhD, St. Bernard Chapter of the LSU Alumni Association Endowed Professor Director, LSU Curriculum Theory Project Louisiana State University

"Hongyu Wang's remarkable Awakenings to the Calling of Nonviolence in Curriculum Studies both assembles and expands upon her decades-long, boundless examinations of complexities and potentialities of nonviolence as an 'everyday practice of education.' Analyzing complex entanglings of divergent theoretical, cultural, historical and social perspectives, Wang consistently incorporates iterations of difference within the ongoing processes of creating, re-forming and renewing nonviolent relationships with self, other, the earth.

Acknowledging nonviolence as a personal calling, one that daily illuminates her cross-cultural pathways, Wang invites her readers to co-travel, to "dream forward" with her as means of enlivening the always-relational, interconnected nature of nonviolence. Via that very invitation, she also enacts the very dynamics of curriculum as lived experience. Writing movingly through both joy and loss in her conceptualizings as well as livings of nonviolence, Hongyu Wang has made a profound contribution to the field of curriculum studies, in particular, and to education, writ large."

—Janet L. Miller, Professor Emerita, Teachers College, Columbia University

Awakenings to the Calling of Nonviolence in Curriculum Studies

Complicated Conversation

A Book Series of Curriculum studies

William F. Pinar.
General Editor

Volume 80

Hongyu Wang

Awakenings to the Calling of Nonviolence in Curriculum Studies

PETER LANG
New York · Berlin · Bruxelles · Chennai · Lausanne · Oxford

Library of Congress Cataloging-in-Publication Data

Names: Wang, Hongyu, author.
Title: Awakenings to the calling of nonviolence in curriculum studies / Hongyu Wang.
Description: New York, NY : Peter Lang, [2024] | Series: Complicated conversation, 1534-2816 ; volume 80 | Includes bibliographical references and index.
Identifiers: LCCN 2023036701 (print) | LCCN 2023036702 (ebook) | ISBN 9781636674896 (paperback) | ISBN 9781636674926 (hardback) | ISBN 9781636674933 (pdf) | ISBN 9781636674940 (epub)
Subjects: LCSH: Nonviolence—Study and teaching. | Peace—Study and teaching.
Classification: LCC HM1281 .W346 2024 (print) | LCC HM1281 (ebook) | DDC 303.6/1071—dc23/eng/20230902
LC record available at https://lccn.loc.gov/2023036701
LC ebook record available at https://lccn.loc.gov/2023036702
DOI 10.3726/ b21283

Bibliographic information published by the Deutsche Nationalbibliothek. The German National Library lists this publication in the German National Bibliography; detailed bibliographic data is available on the Internet at http://dnb.d-nb.de.

Cover design by Peter Lang Group AG

ISSN 1534-2816 (print)
ISBN 9781636674896 (paperback)
ISBN 9781636674926 (hardback)
ISBN 9781636674933 (ebook)
ISBN 9781636674940 (epub)
DOI 10.3726/b21283

© 2024 Peter Lang Group AG, Lausanne
Published by Peter Lang Publishing Inc., New York, USA
info@peterlang.com—www.peterlang.com

All rights reserved.
All parts of this publication are protected by copyright.
Any utilization outside the strict limits of the copyright law, without the permission of the publisher, is forbidden and liable to prosecution.
This applies in particular to reproductions, translations, microfilming, and storage and processing in electronic retrieval systems.

This publication has been peer reviewed.

Dedicated to

My loving aunt, Wang Shaoling

And

Dear friends, Naomi Poindexter and Liesa Smith

CONTENTS

	Acknowledgments	ix
Chapter 1	Awakenings: An Autobiographical, Intellectual, and Pedagogical Journey	1
Chapter 2	Ethics of Nonviolence as a Curriculum Vision (2010)	29
Chapter 3	A Nonviolent Approach to Social Justice Education (2013)	39
Chapter 4	Confucian Self-cultivation and Daoist Personhood: Implications for Peace Education (2013)	61
Chapter 5	A Nonviolent Perspective on Internationalizing Curriculum Studies (2014)	81
Chapter 6	Unteachable Moments and Pedagogical Relationships (2016)	105

Chapter 7	An Integrative Psychic life, Nonviolent Relations, and Curriculum Dynamics in Teacher Education (2019)	129
Chapter 8	Nonviolence as Teacher Education: A Qualitative Study in Challenges and Possibilities (2018)	157
Chapter 9	Curriculum as Mindfully Lived in Relationships (2023) (Hannah Hunter-Lynch, Denise Kimblern, Danny Sexton, and Hongyu Wang)	183
Chapter 10	"Thinking Back through Our Mothers:" A Curriculum of Organic Relationality (2021)	205
Chapter 11	Feminist Approaches to Nonviolence and Curriculum Theory	229
Chapter 12	*Currere* of Nonviolence: Starlight, A Ringing Bell, and Dream Work	255
	Index	267

ACKNOWLEDGMENTS

This book has been written over the span of a decade, and the people I need to thank are too many to include here. First, to my mentors and students. William E. Doll, Jr., who passed away more than five years ago, always took joy and pride in my work, which still inspires my best efforts. William F. Pinar has supported this book project, and his attuned mentorship has been starlight for my journey for more than two decades. The nourishing words of Bill and Bill have played a vital role in my scholarly pursuit and well-being. Janet Miller has always been generous and given me wise advice on things that I feel are difficult to deal with. She has gently nudged me to advocate for myself. With mentors comes the students' impact, also profound and inspiring. My students in the past and in the present have lifted my spirits and energized my commitment to nonviolence education through demonstrating their integrative journeys: Bolliger Wessinger, Jennifer Williams, Jo Flory, Heidi Jenkins, LaKrisa Walker, Mary Kollmorgan, Cathy Bankston, Heidi Massi, Vanessa Jones, Annie Stevenson, and Erin Davis, to name a few.

Second, to my family. The recent, unexpected death of my father was devastating to me, but the pain is also a gift if I am willing to listen to the silence and attend to the gap. My mother, who has sustained her courage, compassion, and creativity in her life, fills me with admiration. My husband and companion, Zuqiang Ke, with his incredible intelligence, insights, patience, and amazing cooking talents brought me happiness in our day-to-day shared life. My thanks to my two nephews, Gu Meizhang, and David Man, for their ability to surprise me with their miraculous flourishing.

Third, to my friends and colleagues. Susan Singh, Marilyn Clarke, Vanessa Adams-Harris, Lesa Magee, and others in a Jungian dream work group have encouraged my nonviolence work and recently helped me with my grieving process. Thanks to Shelbie Witte, my school head, who has supported me and the curriculum studies program. Jennifer Schneider and Jon Smythe have been in a writing group with me and offered valuable suggestions on the first chapter of this book. Their work on aesthetics, place-based inquiry, and ecology brings fresh air and holistic awareness to the curriculum studies program. Special thanks to Nicholas Ng-A-Fook, Samantha Sanders Been-Duke, Jing Lin, Jackie Bach, Molly Quinn, Vanessa Adams-Harris, and Ying Ma, who have given me much-needed encouragement when I have had doubts on the path of practicing nonviolence. Thanks also go to Bonwai Chou, Jenna Min Shim, Xin Li, Lisa Cary, Zhu Huailan, Bao Yanfen, and Wang Xia for their long-time friendship across different continents.

My gratitude also goes to the editor at Peter Lang, Allison Jefferson, for her detailed and thoughtful responses, flexibility, and guidance, and to the publishing team for crafting this manuscript into a book. Thanks also go to my grammar editor, Frances Griffin, for her timely and wonderful work as always.

My aunt, Wang Shaoling, traveled across China, when she was only 16 years old, to help my parents take care of me and my sisters: We are all indebted to her devotion and love. I don't have childhood memories of what it was like under her care, but her calm demeanor must have been comforting to us in a turbulent time (when my family was sent to the countryside for "reform" during the Cultural Revolution). Naomi Poindexter and Liesa Smith, who have journeyed with me on the less-traveled road of nonviolence, have gifted me with much inspiration and joyful companionship. I dedicate this book to these three incredible women with heartfelt and deep gratitude.

· 1 ·

AWAKENINGS: AN AUTOBIOGRAPHICAL, INTELLECTUAL, AND PEDAGOGICAL JOURNEY

Since my trip back to China in 2009 when I was awakened to the call of nonviolence, I have been committed to its formulation as an educational concept and praxis in curriculum studies (Wang, 2010, 2014). In the field of U.S. education, democracy, social justice, and equity have frequently been evoked as our shared aspirations, but we seldom discuss nonviolence that is rooted in a fundamental sense of interconnectedness, often missing in the foregrounding of individual rights. Voices of nonviolence have echoed throughout human history through leaders as diverse as Laozi, Mahatma Gandhi, Jane Addams, Martin Luther King, Jr., Leymah Gbowee, and Desmund Tutu, and the everyday practice of people from all walks of life.

The field of peace education, as a branch of peace studies focusing on international relationships and conflict resolution, often treats nonviolence as a means to the end, rather than introducing its multidimensional energy to fundamentally transform educational systems, climate, and practices. The Western bias of mainstream peace education is noted by both Western and Indigenous scholars (Bajaj, 2010; Te Maihāroa et al., 2022) for its foundation on individualism, deliberation, and rationality, so I prefer the term nonviolence education, which is based upon interdependence, nonduality, and integration of body/mind and self/other with their paramount importance in various Indigenous traditions internationally (including U.S. traditions). Beyond the tendency to approach peace as opposite to war in peace education, this book intends to infuse the energy of nonviolence into the dynamics of curriculum as lived experience, working with tensions to open sustainable pathways.

This book approaches nonviolence as an everyday practice of education in an ongoing process of building nonviolent relationships with the self, the other, and the world. In its interwoven threading of the psyche, society, and culture, it taps into the potential of nonviolence for bridging inner work and outer work to cultivate the mutual flourishing of human beings and of humanity and nature. As an educational concept, nonviolence not only orients interpersonal and intergroup relations, but is also central to the personal cultivation of teachers and students that brings creative energy to both individuals and communities.

Nonviolence as a Personal Calling

Nonviolence is a personal calling for me. It started before I was born, in the heyday of the Cultural Revolution (1966–1976) in China when my mother was pregnant. She believed that her anxiety, fear, and confusion during that chaotic time must have been passed on to me. The Cultural Revolution was a destructive mass mobilization that overthrew authorities and demolished traditions in an ongoing, unpredictable process under the rhetoric of class struggles, manipulated by dictatorship (Wang, 2014). The nation was near collapse economically, socially, and culturally, and violence in a whole range of areas was released during that decade. If the fetus can feel the mother's pain, the call for nonviolence is rooted in my personal unconscious. With the repudiation of both Confucianism and Daoism in China in the twentieth century, elements of nonviolence and the non-dualistic discernment in Daoism were criticized as incompatible with the imperative need for making progress toward modernization. The Chinese indigenous wisdom of inner and outer peace, although still practiced in people's daily lives in one way or another, became buried in the official curriculum for the new generations. Instead, revolutionary violence against enemies was celebrated and political control was solidified in these struggles and nation-building. Ironically, the faces of the enemy kept changing, and no one was safe.

Nonviolence stayed in my unconscious, as I was born into the official ideology of dividing people into either good or bad to justify controlling mechanisms. However, also growing up with the trauma literature about the Cultural Revolution that revealed its categorical thinking (Lin, 1991) and the cruel treatment of those who were different, I was horrified by the unleashing of human brutality and always wished that violence would go away. The desire to end the fighting between persons or groups amicably grew deep in my heart as a child. The years of my youth were during a relatively peaceful time in China, when its economy grew fast and people's lives dramatically changed for the better. However, we were still in the grip of moral, ideological, and political control. Experiencing the personal and national trauma of the Tiananmen Massacre in 1989, when what was right became upside down during my college years, led me to question everything and eventually I came to the United States to witness another way of life (Wang, 2014).

The Curriculum Theory Project at Louisiana State University in which I participated as a doctoral student challenged me more than ever to intellectually, emotionally, and spiritually integrate the self in my cross-cultural journey (Wang, 2023). I was not pressured to be assimilated but to be "placed together" in an ongoing process of transformation (Pinar, 1994, p. 27). During that same period, I began to go back to the Chinese classics to dig into their wisdom. However, upon graduation, when I started to teach at Oklahoma State University in the Fall semester of 2001, September 11 happened and wars against dissidents and perceived enemies marched on. I witnessed how democracy was used repeatedly to justify violence in local, national, and international settings in the post-September 11 age and the No Child Left Behind educational era.

As Ted Aoki (2005) points out, a separate sense of the individual is the foundation of Western democracy. It became clear to me that democracy does not necessarily have an inherent mechanism against violence, and my recent reading of Annelien de Dijn's (2020) historical study of Western democratic freedom confirms that defending freedom through force or even violence started with the Greco-Roman tradition. I can see its link to the Western domination of the world through colonization and neoliberalism. Today's international relations are marked by the arguments for achieving world peace through the use of military force.

Houston Wood (2016) points out that "democratic leaders may choose war more often than autocrats" (p. 100) partly for solidifying people's approval in elections within their own nations while autocrats are not concerned with the people's will. He believes that there will be less war with more and more democratic countries established, since democratic nations do not tend to go to war against one another. If the mechanism of violence against (make-believe) enemies is inherent in Western democracy, I have to ask, on what basis can world peace be achieved? Or is such peace simply another form of domination? Let us not forget that the two world wars in the twentieth century were largely initiated by European countries. Peace studies originated in the West is shadowed by its ethnocentric biases. That is part of the reason that I prefer the term "nonviolence" over "peace" in my work. With my questioning of liberal democracy, I was again on the road of seeking new pathways.

Gandhi's theory and practice of nonviolence surfaced as I was searching. However, not until 2009 did I clearly hear the ringing of the bell for nonviolence. I have detailed this journey in my book, *Nonviolence and Education*, which depicts a qualitative, life history project studying Chinese and American professors' engagements with the counterpart culture and education (Wang, 2014). For this project, I not only listened to those professors' stories, but also listened to my own whisper as a little girl who was longing for nonviolence and compassion, a voice suppressed by the official curriculum, which legitimated violence in various forms. Nonviolence education became a calling for me as I was awakened by its voices from both personal and collective history. Afterward, I quickly discovered Michael Nagler's (2004) inspiring book, *The Search for a Nonviolent Future*, in which he convincingly argues that nonviolence has always existed in human history, and that we must harness its integrative power. My commitment was sealed.

I wrote "Nonviolence as a Zero Space" as an editorial for the *Journal of Curriculum Theorizing* in 2010, right after I had returned from China. The same year I was also invited to make a presentation to the Professors of Curriculum group, where I introduced nonviolence as a curriculum vision. From the beginning of my conceptualization, I have been mindful of being inclusive and not pitting nonviolence against other existing visions, and I use the term "zero" to indicate that "nonviolence is not attached to any particular form except insisting on its nonviolent principle" (Wang, 2010, p. 5) and that it can be compatible with democracy, justice, or Christian spirituality when the nature of relationality is restorative and compassionate. More than anything else, however, I believe, nonviolence has an inherent capacity to counteract violence while restoring broken relationships through compassion for all participants. It is essentially an educational project, as personal cultivation of integrative capacity occurs through education and self-education; and without intentionally developing such capacity, nonviolence cannot play its important role. Since curriculum lies at the center of education, nonviolence becomes its mission as well.

My personal calling started with challenging the normalization of violence in both China and the United States, but in the process of conceptualizing nonviolence as an educational concept, I have learned that nonviolence is a positive force grounded in the interconnectedness of the self, the other, and the cosmos to mobilize relational dynamics that harmonize tensions and differences (Nagler, 2004; Wang, 2014). I have come to believe that this positive, sustainable strength of nonviolence is the foundation for dissolving violence and thus a more fundamental life force. It is from this understanding that I perceive the role of nonviolence education as cultivating loving capacities for bridging divides within the self and between the self and others; building a generative and compassionate community that integrates polarized divisions in schools, colleges, and society; and sustaining the interconnected creativity of humanity and nature.

Nonviolence as a Calling of Our Time

While nonviolence is a personal calling traced back to my childhood and youth, I also believe that it is the calling of our time. Martin Luther King, Jr. (1960/1986) declared, "It is no longer a choice between violence and nonviolence. It is nonviolence or nonexistence" (p. 39). This siren call, issued more than half a century ago, is even more urgent today, as we are in a mode of crisis and survival. At the planetary level, climate catastrophes threaten human and ecological existence in an unprecedented way, and modern science, technology, and human instrumental uses of nature have contributed a great deal to such crises (Bai & Cohen, 2008). At the level of international relations, conflicts, domination, and wars are ongoing. The national politics in the United States and other countries are intensely polarized and nationalistic, while local politics in many states is increasingly oppressive with censorship and exclusive policies. Racial and gender injustice has been intensified, against which the Black Lives Matter and the "Me Too" movements have been contesting.

The expansion of gun rights in the United States is happening at the same time as mass shootings continue to shock the nation and the majority of Americans support gun control. The phrase "gun violence" is so misleading, however, as it hides the human actors. It is true that the military–industrial–political-complex associated with gun production and distribution has made the United States an exceptional country, one that has been ineffective in implementing appropriate gun regulations. However, does a gun shoot itself? Why is the actor in the violence invisible? Why don't we reflect on the conception and practice of hypermasculinity and racism in the United States (Burns, 2018; Pinar, 2001) that is entrenched in the logic of violence? Are there links between mass shootings and state-sanctioned killing in various forms? Why don't we discuss the culture of violence that contributes to the mechanisms of control and mastery that divide the self from the other? Why not address the desperation of younger generations, as the age of mass shooters has gone down? During recent years, school security is framed in many places as increasing surveillance at schools —including arming teachers—where students witness how guns and violence are used to go against (potential) violence. What kind of message is conveyed to the younger generation by doing so?

Recently schoolteachers and librarians have lost their control over what books to use, as school districts in some states can be penalized for only one parent's objection that critical race theory is taught at schools. The intensification of social, racial, gendered, economical, and ecological tensions and fragmentation characterizes our time. Therefore, it has become more urgent to seek pathways that can transcend polarization, heal the divides, and foster compassionate relationships. Nonviolence, which can be found in the best traditions in many different cultures throughout human history, is the starlight that provides guidance in the darkness of our time. Through both nonviolent resistance and nonviolent relationality practiced on a daily basis in schools and community-based education (Romano, 2022), nonviolence holds the promise of shifting relational dynamics toward building a community that can engage dissensus, tensions, and differences to expand new horizons (Miller, 2010; Smith, 2021; Ziarek, 2001).

During the COVID-19 pandemic, the intertwining threads of interdependence and equity, which American individualism had concealed, became much more visible (Poindexter et al., 2021). The virus' disregard of man-made boundaries has made it clear that collaboration and solidarity across differences are necessary for dealing with such a global emergency. We are literally breathing the same air. As Judith Butler (2020) points out, the felt vulnerability is not so much a feeling, as it is a real part of our shared lives, an existential human condition that we must face. On the other hand, the poor, the elderly, Native Americans, African Americans, Latinx, and the urban populations in the United States suffered the most from the pandemic. The virus does not choose whom it targets, but susceptibility to infection and death as well as the damage in its aftermath are unequally distributed to different social groups because of previously existing conditions. These vulnerable populations suffered more from the neglect of public welfare. Ironically, violent protests against mask mandates in the name of freedom of choice also broke out (in contrast to nonviolent protests for racial equality), even if not wearing masks risked spreading infection to others.

In the field of education, social justice education has become more prominent in the recent decade and more so now in confronting many social and political issues. Having been teaching cultural diversity, including teaching historical trauma, the Tulsa Race Massacre of 1921 (previously called the Tulsa Race Riot of 1921)[1] for more than two decades in teacher education, I recognize the aporias, in the Derridian sense, of social justice teaching (Wang, 2005) and the necessity of holding the tensions between conflicting directions. Some of the ongoing questions are: How can students come to terms with their racial identity without categorical thinking? What does it mean to resist essentializing the self along the lines of race, gender, social class, sexuality, or nationality while at the same time telling the truth about the reality of racism, heterosexism, classism, or xenophobia? How do teacher educators teach diversity issues without provoking excessive power struggles in identity politics? How can the instructor's and students' emotional investments in ideas, ideologies, and identities be critically and compassionately examined and loosened up for moving beyond the taken-for-granted?

Pinar (2023) recognizes that identity politics—the combination of racial, gendered, and political discourses, among others—has advanced curriculum studies as a field, but this advancement comes at a cost, "including the erasure of (1) subjectivity as it is reduced to identity, (2) society, as the public good is reduced to one's own good, and (3) history, evident in efforts to rectify injustice by altering the historical record" (p. 188). "Subjectivity" goes into the depths of the human psyche and claims particularity and individuality, while "identity" can be subsumed into the external and collective registers in contemporary cultural politics. While society can offer a space for forming dynamic relations beyond self-interest, identifying with a group with elite leaders as representatives does not necessarily benefit the common good. History, in being truthful, can open new possibilities. While Pinar (2015) uses autobiography as the avenue to engage particularity and "self-difference"

(p. 178) in historical and cultural contexts for subjective and social reconstruction, I also think that affirming nonviolence to the self and the other can go beyond identity politics to transcend a separate sense of the self or a group to shift relational dynamics. Education for cultivating nonviolent personhood works on deconstructing psychic and social violence and points to integrative pathways of transcending power struggles to enable individual and communal transformation.

I do not think that curriculum can be the engine of social and cultural change, as curriculum history has already shown (Kliebard, 2004). Considering curriculum as an instrument for scientific efficiency, economic flourishing, or social reform tends to split the whole of education into pieces, but its fundamental task lies in personal cultivation. Certainly, such a cultivation does indicate a certain orientation, as I am affirming the value of nonviolence in this book. However, education enables individual students to learn, unlearn, and make their own choices. A pedagogy of nonviolence has a built-in mechanism for allowing students to follow their own pathways, even if they do not follow what the instructor advocates. Education invites but does not impose ideas, and nonviolence enables new awareness.

One of the contemporary challenges is how to deal with the issue of difference in a post-colonial, international society, and nonviolence provides a unique answer to it. There are multiple critical approaches in Western scholarship. First, difference is pushed aside, and commonality is considered the only bridge for making connections. This approach often appears in peace education literature that emphasizes shared human connections. Second, difference is treated as a separate entity in a pluralistic way. This approach often appears in multiculturalism literature. Third, difference is essentialized into social identities as opposed to one another. This approach often appears in critical theory and social justice education literature. Fourth, difference is radicalized as unknowable otherness that cannot be assimilated into the self. This approach often appears in queer theory and poststructural discourses literature.

All these approaches can be effective depending on the context. Nonviolence situates difference as an organic part of an interconnected life, informed by Buddhist nonduality, pointing in a new direction (Hershock, 2011; Wang, 2014). In this approach, difference is neither negative nor positive but a component of shared life with great potential to benefit both individuals and communities, so educational engagement with difference is central to curriculum studies. While differentiation can be existentially productive, in nonviolence there are threads underlying separations and oppositions, threads that prevent the proliferation of social divisions and fragmentations. Nonviolent relationality is hospitable to difference and its generative potential but does not radicalize it to unknown alterity. The current polarization in U.S. society feeds into its own cycle of serious self-affirmation with rigid identity. Without playfulness and imagination, the interconnectedness of life can be hidden from our view because what we see are separate entities, of persons or objects. Playfulness is protective of persons while contesting ideas. Nonviolence brings conflicts back into the organic whole by loosening up rigid identities and not attaching the ego to a fixed idea or identity.

Curriculum studies as a field has re-conceptualized curriculum as a complicated conversation, and it is through the attention to this complicated conversation in both curricular content and processes that nonviolence becomes the starlight that shines through the darkness of our time in our daily practice of education. Nonviolence is a less traveled road, but it can open new directions for co-creating a mutually flourishing, shared life in schools, in society, and with the natural environment. Although not without reservations, Native American leader and scholar, Vine Deloria, Jr. (1974), points out, "There is no other way out" than non-violence (p. 7) for social change. My optimism lies in the role of education to cultivate and transform personhood through nonviolence toward nonviolence.

Theoretical Foundations

In this section, I discuss multiple theories that have informed my formulations of nonviolence in curriculum studies. While some fundamental assumptions of each theory are briefly discussed, I focus on what I have taken from them and where I depart from them, rather than providing a comprehensive discussion, which is much beyond the scope of this chapter. Here I briefly discuss international and Indigenous wisdom traditions, Gandhi-King nonviolent social change, psychoanalysis and analytic psychology, poststructuralism, feminist theory, and nonviolence studies, all of which have been interwoven in my work.

International and Indigenous Wisdom Traditions

Nonviolence as a way of life has existed as long as human history and has been shared by many different cultures, including Native American traditions of restorative justice, the African notion of *ubuntu*, Indian *ahimsa* traditions, Daoist *wuwei*, and the peace tradition in Islam (Fiala, 2018; Nagler, 2004; Smith-Christopher, 2007). From the very beginning of formulating nonviolence education, I have drawn upon some of these wisdom traditions to highlight the importance of interconnectedness in life. I approach international wisdom in a broad and mostly philosophical and existential way, and intentionally highlight traditions outside of the West that have been marginalized in the U.S. mainstream education. Going back to their cultural roots, many of these traditions are from Indigenous perspectives that challenge colonialism and its mentality in the contemporary age.

As Kelli Te Maihāroa, Michael Ligaliga, and Heather Devere (2022) point out, "the Eurocentric Western nature of peace and conflict studies" is gendered, with male scholars focusing on studying "violence, war, and conflict, rather than peace" (p. 7), paying little attention to the rich and complex traditional and Indigenous approaches to peacemaking and reconciliation that can be critically engaged (not romantically reified). Non-Indigenous teacher candidates should also engage in truth and reconciliation learning to understand the damages of colonization on Indigenous people and question settler normativity in teacher education (Ng-A-Fook & Smith, 2017). Polly O. Walker (2022) uses the term "eco-relationality in which humans are engaged in relationships of respect and reciprocity with the natural world, ancestors, generations to come and other humans" (p. 43) to describe the many Indigenous worldviews that infuse harmony, balance, and organic relationality into peacebuilding. It is quite telling that "there is no word for 'enemy'" in the Māori language as damaged relationships need to be restored, including coming to peace with "angry friends" (Jackson, 2017, p. vi). In this book, I recursively draw upon the notions of *ahimsa*, *ubuntu*, and Daoist *yin-yang* dynamics, situated in the bigger international Indigenous context, as well as Indigenous mothers' teachings.

Nonviolence is the highest ethical and spiritual principle in Jainism, Buddhism, and Hinduism. Nonviolence is an English translation of *ahimsa*, the Sanskrit term, which means doing no harm in word, thought, and deed to any living beings, including non-human existences (Howard, 2018; Nagler, 2004). *Ahimsa* conveys a positive sense of love and unity, which is often lost in the translation of "non-violence" as a negation (Shastri & Shastri, 2007). While Jainism is the most radical or complete in avoiding all acts of violence at the expense of the self (Howard, 2018), I draw mostly upon the Buddhist notion of interdependence and nonduality, as "the sense of duality or separateness is the root cause of hatred and violence" (Shastri & Shastri, 2007, p. 61).

In Buddhism, inner work through dissolving hatred, greed, and delusion through meditations and outer work for compassionate relationships with others and social change are intertwined. The essential Buddhist notions of interdependence, impermanence, and no-self or emptiness can lead to "a more fluid and open-ended approach to others and to situations, suggesting multiple solutions to human problems and reduction of the likelihood of conflict" (Queen, 2007, p. 21). Nonattachment to any fixed idea, ideology, or dogma prevents the formation of violent thought and action against others and makes it possible to bring parties together from the different sides of the divide. The daily practice of mindfulness in letting go of attachment and developing compassion is essential for dissolving violence and cultivating nonviolence in thought, feeling, and action. Here the sense of a separate individual self found in Western liberalism does not exist. When the dualistic human consciousness that objectifies others and the environment is transformed, the underlying thread of interconnectedness is revealed to anchor nonviolence.

The notion of *ubuntu* in African traditions has gained more attention with the independence of South Africa and its truth and reconciliation efforts in the 1990s. There have been many discussions and debates about the meanings of *ubuntu* for today's post-apartheid educational reform (Le Grange, 2011; Letseka, 2012; Swanson, 2009; Venter, 2004). I first encountered the notion of *ubuntu* through Desmond Tutu's (1999) book and was inspired by the Truth and Reconciliation Commission's work. For Tutu (1999), the notion of *ubuntu* indicates that one's humanity is tied with others' humanity, and as "a form of relational spirituality that connotes the basic connectedness of all human beings" (Battle, 2000, p. 178); affirming of the self and affirming of others go hand in hand and social justice is restorative to all parties in different ways.

Dalene M. Swanson (2009) traces the origin of this concept: "Ubuntu is short for an isiXhosa proverb in Southern Africa, *umuntu ngumuntu ngabantu*; a person is a person through their relationships to others" (p. 11). Restorative social justice as a nonviolent way of nation-building is inspirational for orienting relational dynamics beyond individual rights toward a healing community. Swanson also argues that *ubuntu* "creates a rootedness with the daily, local and lived" (p. 18). In curriculum as lived and its daily work of engaging in a complicated conversation, the underlying tie of *ubuntu* offers a grounding.

In Daoism,[2] *Qi*, which permeates the self and the world, exists in everything and everybody and connects the universe (Wang, 2021). The interactions between *yin* and *yang*—opposite cosmic energies—have a built-in element of being open to the other due to their interconverting capacity. When opposites are interdependent, there is an inherent mechanism for connectedness. Creative harmony—rather than win-or-lose pursuit—unites the means and the end of nonviolence. Daoism's unique emphasis on feminine sustainability in preserving life and the advocacy of *wuwei*—non-dualistic, attuned action rather than pre-determined imposition—illuminate pathways of nonviolence in movement rather than in a fixed ideal.

The Daoist notion of organic healing has informed and shifted my pedagogy (Wang, 2009). In acupuncture informed by Daoism, putting needles into where it hurts may not be the most effective treatment because re-balancing the energy of the whole body is the key to having long-term effects. Similarly, discussing the historical and social contexts of trauma and oppression does not stop at the specificity of an injustice, but situates it in the global context and reveals its underlying general mechanism of control and domination. Often seeing the big picture can support the emotional work of being exposed to what happens in one's own backyard.

There is a clear connection among *ahimsa*, *ubuntu*, and *yin-yang* dynamics through the thread of interconnectedness and interdependence, a thread which is echoed in many Indigenous traditions around the world. And this thread of interconnectedness is missing in the notion of individual human rights in Western liberal traditions. Certainly, emphasizing only the role of interconnectedness without being attentive to the role of individuals may also lead to the establishment and maintenance of hierarchical systems, as such systems indeed have co-existed with these traditions. Inspired by the link to nonviolence in these traditions, I do not intend to set up a new binary, but to acknowledge that the thread of interconnectedness has always been a part of human history that we should embrace in today's education.

As Lesley Le Grange (2011) points out in his constructive critiques of how *ubuntu* is used in South African post-apartheid education, deconstructing and disrupting Western hegemony does not mean "rendering a false dichotomy or moral evaluation between good (African) and bad (Western)" knowledges/cultures (p. 72). There are also historical and contemporary traditions of peace and nonviolence in the West (Lynd & Lynd, 2006; Smith-Christopher, 2007; Zinn, 2002). Nonviolence in various forms is an international heritage that we can all inherit and regenerate. International and Indigenous wisdom traditions often emphasize the function of education in individual and social transformation, so they have profound curriculum implications and are discussed in many chapters of this book.

Gandhi-King Nonviolent Social Change

Influenced by *ahimsa*, arguing for Hindu-Muslim unity, Gandhi practiced nonviolence as a way of life in his diet, meditations, fasting, and family relations, and exercised leadership in India's independence from colonial rule (Easwaran, 1972/1997; Gandhi, 1957/1993). It is important to point out that nonviolence is active: "Practicing nonviolence was to fight against structures of violence—racial, social, and economic—which required active participation" and "positive acts of compassion" for people (Howard, 2018, p. 91). The translation of nonviolence into passive resistance is misleading, as nonviolence is a force that does not rely on coercion but has a sweeping impact.

Unity is an important concept for Gandhi as the foundation for *ahimsa*, which does not do harm, and *satyagraha* (truth-force), which "excludes every form of violence, veiled or unveiled, and whether in thought, word or deed" and holds on to truth that lies in the interconnected life and is not owned by an individual person (Gandhi, 1947, p. 83). He strongly supports the unity between means and end and does not consider any noble end as the justification for violent means. Inner peace, outer peace, and world peace come together for him. Easwaran (1972/1997) describes a snake climbing onto Gandhi, who was meditating, and then quietly climbing off of him due to his inner calm. For Gandhi, peace begins within and "if one cannot change the darkness within oneself, one cannot contribute to transformation in the culture" (Cunningham, 2021, pp. 22–23). His notion of unity opposes hierarchy. As a Hindu spiritual leader, he advocates that Hinduism purge itself of untouchability, to remove "all distinctions of superiority and inferiority, and shed a host of other evils and shams that [had] become rampant in it" (Gandhi, 1957/1993, p. 393). Ultimately, Gandhi (1947) speaks of "an unbreakable heart unity" (p. 244) that enables the force of nonviolence to spread through the web of life.

Influenced by Gandhi's theory and practice of nonviolence, Martin Luther King Jr. (1957/1986) speaks of five points in positioning nonviolence as an alternative to violence in seeking racial justice: First, nonviolent resistance is "strongly active spiritually" (p. 7). Second, it "does not seek to defeat or humiliate the opponent" (p. 7) but to awaken a sense of moral conscience in the oppressors to enable social change. Third, it is the forces of evil—not persons who are doing the evil—that nonviolent resistance opposes. Fourth, it avoids not only physical violence but also internal violence. Retaliating against violence with hatred only increases hate both internally and externally, but the ethics of love on the *agape* level—a Christian notion—can redeem all humanity, including those who are perpetrators of injustice. Fifth, nonviolent resistance is based on faith that God is on the side of truth and justice, so those who struggle for nonviolent social change have "cosmic companionship" (p. 9) and their suffering for social change has a redemptive power.

Later, King (1960/1986) also stated that nonviolence had become more than a method for him: "It became a commitment to a way of life" (p. 38) as well as "the only road to freedom" (King, 1966/1986, p. 54). He asserted that "only a refusal to hate or kill can put an end to the train of violence in the world and lead us toward a community where men [sic] can live together without fear" (p. 58). In leading massive nonviolent resistance in civil right movements, King's political activism is closely tied with his spiritual vision of *agape*, sharing with Gandhi the vision of "redemptive suffering" to seek freedom for all.

These two prominent leaders in nonviolent social change have provided constant inspiration for me to seek pathways of nonviolence in curriculum studies. It is important to note, however, that nonviolent uprisings against colonial rule, social violence, or authoritarianism are political movements, while I approach nonviolence as uniquely educational, promoting personal cultivation for inner integration and relational integration. While education has a political dimension, it is a long-term project that engages students' whole beings in multiple dimensions (intellectual, aesthetic, cultural, ecological, etc.), not seeking immediate effects, even though the current educational climate in the United States demands short-term measurable results (Taubman, 2009). Different from political movements that aim at mobilizing mass action through a unified vision and collective efforts, curriculum as a complicated conversation allows divergence in students' different pathways.

Working from Within

From the beginning of my nonviolence project, I have been committed to building connections between the inner life and social life, influenced by *currere*, psychoanalysis and analytic psychology. "Working from within," as a call from William F. Pinar (1994, p. 7) during the 1970s in U.S. curriculum studies, has become an influential approach worldwide, and *currere*, which he formulated to connect life history and school subjects in educational experience, has led to the flourishing of autobiographical curriculum inquiry (Pinar, 1994, 2019). Most recently he asserts the importance of *currere* in supporting subjective presence against cultural crises (Pinar, 2023). Both psychoanalysis and analytic psychology have informed this approach. I have been particularly drawn to Julia Kristeva's psychoanalytic theory and Carl Jung's work. Throughout this book, the theme of working from within is central and crosses different chapters.

The psychoanalytic notion of the unconscious is that it can never be mastered, although we can learn from it to enrich our lives. In analytic psychology, the notion of the shadow and its projection depicts the damaging effects of not acknowledging one's own unconscious. Julia Kristeva, as a poststructural feminist psychoanalyst, necessarily crosses multiple discourses, and although she does not use the concept of nonviolence, her intellectual influence on me has contributed to my formulation of nonviolence at the intersection of psychoanalysis, poststructuralism, and feminism. Her theory of semiotic/symbolic dynamics in language and in the human psyche opens a space for permanent subjective questioning for renewal and for a community that welcomes the stranger. Building bridges between affects and words through the loving third that allows the semiotic flow to unstablize the symbolic, one works through the difficulty of subjective becoming and thus changes one's actions and interactions to create new forms of subjectivity and community.

Jungian theory goes one step deeper, from the individual unconscious into the collective unconscious, and contemporary Jungians also add a layer, the cultural unconscious, which is particularly helpful for understanding racism, sexism, and classism as projecting the inner shadow onto other cultural groups. Jungian theory, more than classical psychoanalysis, acknowledges that human life is fundamentally connected and proposes the synthetical work of integrating the unconscious through experiential understanding and creative formulations. Jung's (1953) complex notion of the shadow, projection, and multiple channels of seeking psychic integration beyond the intellect has profound implications for engaging in the inner work of nonviolence. Here the nonviolent transformation of emotions such as anger and fear to serve individual and social change intersects with working with the subconscious material through intellectual, artistic, and spiritual formulations. Nonviolence is a whole-being work that necessarily involves the subconscious, the cultural unconscious, and the collective unconscious.

However, there are also tensions between these theories and nonviolence theories. Psychoanalysis assumes the repressive mechanism of civilization and the resistance of the psychic life against society (Freud, 1961), and Julia Kristeva discusses the necessity of matricide for psychic independence (Wang, 2004), but nonviolence theory is based on the existential interconnectedness of life. Some interpretations of psychoanalysis suggest that psychic violence is primary while nonviolence is secondary reparation (Todd, 2003). By contrast, Michael Nagler (2004) argues that nonviolence is a primary force. Containing the tensions in my own formulation, I think that both aggression and compassion exist in the human psyche and society, and education can play a crucial role in cultivating compassion and nonviolence and containing aggression and violence. To do so, we need to understand how psychic aggression works in students and in ourselves; denying its existence is not helpful for creating educative conditions. On the other hand, getting in touch with the vitality of interconnectedness achieves more than negating violence: it releases the creative energy of imagination, intuitive thinking, experiential understanding, and embodied studies.

Affirming that humanity has an inherent capacity for containing destructive impulses and establishing nonviolent relations, I think that interconnectedness is the existential condition for human life, as we are born into it, but the kinds of relationship we choose to develop depend on our choices and how we are educated to make those choices in everyday life. Nonviolence education does not provide the soil for growing *the mechanisms of domination and control in violence*. At the same time, I also think that the different emphases of psychoanalysis on individuality and of nonviolence on relationality are complementary in education. Engaging nonviolence from within is closely connected with engaging nonviolence with others in an ongoing process of individual and social transformation.

Poststructural Theories

William E. Doll, Jr.'s (1993, 2012) postmodern perspectives on curriculum combine philosophy and complexity theory, a combination that was appealing to me even before I came to the United States to study with him. He identifies three features of a postmodern curriculum, also informed by postmodern art and architecture: dialogic and emergent conversation, an eclectic nature, and multiple layers of interpretation. His perspective is more constructive than many other postmodern perspectives, and he sees this approach as playful: "Our own [post-modern] vision is a good deal more doubtful, inherently filled with problematics, rooted in dialogue and history, and continually remade as we interact playfully with ourselves and the environment of which we are but part" (Doll, 2012, p. 152). His sense of playfulness with doubt, uncertainty, loss, and problematics brings a spirit of play into my approach to nonviolence education to counteract the pessimistic view of human nature and the simulacra of reality in the postmodern age.

Poststructural theories provide in-depth critiques of modern Western traditions of metanarrative, essentialism, and universality and elaborate complicated understandings of identity, power, and difference as well as their dynamic relationships. The poststructural theories of identity as nonidentity to exceed normalization and difference as fluid, multiple, complex, and self-contradictory point in new directions for what ethical engagement with difference means for education. As Foucault (1982) points out, the unitary, essential, and universal notion of the modern identity produces exclusion and reproduces domination, and thus, "the relationships we have to have with ourselves are not ones of identity; rather, they must be relationships of differentiation, of creation, of innovation" (p. 16). Self-creation involves intellectually, ethically, politically, and aesthetically crafting one's own life through playing with limits to go beyond the constraints of the normalizing mechanism and categorical thinking while questioning one's own implications in the mechanism.

Poststructural thinkers argue that difference, whether psychic difference or social difference, cannot be erased into perceived commonality because such an erasure itself can become a form of violence. Both the Levinasian theory of the otherness of the other and the Derridian notion of difference emphasize the necessity of not colonizing or assimilating difference into sameness in ethical relationships. Difference, or the alterity of the other, including the psychic otherness within the self, cannot be mastered or reduced, but unsettles a stable notion of identity and opens it up to a radical responsibility to the other, which must go beyond pre-established rules and norms. This poststructural attention to alterity builds in a necessary element of open and dynamic engagement with difference in my approach to nonviolence.

However, the radicalization of otherness in poststructural theories also runs the risk of distancing the self and the other to an excessive degree to make bridging the divides in the psyche and in society difficult. The emphasis on the particular against the universal also can go to the extreme of downplaying the role of relational dynamics. In addition, the imposition of virtual reality in endless simulated copies to the degree of losing touch with reality is incompatible with the need for authentic relationships in nonviolence. The perpetual creation of more differences in the form of variety also contributes to the commercialization of the global society rather than promoting diversity for the well-being of the system (Hershock, 2011).

On the other hand, poststructural theory reminds me of the importance of not reifying nonviolence into a fixed idea or ideal. In Derrida's deconstruction practice, he questions the essentialized Western discourses of democracy, justice, hospitality, forgiveness, and responsibility, among other concepts, but he does so without the intention of replacing these notions by alternative sets of concepts. Rather, he affirms democracy as yet to come (Derrida, 1992) and the necessity for holding aporias to create the possible out of the impossible. It is this notion of dwelling in the opposite pull—reminding me of *yin-yang* dynamics—in order to create something new in a particular situation that keeps my mind open to conceptualizing nonviolence not as an ideal but as an ongoing practice. In this sense, nonviolence cannot fully eliminate violence, but is the daily transformative work of holding tensions to open new possibilities.

Feminist Theories

Women's engagement in daily caring practices and their leadership in nonviolent resistance social activism have had a long history, although their efforts tend to be sidelined in both mainstream feminist thought and social activism scholarship (Gallo-Cruz, 2018). To articulate nonviolence as a feminist project, this chapter traces historical and contemporary feminist scholarship and activism from diverse settings as well as curriculum scholars' work on gendered analysis. A curriculum and pedagogy of nonviolence that enables students to learn, unlearn, and educate themselves is highlighted through the lens of feminist theory.

Within the feminist theory of nonviolence there are different approaches. Several areas of contested sites are highlighted here: First, the role of the maternal. Some value the maternal as an embodied relationship to the other, distinguished from patriarchal manhood, which is dominated by rationality and reason. Others see maternity as a potential site for oppression and for binding women to their traditional role of caretaker. I think these insights and debates contribute to complicated conceptions of maternity that can create nonviolent relationships both within the family and in the world. For women educators, thinking back through their mothers, as Grumet (1988) does, rather than through their fathers, does not mean becoming the same as our foremothers, but is about becoming what we can be through foregrounding women's experiences and voices.

The second site is the tension between a religious/spiritual and a secular basis for nonviolence. Leela Fernandes (2003) argues for a spiritualized feminism so that the positive energy can be released beyond critiques to practice nonviolence for a better world. Acknowledging the restrictions of institutionalized religions on women's rights, she believes a broader sense of spirituality is still necessary for transformative feminist practices. On the other hand, radical lesbian feminist Barbara Deming (1984) provides a secular basis for nonviolence to break the cycle of violence in social change. In addition, the post-structuralist feminist emphasis on the role of alterity is often situated in philosophical formulations that go beyond the realm of religion.

Third, the tension around the roles of self-sacrifice and self-affirmation is also important for a curriculum theorizing of nonviolence. As women have been traditionally positioned as altruistic in their caring practices, the implications of redemptive suffering as Gandhi and King formulated it need to be re-thought for the feminist project of refusing to reinforce patriarchal values that enact violence against women. Some feminists still argue for redemptive suffering, as it serves to radically change the established hierarchical system, including patriarchy. Others argue for not reinforcing self-sacrifice, a male heroic notion of saving the world, but for embracing self-affirmation as the foundation for women's practice of nonviolence in their everyday relationships and in collective action (Deming, 1984; Gallo-Cruz, 2018). I don't think we need to approach self-affirmation and self-sacrifice dualistically, as they are not mutually exclusive, but the gendered nature of this tension needs to be addressed.

While I discuss my perspectives on these contested sites, I also approach the gendered nature of violence and nonviolence in an inclusive, rather than simplistically dualistic way. Nonviolence has been practiced by both women and men historically and contemporarily, and there are women who have been implicated in the system of violence as well as women who have led nonviolent resistance. The social construction and deconstruction of femininity and masculinity need to be balanced with the cosmic dynamics of femininity and masculinity—a Daoist worldview—that exist in all persons to invite everyone's participation in unsettling various forms of gender normativity (Wang, 2021). Ultimately, the commitment to growing the life force of nonviolence can take different modes in specific situations.

Nonviolence Studies and Peace Education

The central contribution of nonviolence studies and peace education to this book is evident throughout all chapters, so here I do not go into detail about how it has shaped my thoughts but point out my tensions with it.

First, Western peace education, which is often framed through international lenses, addressing topics of war and peace, international conflicts, and post-conflict education has produced an impressive body of empirical and theoretical work. While inner peace and ecological peace have emerged from the field (Lin, 2008; Oxford, 2014), the focus on external peace among different social groups or nations remains predominant. However, the intergroup focus seems to miss the daily educational work of integrating body, mind, and spirit that can prevent violence from happening in the first place.

Second, difference is often perceived as an obstacle to overcome for peacemaking and peacebuilding; instead seeking common ground is privileged. This tendency is also present in many nonviolence leaders' messages, such as Mahatma Gandhi, the Dalai Lama, and Michael Nagler, who speak about the basis of nonviolence in unity and commonality. I privilege the role of difference and the necessity of building connections across difference in nonviolence, because social violence often happens to those who are perceived as different in one way or another, and the psychic violence of repressing the unaccepted element of the self often leads to projecting those elements onto others as the carrier of the shadow. We need to find ways of engaging in difference, neither erasing it nor elevating it. What does nonviolent engagement in difference mean for educators? This book labors on this tensioned site in different chapters.

Third, related to the role of difference, nonviolence studies tend to focus more on the universal than the particular. Nagler (2004) makes the argument about addressing the underlying reason for a particular form of violence—for example, anti-Asian hate crimes—rather than "trying to deal with one problem of victimization in isolation" (p. 6). I agree with the necessity to address the underlying mechanism of violence and to make connections across different forms of hatred in the bigger picture. However, naming the specific nature of hatred is also necessary so that the particularity of violence in targeting a certain group can be addressed at the same time. The tension between the particular and the universal can be lived with in an improvised manner, as some situations call for highlighting shared life and other situations call for highlighting difference.

I intend to use this brief review of all these theoretical foundations to provide clarity for my formulation of nonviolence education in the following chapters. While each thread is interwoven into the landscape of a nonviolence curriculum, there are also tensions when all of them are brought together, conveying multidimensional, process-oriented, and improvisational conceptions of nonviolence that dwell in uncertainty, contingency, and non-instrumental pursuits. Nonviolence is not a destination or an ideal to reach, but an ongoing process of daily work to unlearn the mechanism of domination internally and relate compassionately externally to others and to the world. Both the inner work and outer work of nonviolence in and out of the classroom are filled with struggles, tensions, and the effort of working through internal and external difficulties.

In other words, nonviolence is a work of holding tensions and creating possibilities through dwelling in difficulties, with complicated dynamics, generating ever-changing, attuned responses to what situations call for, with the lens of seeing a bigger picture. There are no easy solutions. Non-dualistically integrating body, mind, and spirit in the self, transcending divisions to cultivate compassionate relationships between the self and the other, and building connections across difference from the local to the global community, educational cultivation of nonviolent relations with the self, the other, and the world is situated in creative tensions. In this sense, nonviolence education is not a noun but a verb, mobilizing educational experiences along "polyphonic lines of movement" (Aoki, 2005, p. 209) toward a higher aspiration for a world yet to come, in different places, times, and contexts. Individually and communally, we can make our schools and our lives a bit more loving and a bit more sustainable each day.

Outline of the Book

The chapters are mainly arranged in chronological order, with exceptions for groupings according to topics. Chapter 2 is a revised paper presented at the

Professors of Curriculum annual meeting in 2010, which lays out some fundamental threads in this book: the relationship between nonviolence with the self and nonviolence to others, the questioning of democracy and the pondering of restorative justice, the inherent mechanism of nonviolence in going against violence, the necessity to go beyond "us" versus "them" in intergroup and international settings, and nonviolence as an ethical relationship for renewing curriculum.

Chapter 3 reflects my effort to approach social justice education through the lens of nonviolence, going beyond critical theory and poststructural theory. This chapter defines the concept of nonviolence and illuminates a nonviolent social justice pedagogy in teacher education. Chapter 4 is an elaboration of what Confucianism and Daoism can offer to peace education, which has been pushed aside by both Chinese modernization and Western education. Harmony in difference and tranquility in turbulence are two central tenets for building relationships between differences in one's personhood and establishing interconnections in the conflict-ridden world. Chapter 5 offers more explanation of what nonviolence means for the internationalization of curriculum studies, identifies different approaches to nonviolence education, and discusses nonviolent interactions between the local, the national, and the international levels. All three chapters explicitly draw on international and Indigenous wisdom traditions.

Chapters 6 and 7 discuss the meanings of nonviolence in the inner life of teachers and students through the lenses of psychoanalysis and analytic psychology. In Chapter 6, Julia Kristeva's psychoanalytic insights for intimate revolt are used to inform the process of making sense of breakdown moments to reach a breakthrough in meanings. Echoing Chapter 3's focus, this chapter also addresses social justice pedagogy and the shifts in my teaching approaches, but through a different lens. Chapter 7 explores several important intersections between Carl Jung's transcendent integration of the psyche and cultivating nonviolent relations, including the role of interconnectedness, shadow projection and withdrawal, and multidimensional modes of integrative work, to rethink transformative curriculum dynamics.

Chapter 8 uses a qualitative, teacher research methodology to analyze shifts in students' perspectives on nonviolence and the teacher educator's efforts to create pedagogical conditions for these changes to happen. Chapter 9 is a co-authored article based on three students' experiential projects of mindful relationships, framed largely as students' own perspectives in their writings and conversations. Together, these two chapters demonstrate in embodied ways, from both the educator's and students' viewpoints, how nonviolence and mindfulness can be experienced to facilitate students' meaning-making process.

Chapters 10 and 11 draw on mothers' legacies and feminist theory. Chapter 10 focuses on the notion of organic relationships to reclaim the maternal legacy, including the legacy of nonviolent alliance in working together across differences. Chapter 11 discusses nonviolence education through the lens of feminist theory to highlight gendered approaches to nonviolence on several contested sites.

Chapter 12, as a conclusion chapter, is not a traditional summary, but a poetic, narrative rendering that brings all important themes together in a *currere* style, with the intention to inspire readers' enthusiasm for and commitment to nonviolence work.

From Chapters 2 to 12, my conceptions of nonviolence education have become more complicated with a deepened sense of urgency, enriched by different theoretical orientations and my ongoing teaching experiences. From nonviolence as the antidote to all forms of violence, to the nonbinary notion of violence/nonviolence as a continuum, to nonviolence as holding tensions to cultivate humane relationships, these conceptions keep changing shape and texture. However, there is no linear progression of conceptual changes, as recursive questioning and motifs are embedded in all these chapters, such as the importance of inner work; the role of engaging in cultural difference in pedagogy; relational dynamics at the individual, the national and the international levels; and the implications of gender. They are intertwined threads that weave this book into an organic whole.

My perspectives on a curriculum and pedagogy of nonviolence have also become more nuanced regarding creating conditions for students to experience body/mind, self/other, and inner/outer integrative work in cultivating their non-dualistic understanding, relationships, and awareness. While initially nonviolence was presented as a curriculum vision, nonviolence as everyday practice in education to hold the tensions for it to fulfill its positive potentiality has emerged as an overarching theme. It is an unending work to integrate ongoing splits and divisions in renewing curriculum dynamics at all levels, based upon multi-disciplinary inquiries and creative pedagogical explorations. With these multidimensional, complex, and interdisciplinary layers of nonviolence work in their openness to transformation and creativity, I invite readers to find different entry points into the landscape of nonviolence education to create their own pathways.

Notes

1 When I started to teach in 2001, it was called the Tulsa Race Riot of 1921. However, such a naming does not reflect the systematic and brutal destruction of Black Wall Street by White mobs. Recently it has been re-named the Tulsa Race Massacre of 1921, which more accurately reflects the nature of the tragedy. In this book, several chapters refer to it, and I decide not to update the naming when the previous name was used to remind us of the temporal nature of historical interpretation and the significance of naming.
2 I use the term "Daoism" here to match the pronunciation in Mainland China. It is accepted now in China Studies in the West, although the spelling used to be "Taoism." The spelling in this book uses both, as some of my previous work uses "Taoism." Similarly, *Dao De Jing* and *Tao Te Ching* refer to the same classic book. In general, if there is a variation of terms across chapters, the terms remain consistent within each chapter. Because these chapters were published in different time periods, I decide not to unify everything in this collection.

References

Aoki, T. T. (2005). *Curriculum in a new key* (W. F. Pinar & R. L. Irwin, Eds.). Lawrence Erlbaum.
Bai, H., & Cohen, A. (2008). Breathing Qi (Ch'i), following Dao (Tao). In C. Eppert & H. Wang (Eds.), *Cross-cultural studies in curriculum* (pp. 35–54). Routledge.
Bajaj, M. (2010). Conjectures on peace education and Gandhian studies. *Journal of Peace Education*, 7(1), 47–63. https://doi.org/10.1080/17400200903370969
Battle, M. (2000). A theology of community: The *ubuntu* theology of Desmond Tutu. *Interpretation*, 54(2), 173–182. https://doi.org/10.1177/002096430005400206
Burns, J. (2018). *Power, curriculum, and embodiment*. Palgrave Macmillan.
Butler, J. (2020). *The force of non-violence*. Verso.
Cunningham, R. M. (2021). *Archetypal nonviolence*. Routledge.
De Dijn, A. (2020). *Freedom: An unruly history*. Harvard University Press.
Deloria, Jr., V. (1974). Non-violence in American society. *Katallagete*, 5(2), 4–7.
Deming, B. (1984). *We are all part of one another* (J. Meyerding, Ed.). New Society Publishers.
Derrida, J. (1992). *The other heading* (P. Brault & M. B. Naas, Trans.). Indiana University Press.
Doll, Jr., W. E. (1993). *A post-modern perspective on curriculum*. Teachers College Press.
Doll, Jr., W. E. (2012). *Pragmatism, post-modernism, and complexity theory* (D. Trueit, Ed.). Routledge.
Easwaran, E. (1997). *Gandhi the man*. The Blue Mountain Center of Meditation. (Original work published 1972)
Fernandes, L. (2003). *Transforming feminist practice*. Aunt Lute Books.
Fiala, A. (Ed.). (2018). *The Routledge handbook of pacifism and nonviolence*. Routledge.
Foucault, M. (1982). Sex, power, and the politics of identity. In P. Rabinow (Ed.), *Ethics* (pp. 163–173). The New Press. (Original work published 1997)
Freud, S. (1961). *Civilization and its discontents*. W. W. Norton.

Gallo-Cruz, S. (2018). American mothers' nonviolence. In H. J. McCammon & L. A. Banaszak (Eds.), *Years of the nineteenth amendment: Appraisal of women's political activism* (pp. 273–294). Oxford University Press.

Gandhi, M. K. (1947). *India of my dreams*. Navajivan Publishing House.

Gandhi, M. K. (1993). *An autobiography* (M. Desai, Trans.). Beacon Press. (Original work published 1957)

Grumet, M. (1988). *Bitter milk*. The University of Massachusetts Press.

Hershock, P. (2011). *Valuing diversity*. State University of New York Press.

Howard, V. R. (2018). Nonviolence in the Dharma tradition. In A. Fiala (Ed.), *The Routledge handbook of pacifism and nonviolence* (pp. 80–92). Routledge.

Jackson, M. (2017). Foreword. In H. Devere, K. Te Maihāroa, & J. P. Synott (Ed.), *Peacebuilding and the rights of Indigenous peoples* (pp. v–vi). Springer.

Jung, C. G. (1953). *Two essays on analytical psychology* (R. F. C. Hull, Trans.). Princeton University Press.

King, Jr., M. L. (1986). Nonviolence and racial justice. In J. M. Washington (Ed.), *The essential writings and speeches of Martin Luther King, Jr.* (pp. 5–9). Harper One. (Original work published 1957)

King, Jr., M. L. (1986). Pilgrimage to nonviolence. In J. M. Washington (Ed.), *The essential writings and speeches of Martin Luther King, Jr.* (pp. 5–9). Harper One. (Original work published 1960)

King, Jr., M. L. (1986). Nonviolence: The only road to freedom. In J. M. Washington (Ed.), *The essential writings and speeches of Martin Luther King, Jr.* (pp. 54–61). Harper One. (Original work published 1966)

Kliebard, H. M. (2004). *The struggle for the American curriculum, 1893–1958* (3rd ed.). RoutledgeFalmer.

Le Grange, L. (2011). The philosophy of ubuntu and education in South Africa. In W. Veugelers (Ed.), *Education and humanism* (pp. 67–78). Sense Publishers.

Letseka, M. (2012). In defense of *ubuntu*. *Studies in Philosophy and Education, 31*, 47–60. https://doi.org/10.1007/s11217-011-9267-2

Lin, J. (1991). *The Red Guards' path to violence*. Praeger.

Lin, J. (2008). Constructing a global ethic of universal love and reconciliation. In J. Lin, E. J. Brantmeier, & C. B. Bruhn (2008), *Transforming education for peace* (pp. 301–315). Information Age Publishing.

Lynd, S., & Lynd, A. (Eds.). (2006). *Nonviolence in America*. Orbis Books.

Miller, J. (2010). Communities without consensus. In E. Malewski (Ed.), *Curriculum studies handbook* (pp. 95–100). Routledge.

Nagler, M. (2004). *The search for a nonviolent future*. Inner Ocean Publishing.

Ng-A-Fook, N., & Smith, B. (2017). Doing oral history education toward reconciliation. In K. R. Llewellyn & N. Ng-A-Fook (Eds.), *Oral history and education* (pp. 65–86). Palgrave Macmillan.

Oxford, R. (2014). *Understanding peace cultures*. Information Age Publishing.

Pinar, W. F. (1994). *Autobiography, politics and sexuality*. Peter Lang.

Pinar, W. F. (2001). *The gender of racial politics and violence in America*. Peter Lang.
Pinar, W. F. (2015). *Educational experience as lived*. Routledge.
Pinar, W. F. (2019). *What is curriculum theory?* (3rd ed.). Routledge.
Pinar, W. F. (2023). *A praxis of presence in curriculum theory*. Routledge.
Poindexter, N., Smith, L., & Wang, H. (2021). Heightened consciousness and curriculum in a time of crisis. *Prospects: Comparative Journal of Curriculum, Learning, and Assessment, 51*, 47–61. https:/doi.org/10.1007/s11125-021-09542-0
Queen, C. S. (2007). The peace wheel: Nonviolent activism in the Buddhist tradition. In D. L. Smith-Christopher (Ed.), *Subverting hatred* (pp. 14–37). Orbis Books.
Romano, A. (2022). *Racial justice and nonviolence education*. Routledge.
Shastri, S. Y., & Shastri, Y. S. (2007). Ahimsa and the unity of all things. In D. L. Smith-Christopher (Ed.), *Subverting hatred: The challenge of nonviolence in religious traditions* (pp. 57–75). Orbis Books.
Smith, L. (2021). *Curriculum as community building*. Peter Lang.
Smith-Christopher, D. L. (Ed.). (2007). *Subverting hatred*. Orbis Books.
Swanson, D. M. (2009). Where have all the fishes gone? Living ubuntu as an ethics of research and pedagogical engagement. In D. Caraccioli & A. M. Mungai (Eds.), *In the spirit of ubuntu* (pp. 3–21). Sense Publishers.
Taubman, P. (2009). *Teaching by numbers*. Routledge.
Te Maihāroa, K, Ligaliga, M., Devere, H. (Eds.). (2022). *Decolonising peace and conflict studies through Indigenous research*. Palgrave Macmillian.
Todd, S. (2003). *Learning from the other*. State University of New York Press.
Tutu, D. (1999). *No Future without Forgiveness*. Doubleday.
Venter, E. (2004). The notion of ubuntu and communalism in African educational discourse. *Studies in Philosophy and Education, 23*, 149–160. https://doi.org/10.1023/B:SPED.0000024 428.29295.03
Walker, P. O. (2022). Restoring balance and harmony to peace and conflict studies. In K. Te Maihāroa, M. Ligaliga, & H. Devere (Eds.), *Decolonising peace and conflict studies through Indigenous research* (pp. 41–56). Palgrave Macmillian.
Wang, H. (2004). *The call from the stranger on a journey home: Curriculum in a third space*. Peter Lang.
Wang, H. (2005). Aporia, responsibility, and im/possibility of teaching multicultural education. *Educational Theory, 55*(1), 45–59. https://doi.org/10.1111/j.1741-5446.2005.0004a.x
Wang, H. (2009). Introduction. In H. Wang & N. Olson (Eds.), *A journey to unlearn and learn in multicultural education*. Peter Lang.
Wang, H. (2010). A zero space of nonviolence. *Journal of Curriculum Theorizing, 26*(1), 1–8.
Wang, H. (2014). *Nonviolence and education*. Routledge.
Wang, H. (2021). *Contemporary Daoism, organic relationality, and curriculum of integrative creativity*. Information Age Publishing.

Wang, H. (2023). Transcendent integration in the everyday practice of curriculum. In M. Quinn, P. Munro Hendry, J. Bach, & R. Mitchell (Eds.), *Curriculum histories in place, in person, in practice*. Routledge.

Wood, H. (2016). *Invitation to peace studies*. Oxford University Press.

Ziarek, E. P. (2001). *An ethics of dissensus*. Stanford University Press.

Zinn, H. (Ed.). (2002). *The power of nonviolence*. Beacon Press.

· 2 ·

ETHICS OF NONVIOLENCE AS A CURRICULUM VISION (2010)

Nonviolence as a curriculum vision emerged from my cross-cultural life history and a decade of teaching multicultural education classes on a predominately White campus in Oklahoma. Only recently have I begun to theorize this notion in the context of curriculum studies, so it is a work in progress. Here I introduce the orientation of nonviolence into ethical engagement with difference within the self and with the other in education. How can self-self and self-other relationships be re-imagined to dissolve violence in contemporary life? This is a burning question for me as I travel across two countries that are culturally and politically quite different and witness violence in different forms. My own most recent answer is that *only* nonviolence in its broad sense as an educational project can undo violence in its various forms and create a space for developing both creative individuality and compassionate relationality. As a project, nonviolence education works on the cultivation of personhood and community in an ongoing process in order for humanity to rise above the desire to dominate and control and to pursue fellowship for the welfare of all, ranging from the individual to the biosphere.

As I envision nonviolence as an ethical project of curriculum, I make connections between nonviolence to the self in the psychic life and nonviolence to the other in the social life and in the international context, using key concepts from nonviolence studies, mediated through the Kristevian (1991, 1993) notion of "stranger to ourselves" and "nations without nationalism" to release my imagination for a better world. I also draw upon international wisdom resources for engaging in cross-cultural dialogues (Eppert & Wang, 2008) and curriculum as a complicated conversation (Pinar et al., 1995) to illuminate educational pathways toward nonviolence.

Why nonviolence? In the contemporary age nonviolence is usually associated with Gandhian nonviolent resistance against colonialism for the independence of India and with civil rights movements led by Martin Luther King Jr. in the United States; but as a way of life, its principle has existed for thousands of years throughout human history in many different cultures and traditions, in practices such as not doing harm and resolving conflicts in a peaceful way. While the political and social movements led by Gandhi and King symbolize grassroots social action against the hierarchy of oppression, in the opposite direction, nonviolent governing from the top has also existed historically. Michael Nagler (2004) in *The Search for a Nonviolent Future* gives several examples of nonviolence from the top rather than from below, including William Penn who declared his "resolution to live justly, peaceably, and friendly with" Delaware Indians in 1681 (quoted in Lynd & Lynd, 1995, p. 2), which was followed by 70 years of nonviolent governance. It is paradoxical to describe Penn's relationship with the Indigenous tribe in this way as it was embedded in the system of the colony, but it does point out alternatives in the past and that the brutality of colonization was not historically inevitable. When colonizers first settled in North America there were examples of peaceful coexistence between the British and the Indigenous people, including settlements absorbed into the Native society, but these stories suggesting "the possibility that British settlers had survived by merging with Native Americans" (Loewen, 1995, p. 120) have been completely erased from textbooks because they do not fit into the official storyline. Thus, the colonial legacy of conquest and domination by war as the only way to solve conflicts is reinforced as the indicator of historical progress.

Taoist *wuwei*, nondual action which leads to the transformation of everything but does not force any change, is oriented by nonviolence that does not dominate others or the world. *Tao Te Ching* advocates it as the governing principle for sages and kings while *Zhuangzi* approaches it more as a way of life. I frame the educational notion of nonviolence in a broad sense existentially as a way of life that relates to but goes beyond its political sense. In a commonsensical definition, violence and nonviolence are often approached as doing or not doing physical harm, but both concepts involve much more extensive realms, including intellectual, emotional, social, cultural, and spiritual, in addition to their political meaning. In education, it is important to acknowledge various forms of violence: intellectual imposition, labeling and tracking, emotional restriction, socialization of hypermasculinity, cultural practices of racism and sexism, or spiritual suffocation (Wang, 2010). Nonviolence not only goes against all forms of violence but is also constructive, cultivating inner peace and promoting a compassionate community through shifting relational dynamics within the self and with the other. Nagler (2004) considers it a positive force to transform individuals and society.

My nine years of teaching multicultural education courses on a predominately White university campus have made me realize that we need to find more positive resources to support students' process of working through difficulty. One of the challenges that I have continually experienced in teaching difficult knowledge is how to work, without pedagogical imposition, with students' emotional intensity in unlearning their fundamental assumptions and how to lead students to work through white shame and guilt to take on educational responsibility (Wang, 2005, 2008). The root of social and political hierarchy is the mechanism of domination and control, and racism, sexism, classism, homophobia, and other forms of social violence are symptoms of domination that desire to control or erase the other in order to preserve the self. However, when the other is erased, the self cannot be sustained; Indigenous and international traditions teach us that we are all connected to one another and connected to the land and the cosmos. To treat such symptoms, we must treat the root problem of seeing the self as split, with the mind taking control, and as separate from the other, and we must see nonviolence as going against violence yet not following any route of violent means and thus dissolving the mechanisms of control within and without. It has gradually become clear to me that nonviolence based upon organic interconnections and responsible personhood can undo the legacy of White supremacy, heterosexism, class oppression, and other forms of social violence while not falling into a simplistic identity politics in which the fixation on identity can still be implicated in the desire for mastery and control over the self and the other. Thus for the past decade, I have searched for various nonviolent means in teaching against social violence.

While we in the field of education have critiqued multiple dimensions of violence, we have not yet discussed nonviolence in any substantial way. Sometimes we talk about anti-violence along with anti-oppression, but even the gesture of "anti" implies that aggression is used against the aggression that it intends to dissolve. Democracy is a cherished educational ideal for American educators, yet 14 years of living in this country has not convinced me to embrace democracy wholeheartedly when American political leaders have repeatedly evoked the ideal of democracy to justify bombing another country, which the mainstream American public is ready to accept, or when the banner of democracy is used on a smaller scale in the academic community to exclude difference in a violent way. On the other hand, have we *ever* heard any political leader evoke the principle of nonviolence to arm a nation to go to war? Democracy or peace (peace through strength) can be manipulated as a weapon for warfare or to impose the will of the powerful, but only nonviolence *cannot* justify any violence, whether it is individual or collective. "Violence begets violence" while "nonviolence begets nonviolence" (Nagler, 2004). Jane Addams understood it well a century ago when she campaigned for peace during the time of war, even though her courageous act provoked strong backlash from colleagues and the public. Her painstaking and inspiring work at Hull House also demonstrated that active pacifism was embodied in the daily practice of seeking room for women, the poor, and immigrants to live together nonviolently (Hendry, 2011).

I have been teaching Tutu's (1999) book *No Future without Forgiveness* to students in teacher education in a multicultural diversity issues class for two years. The book tells profoundly moving stories about the work led by South Africa's Truth and Reconciliation Commission in the 1990s to pursue a new, restorative alternative to both victor's justice and national amnesia in confronting the injustice of the apartheid system and healing the collective trauma. The Indigenous notion of *ubuntu* in the interconnectedness of humanity was drawn upon for the foundation for rehumanization and repairing relationships in the difficult labor of seeking truth, making confession, redressing the wrong, taking responsibility, and enabling forgiveness and reconciliation. Reading story after story about how low people could sink in an inhuman system and how people could also rise above anger and pain to readily welcome back into their community the perpetrators after their confession of wrongdoing with authentic apologies, my students, who are mainly in-service teachers, have often been profoundly moved, but they keep saying that nonviolence would not work for Americans and that they cannot neglect the well-being of their family or their loved ones by being so forgiving. Having grown up in China, I do not find it difficult to envision that restoring individual peace is intimately related to restoring the peace of the community, but my students find it difficult to imagine a world in which nonviolence can be extended beyond their immediate circle and justice can go beyond the dualism of self and other. If our notion of democracy and justice cannot reach such transcendence, nonviolence is indeed not possible.

The sense of a person, a group, or a nation as separate, as in American individualism, reinforces the split between the self/friend and the other/enemy. However, the psychoanalytic notion of "the stranger to ourselves" (Kristeva, 1991) undermines such a separation, turning it around to reveal a crucial question: What if the enemy is within the self as the unwelcome stranger? The possibility of forming nonviolent relationships with both the self and the other depends on our answer. The stranger within, for Kristeva, is the semiotic element of both language and psyche in its dynamic relationship with the symbolic element. Sensory experiences forming the unconscious basis of the psyche must be translated into words to connect the semiotic and the symbolic. In other words, enlightenment is not about moving *away* from the darkness in Plato's cave but is a dance with the shadow embodying both elements for the vitality of life.

Kristeva (1993) invites us "to recognize ourselves as strange in order better to appreciate the foreigners outside us instead of striving to bend them to the norms of our own repression" (p. 29). In other words, the stranger within the self is the bridge for connecting with and doing no harm to the stranger in the outside world who does not accept our norms that actually do harm to ourselves. She also argues that the ethic of a compassionate self-other relationship is enabled by our capacity and willingness to be with others through recognizing the weakness and vulnerability of the other, so that we "refuse to see in the other an enemy" (Kristeva, 1996, p. 41). This link with others through suffering and refusal to see the stranger as an enemy is "a basis for a form of morality" (p. 41), an ethics not based upon the dualism of moral superiority/inferiority, but based upon the relationship between self and other mediated through welcoming the stranger within. To refuse to see in the other an enemy is also inherent in the Taoist *yin-yang* dynamics, Buddhist nonduality, and African *ubuntu*.

In her later works, Kristeva directly addresses the issues of politics at national and international levels. Kristeva (1993) argues that psychoanalysis "invites us to come back constantly to our origins (biographies, childhood memories, family) in order better to transcend them" (p. 4). Such origins for us to transcend also include national origins. Here the reiterative return is not for reinforcing the origin as it is but for working through to generate new possibilities. Kristeva asserts "a transnational or international position situated at the crossing of boundaries… against origins and starting from them" (p. 16). A nation provides a boundary for protection and identification but at the same time dissolves the fixation of its own identity, "eventually appearing as a texture of many singularities—confessional, linguistic, behavioral, sexual, and so forth" (p. 32). The dynamic interplay between the singular and the general requires a notion of *nation* without its attachment to nationalism. At the boundaries, "nations without nationalism" can form nonviolent relationships both within their borders and with each other across borders. She also argues for not being ashamed of European—and I would add European-American—culture, "for it is by developing it critically that we have a chance to have foreigners recognize us as being foreigners all, with the same right of mutual respect" (p. 38). In other words, the boundary of the nation helps us get in touch with the foreigner within so as to always open up rather than close down potentiality.

The dualism of "us" versus "them" has played a violent role in international relationships, and the possibility of moving beyond such a fixed boundary depends on our capacity for refusing to dehumanize the other, both the friendly other and the hostile other, to dissolve violence. Michael Nagler (2004) tells a story of how a courageous and compassionate individual can embody such a spirit of nonviolence involving international relationships. In 1989 Karen and other international volunteers were arrested by the Salvadoran National Guard. Karen, who was Canadian, and her friend Marcela, who was from Columbia, were left in prison. When Karen was released and walking out to meet a Canadian official, she saw her friend, face to the wall in the next room, in an image of dehumanization. She could not walk out on her friend and suddenly stopped and walked back. The soldiers were in shock and handcuffed her again.

> They talked to Karen, despite themselves, and she tried to explain why she had returned: "You know what it is like to be separated from a *campanero*." That got to them. Shortly after, they released Karen and Marcela. The two women walked out together under the stars, hand in hand. (p. 28)

Nagler continues, "The fact is, our usual way of thinking about conflict offers no ready explanation for such an occurrence" (p. 28) but it reflects one of our strongest needs, the need "for integration, for acceptance, community, [and] fellowship" (p. 29), and how capturing and connecting such needs can play a dramatic role in changing situations. "It is by this law of nature an act like

Karen's has power, because she both opened the soldiers' eyes to Marcela's humanity and offered them an escape from their own hostility" (p. 30). She affirmed the need for her own bonding with a friend and colleague while offering an opening to the soldiers' own humanity.

Karen risked her life to rehumanize the image of Marcela as a person in the midst of violence and offered a moment of escape for the soldiers from the act of dehumanization that had turned Marcela into an object of hatred. Is not her courage a shining light in the darkness of violence? Does not her attunement to the human need for affiliation and her capacity to draw out such a yearning from the "enemy" open up our eyes to the integrative power of nonviolence? Is not the starlight of nonviolence embodied in Karen's words, thought, and action so illuminating that the power of an army can be overshadowed? We glorify soldiers' patriotic sacrifice, but as Jane Addams (1922) compassionately claims, young soldiers are the war's "most touching victims" (p. 94). What is so glorifying about militant nationalism's demand to kill at the cost of soldiers' humanity? This story shows both the cruel and compassionate sides of humanity, and how evoking the integrative power of nonviolence has enabled the uplifting journey of humanity, just as those stories in the Truth and Reconciliation Commission's work in South Africa (Tutu, 1999) also reveal.

Nagler (2004) argues that this awakening to rehumanization is "the highest kind of education" (p. 51) in which we need to engage in our daily work. If we approach nonviolence as an educational project and make our best efforts to cultivate compassionate personhood and integrative relationships, the destructive force of violence will not be formed in such an accumulating way in the first place. In today's world, the international is not an abstract concept but is embedded in the daily fabric of our lives, as migration and transnational movement becomes more common. The internationalization of curriculum studies calls upon a nondual notion of nation so that both the protective function of identification and the necessity of border-crossing are affirmed for building a polyvalent compassionate community. As educators, we have our pedagogical responsibility to cultivate in the classroom the ethics of nonviolence that embody the social and the international relational dynamics of mutual flourishing to uphold the most loving and creative expression of humanity individually and collectively.

Michael Nagler's vision for nonviolence as education is informed by the Buddhist notion of nonduality and relational ontology, an interconnected worldview in which the duality of the subject versus the object and the self versus the other no longer exists. Peter Hershock (2009) also explains that we need to relinquish the dualistic view that "difference is the simple opposite of sameness" (p. 160) but see it as "the basis for mutual contribution and the realization of sustainably shared (not simply common) commitment to welfare and flourishing" (p. 161). Such a nondual perception takes away the foundation for treating the self and the other as separate entities with its sense of mutuality that prevents seeing the other as the enemy. Kristeva's notion of connecting with the semiotic flow within the self and connecting with others who are different to support the individual's independence through interdependence also transcends the dualistic notion of the individual (person, group, or nation) as against the other. After all, nonviolent work must engage the subconscious and even the unconscious to evoke the compassionate and integrative side of humanity so that the hard core of violence can be dissolved. Such work is a whole-being experience, and the possibility of nonviolence depends on whether one can sustain the tensionality within the self as one reaches out for the other with compassion at both individual and collective levels.

To briefly speak about nonviolent relationships both horizontally among different schools of thought and vertically intergenerationally in the field of curriculum studies, I suggest that, confronting and challenging the violence of educational standardization, political domination, and cultural control, we must question our own embeddedness in any dualistic way of thinking and educating that excludes the stranger. Competitions among different camps to elevate one's positioning above others, without contextualizing one's own investment, often lead to the proliferation of fragmentation rather than mutual flourishing. When the pursuit of differing for the community of curriculum studies is stronger than the pursuit of differing from others for self-interest, the advancement and well-being of the field for shared commitment and opening of new possibilities becomes possible. Intergenerationally speaking, giving younger generations a space to release their own creativity is necessary, and the normalization of the old, if suffocating the young, must be interrupted. On the other hand, when the younger generation is expected to break away from the old to pursue its independence and to claim singularity through separation rather than interdependence, fragmentations and splits from the relational nature of curriculum as an intergenerational conversation are produced. When either direction goes to the extreme, intergenerational violence breaks the fabric of our shared educational life.

In short, in multiple, intertwined dimensions of psychic, social, political, and national and international relationality, opening up nonviolent possibilities lies in our day-to-day educational work. It is a high calling, one that disrupts many of our taken-for-granted assumptions and habits: Are we ready to take the challenge?

References

Addams, J. (1995). Personal reactions during war. In S. Lynd & A. Lynd (Eds.), *Nonviolence in America* (pp. 91–99). Orbis Books. (Original work published 1922)

Eppert, C., & Wang, H. (2008). *Cross-cultural studies in curriculum*. Routledge.

Hendry, P. M. (2011). *Engendering curriculum history*. Routledge.

Hershock, P. (2009). Ethics in an era of reflexive modernization. In J. Powers & C. S. Prebish (Eds.), *Destroying Mara forever* (pp. 151–164). Snow Lion.

Kristeva, J. (1991). *Strangers to ourselves* (L. S. Roudiez, Trans.). Columbia University Press.

Kristeva, J. (1993). *Nation without nationalism* (L. S. Roudiez, Trans.). Columbia University Press.

Kristeva, J. (1996). *Julia Kristeva: Interviews* (R. M. Guberman, Ed.). Columbia University Press.

Loewen, J. W. (1995). *Lies my teachers told me*. Touchstone.

Lynd, S., & Lynd, A. (Eds.). (1995). *Nonviolence in America*. Orbis Books.

Nagler, M. (2004). *The search for a nonviolent future*. Inner Ocean Publishing.

Pinar, W. F., Reynold, W., Slattery, P., & Taubman, P. (1995). *Understanding curriculum*. Peter Lang.

Tutu, D. (1999). *No future without forgiveness*. Doubleday.

Wang, H. (2005). Aporias, responsibilities, and im/possibility of teaching multicultural education. *Educational Theory, 55*(1), 45–59.

Wang, H. (2008). "Red eyes": Engaging emotions in multicultural education. *Multicultural Perspectives, 10*(1), 10–16.

Wang, H. (2010). A zero space of nonviolence. *Journal of Curriculum Theorizing, 26*(1), 1–8.

· 3 ·

A NONVIOLENT APPROACH TO SOCIAL JUSTICE EDUCATION (2013)[1]

Social justice education has increasingly gained attention in the field of education, calling for transforming and reconstructing social, cultural, and educational systems, structures, and processes to address social inequality for equitable redistribution of educational resources and outcomes. In social justice education, we often evoke the ideals of democracy, justice, human rights, equality, and equity; however, we seldom discuss nonviolence in its noncompromising, powerful stand against any violence and its compassionate call for humane interconnections, even though nonviolent principles have existed for a long time (Addams, 1906/2007; Lynd & Lynd, 1995). I argue in this article that no other ideal can play the same role as nonviolence in dissolving the very mechanism of control and domination that leads to violence while not enacting another form of imposition or coercion. During a decade of teaching multicultural education classes on a predominately White campus, I have gradually come to realize that the means and end of education must be united through nonviolence to treat the root problem of social violence in its various symptoms (racism, sexism, classism, and homophobia, to name a few) and to

---

1 This chapter is reprinted with permission of the publisher (Taylor & Francis Ltd, http://www.tandfonline.com). Wang, H. (2013). A nonviolent approach to social justice education. *Educational Studies*, 49(6), 485–503.

transform relational dynamics toward a compassionate community in which differences are contributors to the collective good.

In my journey to embracing nonviolence education, international wisdom traditions have played an important role, including *ubuntu*, Buddhist nonduality, and Taoist *yin-yang* dynamics. A systematic discussion of these traditions is beyond the scope of this article, so I only interweave the most relevant principle of each tradition with a pedagogy of nonviolence. *Ubuntu* emphasizes the power of organic interconnections in healing wounds; Buddhist nonduality suggests that the fundamental source of violence is the dichotomy between body and mind and between self and other, so we need to unlearn dualism; and Taoist *yin-yang* dynamics bring the tensionality of conflicts back into the whole and emphasize the importance of not-forcing in leadership. All of them adopt an interconnected stance in valuing the ecological health of both individual and community, and thus offer fresh lenses for all involved parties to see through conflicts and fragmentation for a bigger picture. To crossculturally blend these notions with social justice education literature, I intend to explore pathways of cultivating nonviolent relationships at multiple levels in teaching difficult knowledge.

First, this article reviews social justice education literature, particularly focusing on two contrasting and influential approaches: critical theory and poststructural theory. The limitations of these two approaches are discussed and a nonviolent approach is proposed as an alternative. Second, to lay ground for further discussion, the notions of social justice and nonviolence are (re)examined to reveal their similarity and differences in understanding the relationship between the self and the other. After the significance of nonviolence is affirmed, its facets are discussed: relational dynamics, inner peace, and nonviolent means. Third, these facets are translated into important aspects of working toward a pedagogy of nonviolence: Integrating the inner and the outer work, shifting the struggles of opposites to the interdependence of differences, and improvising and using nonviolent teaching strategies. Throughout the article, students' resistance to learning difficult knowledge and nonviolent pedagogical responses is another thread.

Approaches in Social Justice Education

The approach to social justice education is not unitary, as demonstrated well by North's (2008) comprehensive analysis of the tensions and contradictions inherent in various perspectives. This article does not use categories that North uses in her analysis, but due to its central concern with transforming relational dynamics through nonviolent principles, here I highlight the issue of identity and social differences in two influential, contrasting approaches in order to situate a nonviolent approach.

First, an influential approach that is oriented by critical theory intends to raise critical consciousness, or in Freire's (1970/1997) term, "conscientização" (p. 104), and to help marginalized groups and individuals resist social oppression and actively pursue cultural transformation. There has been a proliferation of educational literature highlighting racial, ethnic, gendered, and class minority groups, among other layers of cultural diversity, and their struggles for educational equality and equity. Related to this orientation, teachers are encouraged to promote culturally responsive or culturally relevant teaching (e.g., Gay, 2010; Ladson-Billings, 1995; Sleeter & Cornbleth, 2011), suggesting that students'—especially minority students'—cultural backgrounds have certain characteristics that must be considered for successful teaching and learning. Such a critical orientation is necessary to expose the unequal and unjust social and pedagogical reality of marginalization, to advocate redistribution of power and wealth, and to promote social activism for a better world. However, it runs the risk of setting up the camps of *minority us* against *majority them*, although the categories of minority and majority are slippery concepts and are context dependent. The dualistic distinction between the self and the other, both within and across social identity, leads to social violence in the first place, so another way of categorizing *us* versus *them* does not necessarily undo the mechanism of objectification and domination. Different foci within critical theory often compete for establishing class, or race, or gender as more fundamental than other factors in shaping social reality. Such debates address particular social manifestations of violence rather than uncovering and further treating the root of social violence.

With the influence of postmodern and poststructural approaches, social differences are perceived as fluid, multiple, ever-changing, and conflicting; and any universal and essential project of emancipation is under question. In this framework, both self and other become complicated beyond the dualism between the oppressor and the oppressed, indicating greater potential for addressing the complexity, uncertainty, and ambiguity of cultural diversity (e.g., Martusewicz, 2001; Parkes et al., 2010; Todd, 2003; Trifonas, 2003). The notion of identity, itself, is problematized because of the inherent confining effect of categorization.

There are important differences between critical theory and poststructural theory, but for the purpose of this article, I discuss only two. First, critical theory has a clearly defined notion of marginalized groups and positions their struggles as against domination; in other words, the marginalized other becomes the subject of emancipation. However, in the poststructural notion of the otherness of the other, especially in Levinasian and Derridian discourses, the effort to define the other is resisted, so that the other always has a capacity to surprise, which requires the self to be receptive to the other's radical difference. Second, critical theory is based upon a collective identity: Whether it is class, race, gender, or when multiple identities are acknowledged, the emphasis is on the coalition among oppressed groups in working together to achieve social justice through structural changes. However, in the postmodern Foucaultian reformulation of power relationships, it is the individual's exercise of power in a specific and localized situation that holds the potential for enacting social change. Foucault further positions the individual against social and institutional constraints and argues for nonidentity to radicalize the necessity for self-creation (Wang, 2004). Although, theoretically, I align more with poststructural discourses, I also find their radical emphasis on the otherness of the other and individual singularity problematic. In radicalizing the distinction between the self and the other to not lose the novelty and alterity of the other, the poststructural vigilance against assimilating the other into the self runs the risk of distancing the self and the other to such a degree that it becomes difficult to weave self and other back into the whole. The necessity for respecting the other's difference is the basis for making meaningful interrelationships, but such a connection is difficult to accomplish if the other is positioned in the realm of the unknown. Furthermore, the postmodern emphasis on the singularity and creativity of the individual, however contingent and fluid, rather than on the social and the individual as interdependent, still reinforce the problematic tendency of setting individuality against society (Wang, 2004).

If we listen to students' stories in their responses to social justice education, their resistance to learning "difficult knowledge" (Britzman, 1998, p. 2) has been under discussion for more than a decade across various disciplines (e.g., Chan & Treacy, 1996; Chizhik, 2003; Jakubowski, 2001; Pipino, 2005; Rhone, 2002). Different pedagogical approaches to deal with this issue have also been proposed. In those proposals, however, the starting point is usually the instructor's perceptions and perspectives, and it is the students, more or less, who must overcome the difficulties. In other words, students are pedagogical objects to be enlightened. But doesn't students' resistance also indicate the need to question our own desires as educators to transform students in a particular direction? Elizabeth Ellsworth (1997) argues that there is a third participant in the student–teacher relation: the unconscious of both students and the teacher. Without awareness of such an indirect participation, the teacher's direct routes of teaching difficult knowledge often meet students' "passion for ignorance" (p. 63).

Herbert Kohl (1991) discusses how students' "active not-learning" (p. 13) is a choice against institutionalized schooling that reinforces various forms of social injustice. So he makes efforts to invite students into a teaching–learning relationship. His stories are largely about learning from minority students' resistance against official knowledge. I also think that we need to learn from White students who have a difficult time with the notion of White privilege that is becoming the mainstream knowledge in multicultural education. Students' unreceptiveness to difficult knowledge does not simply suggest mainstream students' desire to preserve their privileged identity (or minority students' wish to be assimilated in order to belong), but their refusal to learn may also indicate their desire to resist the pedagogical objectification that portrays them as lacking critical consciousness and being subject to "conversion" (Jupp & Slattery, 2010, p. 457). We need to be mindful of not setting up a dualism between teacher educators as critical pedagogues and students as resistant learners.

Therefore social justice education needs to be attentive to its own tendency toward polarizing sameness/difference, self/other into irreconcilable or distant opposites in the existing discourses, assumptions, and practices. Although not negating the usefulness of critical and poststructural approaches in certain contexts, this article argues for a different, organic, nonviolent pathway that undermines modern dualism in various forms, addresses the root of social violence, and redirects the relational dynamics away from individual's or group's struggles against one another but toward an interdependent viewpoint in which all parties contribute to the well-being of society.

Nonviolence is centrally concerned with the nature of relationality, although it also emphasizes the role of the individual, who remains as an essential site for dissolving violence and practicing nonviolence, and the role of institutions, which provide the structural support for containing violence and promoting nonviolence. Critical theory is more concerned with structural changes and collective struggles, although poststructural theory is more concerned with individual creativity and singularity, albeit socially and historically situated. By contrast, nonviolence works at the site of relationality within and between individuals or groups or institutions to work through difficulty and transform both individuality and communality. Furthermore, the nature of relationality in nonviolence is different from that in both critical theory and poststructural theory: Through nonduality, nonviolence goes beyond dualism in critical theory; through interdependence, nonviolence mediates the poststructural distance between self and other. Relationality in nonviolence refers to interpersonal/intrapersonal, intergroup/intragroup, and intercultural/intracultural relationships, so the relationship between the self and other is not individualistic but multidimensional. What, then, can a nonviolent approach bring to social justice education? Before answering this question, I need first to lay the ground for further discussion by examining the notions of social justice and nonviolence.

Social Justice and Nonviolence

I used Tutu's book (1999) *No Future without Forgiveness* in my multicultural education classes. The book describes the inspiring work of South Africa's Truth and Reconciliation Commission after South Africa's independence from colonialism in following the third way to heal the terrible trauma inflicted by the apartheid regime. One central notion of the book is restorative justice in the spirit of *ubuntu*, which focuses on restoring broken relationships through a process of rehumanizing both the victims and the perpetrators, rather than on retributive justice which punishes the perpetrators. My students, mainly in-service teachers, were profoundly moved by the book, but they kept saying that such a principle would not work in the United States. So I asked them: "Then what does justice mean in the US?" They quickly replied: "An eye for an eye." My students perceived justice as *us* against *them* and found it difficult to imagine how restoring individual peace is based upon restoring the peace of community. Ironically, Americans Jane Addams and Martin Luther King, Jr. are both renowned for their advocacy for nonviolence and peace. When a separate sense of the individual, or by extension a group or a nation, is elevated above the human and cosmic shared relationality, transcending one's own boundary for the bigger collective good remains difficult. If the notion of justice in today's conflict-ridden society does not unsettle the dualism between the self/us and the other/them, social justice education can hardly lead us out of the cycle of blame, guilt, and defense to a less violent world.

Social justice has different meanings for different people, and often hosts internal contradictions (North, 2008). Zajda, Majhanovich, and Rust (2006) trace the epistemology of social justice back to Plato, Aristotle, and Kant philosophically, and locate its direct source in social reformers' efforts to attend to the needs of uprooted peasants at the end of the nineteenth century. They point out that "most conceptions of social justice refer to an egalitarian society that is based on the principles of equality and solidarity, that understands and values human rights, and that recognizes the dignity of every human being" (p. 1). This commonly used idea of social justice is based upon the notion of the individual person, each person with individual rights forming a collective to decide what is most beneficial to all (or at least to the majority). As Aoki (2005) suggests, most important Western concepts such as right, democracy, freedom, autonomy, or privatization are based upon the notion of the individual. When an individual (or a group) is considered an entity in itself, separate from others, social justice in its emphasis on the social welfare of all participants as equals does not necessarily lead to better social relationships but may slip into another version of the (group) self in the name of the collective. The conception of critical theory-oriented social justice, although emphasizing the collective, tends to separate groups; and in oppositional struggles, social identities can become self-contained and a particular collective becomes exclusive of others.

As Hershock (2009) argues, it is a fallacy to assume that "whatever is good for each and every one of us [individually] will be good for all of us [communally or ecologically]" (p. 156) because, as we have witnessed, what is good for the local may become detrimental to the ecological or the global. We need a more interconnected approach to think about social justice issues.

Taking a poststructural turn, Todd (2003) loosely defined social justice education as:

> a wide range of pedagogies that seek to ameliorate social harm wrought through inequitable practices and structures. Social justice education has been and continues to be marked by a moral concern with those who have been "Othered" and marginalized through discriminatory relations that are seen as violent, both in symbolic and material terms. (p. 1)

This moral concern with the marginalized others shares a similarity with critical theory, but Todd's notion of the "Other" is based upon the "Levinasian understanding of the Other as infinitely unknowable" (p. 3). This ethical call to deobjectify the other and preserve the alterity of the Other is important for the shift from learning about the other to learning from the other, making moments of nonviolent learning possible. The remaining question, however, is whether such a radical commitment to the other can bring both the self and the other back into the interwoven fabric of life.

Facets of Nonviolence

Not incompatible with the notion of social justice, nonviolence is also fundamentally concerned with not doing harm to others, especially those who are marginalized, but its underlying basis is the mutual embeddedness of everything and everybody in the cycle of life. Philosophically and spiritually, nonviolence as a notion and a practice has existed for thousands of years in different traditions throughout the world (Nagler, 2004; Smith-Christopher, 2007). Politically, it has become widely recognized due to anticolonial and civil rights movements in the contemporary age, particularly the nonviolent movements in India led by Gandhi. Here *nonviolence* refers to using nonviolent means in collective struggles against colonization or social injustice. In other words, it refers to grassroots social and political movements. Nagler (2004), however, convincingly argues that nonviolent governing both in the United States and in the world has also had a long history. The possibility of practicing nonviolence top-down is particularly informative for teacher educators, who hold institutional and pedagogical authority in the classroom, in moving toward a pedagogy of nonviolence. Although the historical and structural forces influencing nonviolence education are paramount, this article does not highlight these structural issues because its focus is on nonviolent pedagogical relationships in teacher education. Although a pedagogy of nonviolence is constrained by educational institutions and social systems that are currently not supportive but suppressive of nonviolent relational dynamics, such a pedagogy can also contribute to nonviolent political and social change by teaching against the grain.

When we talk about violence and nonviolence, we usually first associate violence with physical aggression, but the realm of both violence and nonviolence is much broader, involving conceptual, intellectual, emotional, cultural, and political dimensions, among others (Wang, 2010). Within and across these dimensions, several facets of nonviolence are particularly important for social justice education. First, nonviolence initiates and sustains a relational dynamic that draws out the compassionate and loving side of humanity to rise above human cruelty and hatred. Second, a nonviolent relationship with the other goes hand in hand with a nonviolent relationship with the self. Third, the means and end are united through nonviolent principles that do not use any form of imposition and coercion. I discuss these aspects briefly as follows.

Relational Dynamics

The power of nonviolence lies in the relational dynamics that go beyond modern dualism and a win-or-lose mentality to situate the relationship between the self and the other—individually or collectively—as mutually beneficial in the picture of the whole. Although dealing with cultural differences is crucial to social justice education, Hershock (2009) draws upon the Buddhist notion of nonduality to argue for "a concerted shift from considerations of how much we are the *same* or *different from* each [sic] another to how we might best *differ for* one another" (p. 160; emphasis in original). In a non-dualistic view, subject and object, body and mind, and self and other exist interdependently. The importance of difference lies in enriching an intricate interconnectedness of life, rather than asserting the value of the singular over the network. Such a shift to perceiving differences as essential for mutual contribution and shared welfare, as neither needing to be erased (or merely tolerated) nor needing to be elevated or preserved, but as a part of a relationship network, is a shift not only away from the liberal notion of the individual, but also from the identity politics of static diversity or the postmodern radicalization of singularity. When social and cultural differences are viewed in this way, the underlying task of social justice education is to create educational conditions for such relational dynamics of *differing for*, rather than *differing from* to flourish. Although particular differences such as racial or gendered differences must be discussed, the discussions are not only for solving one particular issue, but for changing our ways of relating to others so that we can practice nonviolence in other situations as well.

Nonviolence changes the nature of the relationships in which all participants are involved and evokes all parties' feelings for the connectedness of humanity (and of humanity and nature). The underlying basis of nonviolence is the mutual embeddedness of everything and everybody in the cycle of life, which the notion of *ubuntu* expresses well. *Ubuntu* is tied to African orality and tradition (for instance, the saying "A person is a person through other persons"), although not particularly to any authoritative text, and connotes a complicated sense of connectedness in which a person is in relation to others horizontally in a community and vertically to ancestors and offspring (van der Walt, 2010; Venter, 2004). Venter (2004) also points out that such an

African community, similar to the Buddhist community, is connected with the universe through sharing the earth, mountain, and sky "with the unborn, [and] the living spirits of the dead" (p. 151). Nonviolence is not about power struggles but about social, moral, and spiritual imaginations for the oneness of body/mind and self/other in a local, national, or international community.

The belief in nonviolence is also a belief in humans' capacity for compassion and love that can dissolve aggression and hatred. Many moving stories in Tutu's (1999) book demonstrate the power of forgiveness and love in transforming pain and hatred. To dissolve social violence, we as educators must have such a profound faith in students and be able to discern what is good in them and let it out. The duality between critical pedagogues and resistant students implies teacher educators' lack of trust in students' own capacity to work through difficulty for critical awareness. If we can enact nonviolent relational dynamics in the classroom, students become participants in building a productive community, and they are more likely to demonstrate their best potential and less likely to respond in self-defensive ways (see students' own stores in book chapters edited by Wang & Olson, 2009).

Inner Peace

Not doing violence to oneself is also important for forming a nonviolent relationship. Both Buddhist and Taoist notions of nonviolence require cultivating inner peace as an important step. To be able to interact with the other nonviolently, including both friendly others and hostile others, one must engage in the inner work of transforming anger, hatred, fear, and greed into positive relational orientations. Being able to negotiate conflicts within makes it possible to negotiate conflicts in the outside world, although the inner work and the outer work are usually intertwined and mutually enhance each other.

Jane Addams (1906/2007), who was able to question the social and family expectations for a woman of her time and work through her internalized gendered norms to pursue a public life according to the "newer ideals of peace" (p. 5), is an example of such an extraordinary work of integration (see Pinar, 2009, Chapter 5, for details). For Mandela (1994/2003), decades of prison life did not intensify his hatred of enemies but transformed his anguish, despair, and anger into a vision for South Africa's independence through negotiation and peace. Both leaders cultivated inner peace to reach outer peace. Their stories are particularly inspiring for students from historically marginalized groups. But inner work is equally important for the mainstream White students, although the emotions and feelings that they need to work through might not be the same as those of the minority students. For instance, guilt and shame often emerge during the process to lock students into defensive mechanisms. Here Howard's (2006) journey of working through difficult knowledge and difficult emotions to become a transformative White teacher and teacher educator is particularly illuminating. Many White students related to his journey in different ways (see students' chapters in Wang & Olson, 2009). Only when White students integrate conflicting thoughts and emotions provoked in confronting privilege and their own implications in a system of injustice can they achieve a certain sense of integration to contribute to developing nonviolent relationships in the community.

Teacher educators are not free from such a need for a rigorous process of inner work. We must ask what is behind our own passion for social justice education and our adoption of particular modes of pedagogy. For instance, as a gendered, national, racial minority teaching in American teacher education, I have had to work on myself as I work with my students. It has taken me years to understand how my own implicit sense of loss interacts with my teaching, and such an inner work has continually changed the trajectories of my pedagogy from a more confrontational mode to a more nonviolent mode of teaching (Wang & Olson, 2009).

Nonviolent Means

The key to nonviolence is to use nonviolent means to transform the nature of relationality, as Gandhi declares: "I do not believe in short-violent-cuts to success ... I am an uncompromising opponent of violent methods even to serve the noblest of causes" (quoted in Easwaran, 1972/1997, p. 43). Especially in a conflicting situation, transforming the win-or-lose mentality to enable the cooperation of all parties cannot be achieved by imposing one's own agenda. Nonviolent principles of relying on persuasion, emotional resonance, experiential understanding, or personal examples operate not only at the conscious level, but also at the subconscious level to influence the whole person. Taoism is well known for enacting nonviolent dynamics in a community, which I will discuss further later.

Violence is the result of the collapse of relationality, whether the relationship is human or ecological, physical or psychic, material or spiritual. In other words, racism, sexism, classism, homophobia, and all other forms of social violence are symptoms of the domination mechanism which desires to erase the other, however the other is defined, in order to preserve the self. To treat such symptoms and achieve the end of a nonviolent world, the pedagogical means we use cannot be impositional, even when students disagree with our vision of social justice. Otherwise, students may experience the pedagogical demand for change as another form of authoritarian control. In pedagogical situations, teacher educators have a unique opportunity to practice nonviolence from an authority position and thus to model how to establish nonviolent relationships. Nonviolent means, however, do not shy away from challenging students to unlearn the taken-for-granted assumptions in a disciplined way, because the core of nonviolence education is to dissect the norm of violence and carve out compassionate understandings and commitments.

Toward a Pedagogy of Nonviolence

Three facets of nonviolence show a fundamental shift in our view about the nature of relationship: Neither the self nor the other can exist without relationality. A nonviolent approach is not about privileging either the self or the other; it is about reexamining the relational dynamics and reorienting the relational changes to promote the mutual contribution of all to the whole which in turn supports nonviolent and creative individuality and communality. Relationship here becomes organic because it is based upon internal connections across differences and the whole is not an addition of separate equal entities but achieves its integrity by an intricate interweaving of all parts in various shapes.

A decade of teaching multicultural education classes has convinced me that students are more willing to respond with compassion, courage, and the capacity to move forward when nonviolent principles underlie pedagogical arrangements. Embodying the different facets of nonviolence, we need to pay attention to the following aspects to move toward a pedagogy of nonviolence: Integrating the inner and the outer work; shifting from the struggle of opposites to the interdependence of differences; and improvising and using nonviolent teaching strategies. I briefly discuss these aspects here.

Integrating the Inner and the Outer Work

In social justice education, integrating the inner and the outer work is seldom a rational knowing process. More often than not, when learning is arrested, when students refuse to move forward with more understanding, or when students openly challenge the teacher's authority, it is not because they don't have enough knowledge, but precisely because they cannot afford to feel the burden of knowledge. It is not knowing that is at stake; it is students' emotional dissonance that underlies resistance.

Many strong emotions are evoked when students engage in social justice literature, including anger, outrage, shame, guilt, shock, fear, sadness, or ambivalence and inner conflicts. Teaching the Tulsa Race Riot of 1921 at Oklahoma State University has been full of emotional dramas for my multicultural education class because the Riot happened right here on the site of the OSU-Tulsa campus, yet few students know about it in detail. Various strong emotions surface during the process of learning from what happened so close to home. As the instructor, I have found it difficult to witness students' emotional responses and to simultaneously deal with my own feelings evoked by confronting the historical trauma. Despite my best efforts to lead students beyond guilt so that they can take on "responsibility without guilt" (Howard, 2006, p. 104), the shame and guilt many White students experience remain, articulated or unarticulated, throughout the course. I have gradually realized that a nonviolent relationship with difficult emotions involves letting students stay with or/and express them. Teacher educators need to be open, nonjudgmental, and receptive in such situations, rather than trying to push those emotions away. As some scholars (Boler, 1999; Martusewicz, 2001; Todd, 2003) argue, such discomfort should become the very site of education. After all, the denial of guilt and the evasion of responsibility can have devastating personal and social consequences.

On the other hand, I argue that the organic interconnectedness permeating life is prior to individual experiencing of guilt, so once the power of integrated life energy is tapped and released, social violence can be addressed through organic relationality without necessarily evoking social guilt. If violence comes from a dualistic, objectified consciousness that dominates and controls the other and the world (Bai & Cohen, 2008), then the target of our critique is the dualism that causes human alienation and misery, not any person or group. As Nagler (2004) points out, blaming somebody or a certain group for wrongdoing cannot lead to any enlightenment but usually traps the blamed party in a defensive position. In a multicultural class, for example, it is not unusual for White students to feel blamed when racism is discussed or male students to feel blamed when sexism is discussed. Key to the issue at hand is what, rather than who, leads to violence so that the mechanism of violence can be treated. When students can both separate themselves from the blame and understand their implication in the system of domination, they are more likely to be committed to working against social violence.

An organic approach of healing can be helpful for working through difficult emotions. In the art of Chinese acupuncture, strongly influenced by the Taoist philosophy, needles are not necessarily put into the area that hurts. Needles can be put into another part of the body to relieve the symptoms, and such a treatment away from the problematic area can have long-term effects. This principle is based upon the inner connectedness of the body, as well as its connections with the external environment; therefore, restoring the circulation of *qi*—the vital energy of life—through the whole body is healing. For pedagogical considerations, an identity-based categorical dichotomy between White and Black/people of color, man and woman, poor and rich, straight and queer, and so on, can easily induce shame and guilt and provoke defensive mechanisms. But if we rely on the integrative power of nonviolence to enable students to get in touch with their connectedness to the other and to the world, if we engage students with whole-being experiences to move them out of their comfort zones, if we situate issues in larger contexts so that students don't feel blamed personally, they are much more willing to initiate new learning.

One of my examples is teaching the book *No Future without Forgiveness* by Desmond Tutu (1999) in juxtaposition with teaching about the Tulsa Race Riot of 1921. Students are touched to see how so much pain can be addressed through an interconnected sense of humanity and an integrated sense of community in the South African situation. After reading and discussing this moving book, students are confronted with what happened in their backyard. Such a pedagogical arrangement of bridging knowledge and emotions and of situating our own racial scar in the global struggle is an approach to healing the pain through the circulation of life energy, rather than by paying attention only to the isolated area that hurts. Even though the book directly challenges students' individualistic sense of the self, and some students remain skeptical, they are opened up to another possibility for redressing social wrongs. As they felt strongly about what they were learning, some of them also engaged their families, coworkers, and their own students with discussions about the Tulsa Race Riot and the African notion of *ubuntu*. After the class, some students also chose to teach the Tulsa Race Riot themselves, or create Web sites to spread the influence, or use *ubuntu* as the topic of their master's degree final projects. Such an integration of thought, emotion, and action led to transformations more integrative and less painful.

Getting in touch with interconnectedness, however, may not always protect students from pain. Sometimes, uncovering the intricate and complex connections that have been invisible to students can be shocking, as such a *seeing* may turn their taken-for-granted world upside down. For instance, Loewen's (1995) historical discussions about Native Americans' direct contributions to the American political system of democracy hit right at students' blind spot because the conventional assumption was that the White founding fathers created American democracy single-handedly. Recovery of such stories at the intersections of different cultures is important because when the undercurrent of mutual influence within and across cultural differences is made visible, the domination of one party can no longer hold firm. On such occasions, we cannot avoid pain as it emerges in teaching and must make pedagogical use of it. If students are able to express their strong emotions in a supportive class community and discuss their affective reactions so that words and feelings can be connected, they are less likely to project their own difficulty onto others. And it cannot be overemphasized that teacher educators must continually engage their own inner work throughout the process to accompany students' integrative inner and outer work.

Shifting From the Struggle of Opposites to the Interdependence of Differences

Relational dynamics is a key aspect of a pedagogy of nonviolence. The *yin/yang* dynamics in Taoism are informative here. *Yin* and *yang* are opposite yet complementary cosmic forces, the interaction of which gives birth to all the phenomena of the universe. *Yin* signifies darkness, softness, passivity, and femininity; *yang* signifies brightness, hardness, activity, and masculinity. What underlies *yin/yang* dynamics is the mutual transformation of opposites based upon the interdependence of differences. In the *Tai-ji* symbol demonstrating this dynamic, there is a smaller dot of *yang* within the realm of *yin* and a smaller dot of *yin* within the realm of *yang*. When *yang* goes to the extreme, *yang* can be changed into *yin*, and vice versa. Due to this built-in element of openness to the opposite, opposites are prevented from becoming enemies to each other but are inherently connected. The *yin/yang* interplay is the basis not only for the Taoist interconnected worldview, but also for Taoist leadership by not forcing change. When a leader follows the *Tao* to accomplish a task, it happens "naturally" without effort (*Tao Te Ching*, Chapter 17, author's translation). If accumulated masculine (in both men and women) aggression leads to its downfall and accumulated feminine (in both women and men) gentleness leads to sustaining strength, then nonviolence is the key to the secret of sustaining life energy for individual well-being, social welfare, and ecological harmony.

In social justice education, categorical distinctions often lead to opposite pairs struggling against each other. A strong sense of a power struggle often marks students on the either side of the struggle. Although various forms of unequal power relationships must be disrupted, a Taoist approach is not for one side to win the battle; the approach is to demonstrate the mutuality of opposites and the changeability of conflicting sides and to reveal the fatal vulnerability of the forceful to prevent aggression from becoming harmful. In the broader context, the win-or-lose mentality has been intensified by external attacks on public education and internal complexity with identity-based competition for a representative presence. Being able to see conflicting directions at the same time, to come up with adaptive responses to facilitate the flow beyond conflict, and to pull tensionality back into the whole becomes even more important. The Taoist interplay between *yin* and *yang* is enabled by an inherent bridge between opposites, and a pedagogy of nonviolence is dependent upon building internal connections between and among differences. Such a relational, fluid, and interdependent view goes against violence by dissolving its basis in the domination of one side over the other side.

Enacting such relational dynamics requires rethinking the notion of identity from an interdependent viewpoint. Like an animal shedding its skin for a new birth, a Taoist leader's wisdom is not achieved by intellectual or emotional attachment, but by dissolving attachment to any narrowly defined identity, layer by layer, to achieve insights into the whole of intricate interconnections. The notion of no-self in Buddhism also suggests that there is no fixed essence or identity because all existence is impermanent, in flux, and relational. Transcending a separate sense of the self to reach a state of no-self involves a lifelong process of personal cultivation toward enlightenment and compassion. The Taoist and Buddhist nonattachment to a rigid sense of identity not only directly challenges identity politics but also invites us to rethink the issue regarding the identity-building of marginalized students and the identity awareness of mainstream students. For instance, if a White male student with rich diversity experiences does not identify with the mainstream culture but chooses to start with a sense of interconnectedness when approaching racial issues, should he be redirected to critiquing Whiteness as the starting point? Critical multicultural educators' categorical demand that White students critique Whiteness and that minority students embrace coloredness may block the multiple potentiality and pathways of nonidentity and no-self in engaging nonviolent social change. Identity-building in social justice education from the different vantage points of students can be helpful under certain contexts, but we need to avoid categorical claims. We also need to work with students to complicate and destabilize social identities to build an element of opening within to what is different outside. Tutu's (1999) definition of *ubuntu* also demonstrates well such a relational ontology:

> A person with *ubuntu* is open and available to others, affirming of others, does not feel threatened that others are able and good, for he or she has a proper self-assurance that comes from knowing that he or she belongs in a greater whole and is diminished when others are humiliated or diminished, when others are tortured or oppressed, or treated as if they were less than who they are. (p. 31)

Such an interdependent view of humanity forms a stark contrast to a competitive mentality; it sees what is affirmative to the other as affirmative of the self and what is damaging to the other as damaging to the self. In such a view, differences are for enriching a community, not for competing against others. To connect students with such a spirit of *differing for one other*, rather than *from each other*, teacher educators can select materials embodying the interconnectedness of life and let students' engagement with texts and with one another initiate the process of unlearning and learning. In addition to using emotionally appealing materials, theoretical works can also serve a similar purpose. I have been using Nagler's (2004) *The Search for a Nonviolent Future* for two years, challenging students to understand social justice from an interdependent view and envision their own multicultural teaching from a nonviolent approach. Students' discussions of this text have led to intriguing and heated debates among students from various angles. The emotional resonance/dissonance of *No Future without Forgiveness* and the provocative ideas of *The Search for a Nonviolent Future* both have served well in inviting students to see the world differently even if they disagree. When such materials were combined with students' local investigation of the Tulsa Race Riot of 1921, students were invited to see relational dynamics through the view of interconnectedness.

Improvising and Using Nonviolent Teaching Strategies

Teacher educators can adopt various teaching strategies to infuse the interconnected energy into learning, not to force change by conversion, but to engage students in a heartfelt process of experiencing, understanding, and acting upon the world differently. Such a process is usually uncertain, ambiguous, and full of surprises, and students need compassionate guidance in their journeys. As I have discussed, choosing materials that embody the integrative power of life (literature, film, local history, or theories promoting dynamic relationships) and using activities that encourage students' whole-being experiences (writing autobiographies, role-playing nonviolent social interactions, engaging in community actions or local investigation projects, or sharing peers' multicultural journeys) can be effective in moving students toward the integration of body/mind, self/other, and inner/outer works. No specific method holds the key to enacting nonviolent dynamics in teaching, but the underlying orientation of nonviolence can make many strategies successful. Without any set formula for enacting nonviolent principles in teaching, teacher educators' ability to improvise situation-specific pedagogical responses becomes important. The pedagogical relationship itself can become a nonviolent means.

Social justice education in general advocates a proactive stance toward changing the world, but social action and meditative unlearning need to be combined to achieve the integration of the inner and outer work and enact nonviolent relational dynamics. Meditation, *Tai-ji*, and yoga are well-acknowledged practices for inner peace; if we cannot use these practices directly in the classroom, we certainly can encourage students to engage in contemplative, whole-body, whole-being experiences in other forms. *Currere* (Pinar, 1994), as a particular form of autobiographical study, combines meditative sensitivity and critical reflection. When I used it in my class as a whole-semester self-study project with social and cultural differences as the focus of reflection (Wang & Olson, 2009), it proved effective in not only bringing clarity and insights but also in promoting productive emotional work to reach a new level of multicultural awareness.

Another useful method is to role-play conflicting situations with the purpose of finding alternative paths out of conflicts. I used small group studies of cases, which were either taken from casebooks or happened in students' educational work, and asked students to address the needs of each participant in a conflicting situation. Students discuss what basic needs of each party in the conflict are reflected in the situation, think about how to negotiate and meet each person's needs without anybody taking out aggression against others, and write up an agreement among all parties to live together more peacefully. This method can be enriched by Rosenberg's (2003) nonviolent communication process, which involves four components: observing, feeling, uncovering needs, and making a specific request. The self expressing these components and receiving them from the other leads to a cycle of communication and mutual understanding. In such a process, one does not impose one's own agenda because one is working on the self, rather than blaming the other; however, neither does one assume that the other is unknown either but invites the other to participate in such a communication. Teacher educators can also learn specific techniques from Rosenberg's strategies about particular ways of questioning that encourage students to go beneath their defensiveness or aggression to understand their own needs and desires.

To establish nonviolent pedagogical relationships, the teacher educator's responsive and responsible connectedness with students is crucial to providing both support and challenge. As a responsive loving guide, the teacher educator accompanies students' difficult journey and holds on to their struggles. As a responsible, compassionate critic, the teacher educator is not afraid of being interruptive, as learning happens at the site where one resists learning. Such attentiveness to bringing the unaware potential into existence may not be pleasant immediately, but the teacher's nonviolent stance is not about being nice, but about being educative for the long-term effects of teaching–learning relationships. In my classes, the instructor and students establish discussion guidelines and expect an uncomfortable learning space from the beginning, and we work on accepting difference and dissonance as a natural element in a nonlinear curve of learning throughout the semester. I also make efforts to maximize the interactions between students and texts and among students throughout the class, to decenter the teacher's authority. I firmly believe in students' ability to unlearn the legacy of violence and construct nonviolent social relationships even if they resist my pedagogical efforts. As I improvise my teaching strategies according to students' need and the pedagogical situation each day, I have learned to hold on to students' learning curves through "pedagogical thoughtfulness" (Aoki, 2005, p. 196). Even when shutdown moments happen, I still choose to open up conversations that may not be effective at the time of eruption, but may sink in later.

It is worthwhile to mention here that a pedagogy of nonviolence is not a given ideal for others to follow; it is a rigorous process of both inner and outer work in which teacher and student must be willing to engage individually and communally to work out their unique pathways. There is no step-by-step model to follow, and the specific means, as long as they follow nonviolent principles, can be various but effective. Moreover, nonviolence usually shows its effect in the long run, so it may not work immediately in teaching situations, and when teacher educators have students for just one semester, results might not be visible at the end of the class. But over time and collectively, social justice education can be better served by a pedagogy of nonviolence.

In summary, this article critically examines the dualism in critical theory and the radicalization of the otherness in postmodern theory and proposes a nonviolent approach to social justice education with its emphasis on non-dual relationality. This approach challenges both teacher educators and (pre-service or in-service) teachers to go beyond any separate sense of the self, whether in a personal or a group sense, layer by layer, to get in tune with the interconnected pulse of life. Informed by the wisdom of *ubuntu*, Buddhism, and Taoism, I identify three important facets of nonviolence: relational dynamics of differing for one another, inner peace as the basis for outer peace, and the necessity of nonviolent means. To enact a pedagogy of nonviolence based upon such a conception of nonviolence, I address the following important aspects of educational work: The inner work of transforming difficult emotions into life-affirmative energies go hand in hand with outer work of social action; The mentality of competitiveness is dissolved for an interconnected approach to social differences; The educational means of nonviolent strategies are improvised and used to accompany students' ongoing process of learning difficult knowledge. I argue that racism, sexism, classism, homophobia, and other forms of injustice are symptoms of social violence. To heal these symptoms, we must treat the root of violence, and it takes nothing less than committed and consistent efforts to engage nonviolence pedagogy in social justice education to empty out the metanarrative of domination and to co-create a more compassionate world.

References

Addams, J. (2007). *Newer ideals of peace*. University of Illinois Press. (Original work published 1906)

Aoki, T. Ted (2005). *Curriculum in a new key: The collected works of Ted T. Aoki* (W. F. Pinar and R. L. Irwin, Eds.). Lawrence Erlbaum.

Bai, H., & Cohen, A. (2008). Breathing qi (ch'i), Following Dao (Tao). In C. Eppert & H. Wang (Eds.), *Cross-cultural studies in curriculum* (pp. 35–54). Lawrence Erlbaum.

Boler, M. (1999). *Feeling power*. Routledge.

Britzman, D. P. (1998). *Lost subjects, contested objects*. State University of New York Press.

Chan, C. S., & Treacy, M. J. (1996). Resistance in multicultural courses. *American Behavioral Scientist, 40*, 212–221.

Chizhik, E. W. (2003). Reflecting on the challenges of preparing suburban teachers for urban schools. *Education and Urban Society, 35*, 443–461.

Easwaran, E. (1997). *Gandhi the man*. Blue Mountain of Meditation. (Original work published 1972)
Ellsworth, E. (1997). *Teaching positions: Difference, pedagogy, and the power of address*. Teachers College Press.
Freire, P. (1997). *Pedagogy of the oppressed*. Continuum. (Original work published 1970)
Gay, G. (2010). *Culturally responsive teaching: Theory, research and practice* (2nd ed.). Teachers College Press.
Hershock, P. (2009). Ethics in an era of reflexive modernization. In J. Powers & C. S. Prebish (Eds.), *Destroying Mara forever: Buddhist ethics essays in honor of Damien Keown* (pp. 151–164). Snow Lion.
Howard, G. (2006). *We cannot teach what we do not know* (2nd ed.). Teachers College Press.
Jakubowski, L. M. (2001). Teaching uncomfortable topics. *Teaching Sociology, 29,* 62–79.
Jupp, J., & Slattery, Jr., P. G. (2010). Committed White male teachers and identifications. *Curriculum Inquiry, 40,* 454–474.
Kohl, H. (1991). *I won't learn from you!* Milkweed Editions.
Ladson-Billings, G. (1995). Toward a theory of culturally relevant pedagogy. *American Educational Research Journal, 32,* 465–491.
Loewen, J. (1995). *Lies my teacher told me*. Touchstone.
Lynd, S., & Lynd A. (Eds.). (1995). *Nonviolence in America*. Orbis Books.
Mandela, N. (2003). *Long walk to freedom*. Abacus. (Original work published 1994)
Martusewicz, R. A. (2001). *Seeking passage*. Teachers College Press.
Nagler, M. N. (2004). *The search for a nonviolent future*. Inner Ocean.
North, C. E. (2008). What is all this talk about "social justice"? Mapping the terrain of education's latest catchphrase. *Teachers College Record, 110,* 1182–1206.
Parkes, R. J., Gore, J. M., & Ellsworth, W. (2010). After poststructuralism: Rethinking the discourse of social justice pedagogy. In T. K. Chapman & N. Hobbel (Eds.), *Social justice pedagogy across the curriculum* (pp. 164–183). Routledge.
Pinar, W. F. (1994). *Autobiography, politics, and sexuality*. Peter Lang.
Pinar, W. F. (2009). *The worldliness of a cosmopolitan education*. Routledge.
Pipino, M. F. (2005). Resistance and the pedagogy of ethnic literature. *Multi-ethnic Literature of the United States, 30,* 175–190.
Rhone, A. (2002). Effective teaching techniques to overcome teacher resistance. *Contemporary Education, 72,* 43–46.
Rosenberg, M. B. (2003). *Nonviolent communications*. Puddle Dancer.
Sleeter, C. E., & Cornbleth, C. (2011). *Teaching with vision*. Teachers College Press.
Smith-Christopher, D. L. (Ed.). (2007). *Subverting hatred*. Orbis Books.
Todd, S. (2003). *Learning from the Other*. State University of New York Press.
Trifonas, P. (Ed.). (2003). *Pedagogies of difference*. Routledge.
Tutu, D. M. (1999). *No future without forgiveness*. Doubleday.
Van der Walt, J. L. (2010). Ubuntugogy for the 21st century. *Journal of Third World Studies, 27,* 249–266.
Venter, E. (2004). The Notion of *ubuntu* and communalism in African educational discourse. *Studies in Philosophy and Education, 23,* 149–160.

Wang, H. (2004). *The Call from the stranger on a journey home: Curriculum in a third space*. Peter Lang.

Wang, H. (2010). A zero space of nonviolence. *Journal of Curriculum Theorizing, 26*, 1–8.

Wang, H., & Olson, N. (Eds.). (2009). *A Journey to unlearn and learn in multicultural education*. Peter Lang.

Zajda, J., Majhanovich, S., & Rust, V. D. (2006). Education and social justice. In J. Zajda, S. Majhanovich, & V. D. Rust (Eds.), *Education and social justice* (pp. 1–12). Springer.

· 4 ·

CONFUCIAN SELF-CULTIVATION AND DAOIST PERSONHOOD: IMPLICATIONS FOR PEACE EDUCATION (2013)[1]

Introduction

While the contemporary age has brought unprecedented interconnectedness across the globe and in everyday life, it has also simultaneously witnessed fragmentation, conflict, and ethnic and religious warfare. Can Confucianism and Daoism, first formulated in ancient China, be useful for addressing our contemporary concerns about bringing peace out of conflict? This essay argues that the Confucian and Daoist traditions of reaching peace within in order to sustain peace outside offer us important lessons. Building harmonious connections between differences in one's personhood paves a path for negotiating interconnections across conflicting multiplicities in the outside world. In this sense, peace is not merely a diplomatic or political issue but also a fundamental educational issue since it is rooted in personal cultivation.

Peace studies as a formal program was initiated after World War II in the West. As part of it, peace education is concerned with cultivating knowledge, skills, and attitudes that can lead to peace rather than violence by way of a

---

1 This chapter is reprinted with permission of the publisher, Springer Nature. Wang, H. (2013). Confucian self-cultivation, Taoist personhood: Implications for peace education. Frontier of Education in China, 8(1), 62–79.

formal curriculum or community-based activities (Lin et al., 2008; Salomon & Cairns, 2010). Two aspects of peace education are intertwined: negating violence and promoting a culture of peace. Originally dealing with the causes of war and its prevention, peace education has recently evolved to embrace new paradigms that locate unity (Danesh, 2010) or harmony (Brantmeier & Lin, 2008) as the center of attention, shifting the focus toward transforming education for peace. Drawing upon Eastern traditions, Jing Lin (2006, 2008) emphasizes the importance of understanding peace as a process of the dynamic interplay of opposites and as a global ethic of universal love and reconciliation. The essential messages of dissolving violence and advocating peace in Confucianism and Daoism can inform today's efforts in peacemaking, peacekeeping, and peacebuilding.

In this essay, without claiming that Confucianism or Daoism can offer solutions to our contemporary issues, I examine classical writings of both philosophies to discuss what possibilities they may offer as we travel through today's complex landscapes of peace education. In particular, their central concern with personhood as the site of educational and social change is discussed as a way of rethinking peace education. Peace movements in the contemporary age are usually seen as proactive, collective efforts to end wars, challenge social or ecological injustice, or eliminate intergroup conflicts.[1] By contrast, Confucianism and Daoism locate the cultivation of inner peace as the bridge to outer peace. This essay starts with this location, situates it in historical contexts, moves to the relational issues of harmony in difference and tranquility in turbulence, and further discusses the role of leadership and governing to argue for unity between the means and end of peace education. The implications of classical Confucianism and Daoism for peace and peace education are suggested throughout the paper either explicitly or implicitly.

The Site of Personhood Between the Microcosmic and the Macrocosmic

Both Confucianism and Daoism view a person as a microcosmic universe connected with the macrocosmic universe. The movement within the inner world circulates out into the external world and vice versa so the interaction between the micro and macro levels is the key for personal and global welfare. Thus, discussions about world peace need to start with peace within. The West has long claimed the importance of the individual and usually perceived the Chinese tradition as hierarchical and suppressive of individuality; ironically, however, the location of the person as the site for relating to others and governing the world is a deeply rooted Chinese philosophical notion.

It is written in the *Dao De Jing* that "cultivated in the person, its *de* is true; cultivated in the family, its *de* is rich; cultivated in the village, its *de* lasts; cultivated in the nation, its *de* is abundant; cultivated in the world, its *de* is universal" (Chapter 54, author's translation). There are different interpretations of what *De* means in Daoism (Cline, 2004) and one of the contested points is related to whether or not *De* is moral. Some believe it has moral connotations, some believe that it is naturalistic without moral connotations, and others think that it has both moral and cosmic dimensions. In general, however, it is considered as the embodiment and expression of *Dao*, which can be related to an individual thing or an individual person. Fung (1948/1976) explains that *De* is what each individual thing obtains from the universal *Dao*, so "Te [De] is a word that means 'power' or 'virtue,' both in the moral and non-moral sense of the latter term. The Te [De] of a thing is what it naturally is" (p. 100). I think the notion of the Daoist *De* is broader than Confucian morality since it is rooted in the natural way, but there is a certain connection between Daoist *De* and the Confucian virtue based upon internal principles rather than external demands. Personal cultivation is about getting in touch with *De* and achieving *Dao* is coexistent with expressing *De* and reaching *Dao* in the family, the village, the nation, and the world.

The Great Learning, one of the Confucian classics, outlines the steps to self-cultivation in detail:

> When things are studied, knowledge is achieved. When knowledge is achieved, then one reaches sincerity of thought. When one reaches sincerity of thought, the integrity of heart comes. With the integrity of heart, the person can be cultivated. When the person is cultivated, the family life can be regulated. When the family life is regulated, the nation can be rightly governed. When the nation is rightly governed, the whole world can be made peaceful. From the emperor down to the common people, all must consider the cultivation of the person as the root of all. It cannot be that, when the root is neglected, what springs from it will be well-ordered. (1992, p. 1, author's translation)

Dao De Jing and *The Great Learning* clearly echo each other, although the process of self-cultivation in *The Great Learning* is more specifically articulated with a clear sense of flowing from one level to another level until it reaches the broadest level of the whole world, while *Dao De Jing* does not explicitly speak about the extension from one level to another. These steps depicted in *The*

Great Learning became a foundation stone of Confucianism. Moreover, Laozi's *Dao* is firstly cosmic and secondly moral, while early Confucians believed in the moral nature of the universe and elevate humanity to a higher position than other forms of existence. *Dao De Jing* clearly speaks about how *De* and *Dao* take priority over Confucian virtues (Chapter 38). The Daoist connotation of virtue goes beyond humanity since virtue also resides in what a thing naturally is. Partly for these reasons, the concentric linking of person, family, nation, and world is usually regarded as a Confucian concern.

Likewise, while "internal sagehood and external kingship" is usually regarded as a Confucian notion, the phrase first appeared in the *Zhuangzi* (Chapter 33, author's translation). Zhuangzi also radically claims that one needs to achieve authentic personhood first because the true nature of *Dao* is for governing the self, and then what is left is for governing the country and the world (Chapter 28). He privileges personhood over conducting world affairs and believes that only those who attend themselves first can be entrusted with the responsibility of governing the world. This priority of the authentic self, however, is embedded in his underlying principle of forgetting or dissolving the self in order to become one with *Dao* and thus does not indulge in self-centeredness.

The specific focuses of Confucianism and Daoism may have different twists but Confucians and Daoists share a commitment to personal cultivation as essential for both individual fulfillment and societal development. This commitment has important implications for the current concerns with peace education in the contemporary age, an age full of turbulence, conflict, and crisis, not very different from the historical period in which both Confucius and Laozi lived. Peace is usually perceived in the West as between nations or groups, but peace in Confucianism and Daoism is first and foremost about peace within each person, and in this sense, peace education is first of all about personal cultivation for peace within and without. The formulations of classical Confucianism and Daoism were responses to their own historical circumstances, but the seeds they planted are rich for growing our own visions of how to make dynamic interconnections across differences in today's world. Their unique perspectives on achieving harmony, tranquility, and peace despite turbulence offer us illuminating links for education for and through peace at various levels. Before addressing the issue of peace out of conflict, the following sections first discuss the historical contexts in which classical Confucianism and Daoism responded to the call of their time, and then briefly introduce the Confucian conception of self-cultivation and the Daoist conception of personhood.

A Brief Review of Historical Contexts

Confucianism and Daoism emerged in the Spring and Autumn and Warring States Period (770–221 BCE) when the stability of the Zhou Dynasty was lost (Fung, 1948/1976; Li & Ji, 2001; Mair, 1994). This period was also called the Eastern Zhou Dynasty. The Zhou Dynasty initially ruled through the distribution of land among nobility and the regulation of the extended family system. But that system began to break down and nobility gained so much control as to compete among one another for hegemony while the Zhou kings lost control. Gradually the status of nobility according to the bloodline was interrupted as many lost their inherited status due to all the fierce fighting. As a result, a particular class, called *Shi*, emerged and became "an influential group of scholars and political theorists who actively sought to alter the policies of the various dukes" (Mair, 1994, p. xvii). Moreover, *Shi* was composed of people from various social groups, not just the descendants of nobility, but they were all well-educated, and from this intellectual class emerged leaders of various schools of thought.

It was at the end of the Spring and Autumn Period when both Laozi and Confucius appeared on the stage (Laozi is usually considered to have lived a couple of decades earlier than Confucius), along with many other influential leaders. It is important to recognize that there are debates about whether or not Laozi was a real person and whether or not Laozi composed *Dao De Jing*, and there has not been any consensus (Gu & Guan, 1994; Mair, 1994). But the existence of *Dao De Jing* and its founding role in Daoism is beyond dispute. Faced with turmoil in family, society, politics, and culture, different scholars and philosophers expressed their respective social and political ideals and made efforts to practice these ideals when they found the support of any ruler receptive to their ideas. Daoism and Confucianism were just two of these schools of thought, and became highly influential in Chinese society and Chinese culture only in the later part of Chinese history. In a turbulent time, how to restore peace and order out of chaos became a major concern, but answers to such questions were various. Due to the scope and focus of this paper, details of these various ideas cannot be expanded on, but the fact that there were many diverse perspectives responding to similar social and personal issues tells us that historical and social contexts influence but do not determine individual perspectives.

Both classical Confucianism and Daoism were concerned with inner and outer peace as a response to their historical time, and their shared intention, first of all, to influence rulers who could settle the turbulence in the world as sage-kings, if they cultivated inner peace. But the channels to accomplish such a task were not the same between early Confucians and Daoists. This difference might be partially due to which historical heritage they drew upon for further advancement. For instance, Xiaopeng Zhu (2009) argues that Confucianism drew inspiration from the hierarchal and patriarchal society of three ancient dynasties especially the Western Zhou Dynasty, but Daoism went back before the three dynasties to reach into the ancient Chinese matrilineal culture for revelation. Sometimes Confucianism is perceived as *Yang* and Daoism is perceived as *Yin* in Chinese philosophy so they form complementary and interactive dynamics for influencing Chinese society as a whole.

While Confucius and Laozi are usually considered contemporary to each other, so are another pair of leaders in classical Confucianism and Daoism, Mencius and Zhuangzi (there are also debates about Zhuangzi as a historical person). The Spring and Autumn Period led to the Warring States Period in which the larger states formed during the earlier chaos competed through warfare and Chinese society further deteriorated to a state where all traditions were in disarray (Li & Ji, 2001). Mencius and Zhuangzi lived in the middle of the Warring States Period and they were both disgusted by the bloody social conditions of that time. It is significant that both philosophers paid more attention to the individual person than earlier founders of each school, even though their attention was directed toward somewhat different ends. While the *Analects of Confucius* and the *Dao De Jing* both addressed rulers and urged them to become sage-kings who could bring peace to the world, Mencius put more emphasis on common people's individual development (Mair, 1994), and Zhuangzi emphasized the achievement of individual freedom over the governing of society (Ding, 2004). The ruthless governing style of state rulers at that time without any consideration of ordinary people's interests or needs provided a background against which Mencius's further formulation of principles of humane governing for a better society and Zhuangzi's rebellion against any social constrain upon personal freedom were developed.

This brief historical review tells us that the Confucian and Daoist concerns with inner peace and outer peace emerged from one of the most turbulent historical periods in China. Against the existing destructive environment, these masters carved out a basis for initiating engaging social transformation to achieve harmony: personal cultivation. In today's world, facing the threat of unprecedented ecological crisis, social conflict, and nuclear destruction, we may well learn from Confucianism and Daoism that the starting point of peace education is not the world itself, but rather it is within the self. Next, Confucian and Daoist concerns with personal cultivation are discussed.

The Confucian Tradition of Self-Cultivation

For Confucius, the purpose of self-cultivation is to bring peace to others and the whole world (*Analects of Confucius*, 14.42). Becoming a sage inside and becoming a king outside are inherently related, and self-governance goes hand in hand with the governing of the world. While self-cultivation is fundamental, the self is not an isolated entity but is always in social relationships and cosmic interconnections. The relationship between self and the other can be best stated in the following principle: "A *junzi* wishing to be established himself seeks to establish others; wishing to be expanded himself seeks also to expand others" (*Analects of Confucius*, 6.30, author's translation). *Junzi* (translated as nobleman, gentleman, superior man, man of perfect virtue, or exemplary person), is the Confucian ideal of a cultivated person.

Such a relational viewpoint of the Confucian self opens an important gate for reaching peace through connecting with others rather than being at war with others. The reciprocal relationship between self and other requires the avoidance of violence. *The Analects* states, "do not do to others what you do not want done to yourself" (15.24, author's translation). Thus, Confucius not only promotes a mutually advanced relationship between self and other but also refuses to impose the will of the self onto others. As Fingarette (1979) points out, *Junzi* seeks to actualize the Way but does not impose anything so that "an ideal community in which there is no coercion or imposition of one person's will upon another" (p. 136) becomes possible. Confucius speaks directly against using force and military violence (*Analects of Confucius*, 7.21) and advocates peacemaking in conducting affairs between states (*Analects of Confucius*, 14.16). For him, government through *Ren*, through moral virtue, through personal exemplars, is the way to promote peace in the world.

The Confucian framework of personal cultivation involves an extension from the self to the other, from the internal to the external, and from the near to the far. The steps of personal cultivation outlined in *The Great Learning* demonstrate a complicated encircling web of relationships in which knowledge pursuit is integrated with moral consciousness and the extension from the near to the far is coupled with the fulfillment of the near under the far. In fulfilling oneself, the relational potentiality of things, others, and the world is also fulfilled. The fulfillment of the world in turn deepens and advances self-realization. Here individual and society become both means and end for each other.

The interdependent relationship between self and society does not mean the loss of individual integrity in interconnections as criticism of Confucianism often claims. Both Confucius (*Analects of Confucius*, 6.17; 7.16) and Mencius (*Mencius*, 6.2) speak about a strong inner sense of moral mission despite difficulties in external circumstances. It is necessary to follow moral integrity rather than society, especially when the social conditions are incongruent with the Confucian ethical, moral, and political ideals. Both de Bary (1998) and Tu (1985) challenge the common assumption that the Confucian self aims at serving collective intentions and needs. It seems that the debates about whether the Confucian self seeks social harmony or self-realization miss the essential Confucian teaching about the nonduality between self and society. In the long run, social harmony is rooted in internal harmony and self-realization is dependent on the degree to which a society makes it possible, even though self and society can be at odds with each other. Such a Confucian viewpoint was the platform for both personal transformation and societal reform in wartime China.

How can one achieve inner harmony and promote outer peace with others and between states? Confucius advocates both *Ren* (translated as love, humane-ness, reciprocity, benevolence, perfect virtue, and so forth) and *Li* (translated as ritual or propriety). He thinks *Ren* is the core content of *Li* while *Li* carries the best part of historical legacy. Different from Daoism, which perceives humans as natural beings, Confucius believes that humanity has unique and superior qualities and that moral consciousness and the ability to create civilization make human beings different from other forms of existence.

Ren, is central to both Confucius and Mencius as the ideal quality for both *Junzi* and society. For Confucius, practicing *Ren* depends on oneself rather than others (*Analects of Confucius*, 12.1); he also sees it as a task that is accomplishable for anybody who is willing to try: "Is *ren* far from me? I wish to be virtuous, then *ren* comes at hand" (7.30, author's translation). Making an important link between *Li* and *Ren*, Confucius considers a loving filial relationship as the basis of *Ren*, which requires the individual to extend familial feelings to others in the world. Mencius's five human relationships (father and son, ruler and minister, husband and wife, old and young, and between friends) clearly shows that family relationships are the cornerstone of social networks. The filial relationship is listed first. The image of ruler and minister is often evoked as that of father and son, and loyalty between friends is likened to brotherly affection.

Mencius further develops *Ren* as universal human nature and considers the task of practicing *Ren* in a turbulent time as returning to the original source of goodness and restoring peace to the world. Mencius argues that the four feelings of commiseration, shame, reverence, and the sense of right versus wrong are inherent in everybody (*Mencius*, 11.6). Thus *Ren* becomes ontological, and Mencius stresses the imperative of moral cultivation at the personal level in order to change society at large. For both Confucius and Mencius, *Ren* is much more than reason but is an overarching scheme for emotional, ethical, moral, social, and spiritual growth. Touching people's hearts rather than enacting legal regulations or engaging in military competition is their concern.

Confucius and Mencius share fundamental humanistic concerns. Their notion of self-cultivation is intricately linked with societal welfare and its essential moral nature is crucial to achieving inner peace and world peace. The Confucian interdependent relationships between self and other, and between individual and society lay a solid foundation for making nonviolent connections, and this notion of interdependence is an important building block for peace education as both means and end.

The Daoist Tradition of Personhood

Due to their different interpretations of the role of humanity in the universe and the effects of civilization, the Daoist sense of personhood is different from the Confucian self even though both perceive the individual person as the micro-body of the universe. For Laozi, the individual person is a natural being and the highest level of personal achievement is to go back to the original source of life and follow the way of nature. Different from the Confucian view of humans' occupying a superior position in the universe, Laozi lists humanity along with three other important aspects: heaven, earth, and Dao: "Human follows the way of the earth; the earth follows the way of the heaven; the heaven follows Dao; Dao follows the way of nature" (*Dao De Jing*, Chapter 25, author's translation). Here humanity is not more valuable than other aspects but must be in unity with nature. The literal translation of the Chinese for nature is "self-so" or "self-so-ness." To borrow a phrase from contemporary chaos and complexity theory, it is self-organization. This self-so-ness is the Daoist key to everything.

Following the way of nature means respecting and caring for every person and everything and seeking the growth of the whole as well as providing a good atmosphere for the growth of every inanimate and animate thing and human relationship in the family, village, nation, and state. The spontaneity and creativity of self-organization both in the human and natural world is enabled by "the movement of the deep underlying harmony that interfuses and interpenetrates between man and man [sic], between men and things" (Chang, 1963, p. 93). It is this sense of movement that the next section will address to highlight the Daoist possibility for going beyond conflicts to reach peace.

With such a belief in nature, it is not surprising that Daoism questions societal conventions that block the spontaneous movement of nature and rigorously calls for unlearning those ideas and practices. So Laozi paradoxically speaks about learning leading to more knowledge but unlearning getting nearer to the Dao: "The pursuit of learning results in daily increase [of knowledge]; following the *Dao* leads to daily decrease [of convention]" (*Dao De Jing*, Chapter 48, own translation). Different from the Confucian emphasis on moral values and rituals, Daoism challenges all conventional notions regarding strength, achievement, and knowledge and seeks to go beyond all distinctions, for instance, between right and wrong, good and evil. For Laozi, only after *Dao* is lost do *Ren*, righteousness, ritual, intellect, and trustworthiness become important (*Dao De Jing*, Chapter 38). He does not necessarily negate the importance of *Ren*, but rather insists that what is more essential is *Dao*, which cannot be achieved without going beyond *Ren*. Zhuangzi claims:

> If one has high morals without suppressing desires, cultivates the self without talking about *ren* and righteousness, governs the nation without pursuing success and fame, has a free spirit without retreating into sea and river, has a long life without making efforts to improve the blood circulation and to soften the body, one cares for nothing but gains everything with good things coming to his way; this is the Dao of heaven and earth, the virtue of the sage. (*Zhuangzi*, Chapter 15 "Regulating Consciousness," author's translation)

The Daoist sage seems to follow a reverse route to wisdom, leadership, and peace.

Does Daoism have a tradition of personhood? This question can become an issue for debate. Even with Confucianism, it is also controversial whether or not a sense of the self exists. Certainly, it does not exist in the sense of the self that positions the individual person as a separate entity, and the Confucian construction of the individual is not separate from others or the collective but is interdependent with society. With Daoism, it is even more elusive, as Zhuangzi's notion of the authentic person ultimately seeks to dissolve the ego in order to become united with *Dao*. His notion of the self becomes paradoxical: selfless self-realization. But in this nondual sense of the self and the universe lies another perspective of personhood. Laozi's notion of sagehood and Zhuangzi's notion of authentic personhood all speak to a person's enlightenment, although Laozi speaks more about the government of the world and Zhuangzi speaks more about achieving personal freedom (Sun et al., 2004).

Laozi's vision of a sage is that a sage is first to be compassionate, second to be frugal, and third to refuse to be ahead of all in the world. For Laozi, compassion leads to bravery, frugality leads to profusion, and refusal to be the first leads to becoming the chief of all. On the contrary, bravery without compassion, profusion without frugality, and occupying the foremost position without taking the hindmost position lead to death (*Dao De Jing*, Chapter 67). Laozi is well known for his advocacy of softness to overcome strength and of positioning oneself on lowly ground. Doing so, however, leads to success rather than failure. Laozi claims that the sage does not praise himself, does not pursue anything to an excessive degree, and does not compete with others in the world. But precisely because of his non-competition, nobody in the world can compete against the sage who follows the natural course of success (*Dao De Jing*, Chapters 22, 29). This positioning is related to Laozi's dialectic worldview in which opposites go toward each other. From here it is not difficult to discern his position against war, military advances, and man-made force to impose any will upon people and the world. Compatible with such a natural course, peace of mind is not achieved by intellectual understanding or emotional attachment but by achieving insight into things as the way they are. For Laozi, if one follows the way of nature in its movement, opposites become a part of the dance of life and nonviolence is the key to the secret of sustaining life energy for human welfare.

According to Huai Zhen Ding (2004), at least four steps are essential to achieving authentic personhood for Zhuangzi. First, one needs to purify one's heart to reach a state of emptiness and quietude. This requires dissolving worries and concerns so one can return to the way of nature. Second, one needs to sit quietly and forget self, things, and the distinction between self and things so as to gradually get in touch with *Dao*. Here lies the paradoxical state of forgetting the self in order to cultivate the self's compliance to *Dao*. Third, one is no longer influenced by the vicissitude of gain and loss, or sadness and happiness, but can adapt to any change freely. Fourth, one persists in efforts to go beyond the secular world, beyond everything under heaven, and beyond life and death until one reaches the unique *Dao* in the clarity of the morning light. This process is called "tranquility in turbulence," in which one reaches a carefree state in union with *Dao* after passing through all the turmoil. From this sketch, we can see that the effort to go beyond all conventional concerns is simultaneous with a deepened relationship with *Dao*. The inner peace is not accomplished by escaping or retreating from the world but by the rigorous process of liberating oneself from all the external and internal constraints. This rigor is by no means less demanding than the Confucian advocacy for persistent involvement.

Attaining a peaceful state of mind is the basis for bringing peace to the world. With inner calmness, the Daoist sage can settle that which is restless. In a low position, one draws people and enables others to engage in personal and social transformation for peace. Daoist wisdom is not only contrary to the mainstream of modern Western traditions, but is also often seen as backward and ill-fitting for today's China. As the author argues elsewhere (Wang, 2008), however, Daoism has sustained Chinese civilization, and getting in touch with its vital energy is important for today's education. In particular, its teachings about nonviolence are essential for peace education.

Harmony in Difference and Tranquility in Turbulence: Peace Out of Conflict

Their notion of personhood is a microcosmic that embodies the macrocosmic subjects of Confucianism and Daoism to the critique that they submerge individuality in holism and suppress personal freedom. However, in this interdependent viewpoint lies the capacity to see a bigger picture and, rather than repressing difference, carve out of conflict a generative space that makes inner peace and world peace possible. Harmony and peace are often perceived as static rather than dynamic and, in the Western critiques of Chinese philosophy, as serving the collective at the expense of freedom. However, the Confucian notion of harmony in difference and the Daoist notion of tranquility in turbulence present a quite different picture. This section discusses these dynamics in relation to peace education.

Confucius says, "A *junzi* seeks harmony not sameness; an inferior man seeks sameness not harmony" (*Analects of Confucius*, 13.23, author's translation). This sense of harmony, quite contrary to the popular criticism of Confucianism as a centralized and unitary system, incorporates rather than rejects difference and implies variety rather than conformity. According to Chang Chun Wang (2002), this principle of harmony in difference is important to Confucius' thought and marks its essential openness.

Harmony in difference has several aspects that contribute to peace out of conflict. First, harmony is opposite to sameness and does not come from agreement or blind loyalty but from negotiating with difference within and reaching balance between the Confucian Way and current circumstances. When inner balance is achieved within a person by self-cultivation, a Confucian can deal with external conditions in accordance with the Confucian path. Second, harmony is not conformity. The rejection of sameness is a refusal to follow the mainstream customs, practices, and assumptions of a chaotic age when they do not follow Confucian principles. Both Confucius and Mencius urge *Junzi* to cultivate an internal sense of what is good and what is right. When the external conditions do not allow the actualization of inner principles, *Junzi* should not follow others' steps. Third, harmony is dynamic and creative as it moves through differences to achieve balance. In the end, the inner peace of a person may not be compatible with external circumstances. Confucius and Mencius believe that retreat from the public world in order to preserve principle is important, and they also advocate sacrificing oneself for the sake of the Confucian way when necessary. In either case, what cannot be given up is the Confucian way. Harmony does not avoid conflict but works through conflict to set peace in motion.

Laozi also emphasizes the role of harmony, "knowing harmony reaches constancy; knowing constancy brings the illumination of insights" (*Dao De Jing*, Chapter 55, author's translation). Harmony is reached in the dynamics of opposites, or in Zhuangzi's phrase, "tranquility in turbulence." The notion of *Yin* and *Yang* in classical Confucianism is interactive and the privilege of *Yang* over *Yin* was developed later. But in Daoism, the interaction between *Yin* and *Yang* and the creative potential of such an interaction is essential. Quietude, stillness, tranquility of the mind, and peace of the world all come from the interplay between opposite cosmic forces. *Dao De Jing* is full of teachings about how opposites mutually transform each other. Opposites do not become enemies to compete against and win over the other or even eliminate the other. The *Tai-ji* symbol illustrates well an inherently built-in existence of

Yang within *Yin* and of *Yin* within *Yang*. When *Yin* and *Yang* are interconnected in this way, they cannot be at war with each other, as the killing of the other implies the killing of the self. It is the interaction of two opposite forces that holds the key to harmony. In this sense, peace itself is in movement rather than a static state of mind or human affairs. As Edward J. Brantmeier and Jing Lin (2008) argue, "Peace is to be understood as both a process and result of balance and harmony that is negotiated and renegotiated over time. It inherently transcends duality and dichotomy" (p. xv).

Since the Daoist notion of harmony and peace incorporates difference, opposition, and multiplicity, being able to see conflicting sides of the same issue and follow the two courses at the same time in an interconnected web of life is important. When situated in a broader context, what is initially perceived as conflict becomes a connected part of the whole. Zhuangzi's story about the monkey and the monkey trainer is an interesting example:

> Once upon a time, there was a monkey keeper who was feeding little chestnuts to his charges. "I'll give you three in the morning and four in the evening," he told them. All the monkeys were angry. "All right, then," said the keeper: "I will give you four in the morning and three in the evening." All the monkeys were happy with this arrangement. Without adversely affecting either the name or the reality of the amount that he fed them, the keeper acted in accordance with the feelings of the monkeys. He too recognized the mutual dependence of "this" and "that." Consequently, the sage harmonizes the right and wrong of things and rests at the center of the celestial potter's wheel. (*Zhuangzi*, Translated by Mair, 1994, pp. 16–17)

This ability to follow two courses at the same time and thus to bring the freedom to turn to either the left or the right depending upon the circumstances demonstrates a deep insight into the ways things are in the bigger picture and goes beyond the confinement of either right or wrong. When dualism is transcended, the tensionality of conflict is pulled back into the whole to bring peace to turbulence. The situation is solved with a shift of the lens, a lens that sees through problems to bring clarity and open alternatives. This Daoist playfulness with paradoxes and contradictions emanates a sense of humor that relieves the fixation of any orthodoxy, whether it is the conventional notion of ego or the popular norms of the society. Tranquility in the midst of turmoil is full of smiles and laughter; peace and humor go hand in hand.

Harmony in difference and tranquility in turbulence embody the capacity to see through conflicts for shared humanity, but without sacrificing independence and freedom. Peace is not about reaching consensus or a fixed course but about seeing conflicting courses at the same time and searching for a route that leads to win-win situation for all parties. Peace education is not about transmitting fixed knowledge or skills but about cultivating a capacity to understand the dynamic interplay of all factors in a situation in order to come up with interdependent strategies that evoke the peaceful aspects of all parties. In such an approach to peace and peace education, co-creating a shared life is not dependent upon eliminating differences but upon promoting nonviolent relational dynamics that draw out the best part of all participants in a community.

Inner Peace Reaching Outer Peace in Governing and Leadership

The inner peace of Confucian and Daoist sages is brought forth to influence the world through their respective visions of good government. Confucianism advocates government through *Ren* while Daoism advocates government through *Wuwei*. These notions challenge teachers and teacher educators to examine their roles in educating students and, particularly in peace education, to enact peaceful exemplars in their work.

In Confucianism, the moral orientation of *Ren* is inherently related to social progress. Government through *Ren* is accomplished by a Confucian sage who cultivates the supreme virtues within his heart and exercises inner sagacity to meet outer kingliness. This kingly way is the way of moral power. A benevolent government intends to reach out for people and lead by evoking positive responses from people rather than by legal or military force. Influencing people by moral persuasion without coercion is essential to Confucian governing. When Zigong asks about Confucius' choices among three conditions for an effective government—sufficient food, arms for defense, and the common people's confidence in their leaders—Confucius lists common people's confidence as the first priority (*Analects of Confucius*, 12.7). Similarly, for Mencius (*Mencius*, 4.1), opportunities presented by heaven or earth cannot compete with the united power of people, and this unity comes from governing through *Ren*. The control of the state border, the difficult barriers of mountains and rivers, and the strength of arms are, none of them, equal to the effects of governing through *Ren*.

The Confucian avoidance of force not only includes military force but also includes other forms of force such as legal force. For Mencius, caring for people is the most important task for governing; if people do bad things due to poverty but government punishes people legally, such a mode of governing is equal to framing the common people for committing crimes (Mencius, 5.3). When conflicts are dealt with by underlying humane principles of morality, the mutually enhanced relationship between the part and the whole (and among parts) can be promoted to achieve long-term peaceful effects.

Laozi's governing principle is *Wuwei* (see *Dao De Jing*, Chapters 2, 3, 37, 57, & 63). Although *Wuwei* literally means "non-action," it does not mean doing nothing. David Loy (1985) reads it as nondual action. *Wuwei* in *Dao De Jing* is coupled with its opposite, *Wubuwei*, which means being free to do anything (Chapters 37, 48). When a sage governor follows the *Dao* of nature, success comes without imposition. Laozi says, "Dao holds on to *wuwei*; yet through it everything is done. If nobility and kings can keep it, everything will transform itself" (*Dao De Jing*, Chapter 37, author's translation). *Wuwei* leads to the transformation of everything but does not force any change. To accumulate strength, like water flowing downhill, *Wuwei* keeps a low position.

From this position, the Daoist commitment to nonviolence is made evident and Daoism has a unique emphasis on non-possession, tranquility, spontaneity, and gentleness. Both Laozi and Zhuangzi are opposed to the use of warfare in government. Laozi affirms that the Daoist sage cannot rely on the force of arms for governing because such aggression is a curse and will eventually lead to decay. What is against Dao will perish (*Dao De Jing*, Chapter 30). He further claims that victory in battle should be commemorated with a mourning ritual rather than glorified by celebration (Chapter 31) and that "when two armies match each other in force, the one holding compassion will win" (Chapter 69, author's translation).

If conflicts should not be resolved by combat, the Daoist leader enables nonviolence by starting with what the common people want: "The sage does not have a selfish heart; he considers the heart of the people as his heart" (*Dao De Jing*, Chapter 49, author's translation). While the Confucian extension of *Ren* from self to other and further to the world runs the risk of seeing one's own principles and ideals as good for others, Laozi's sage king does not attempt to control the common people but gives them space for personal and social engagements. Laozi envisions the power of the sage as embedded in returning to the original source of nature: "I adopt *wuwei*, yet the people transform themselves; I love quietude, yet the people correct themselves; I do not interfere, yet the people enrich themselves; I do not desire, yet the people return to the state of nature" (*Dao De Jing*, Chapter 57, author's translation). With the nourishing of life as its fundamental purpose, Daoism enables inner and outer peace through a path less traveled.

The Confucian and Daoist styles of leadership teach educators important lessons about uniting the means and end in peace education. When educating for peace is not engaged through peaceful means, the message cannot fulfill its own potential. In schools and educational settings, various forms of violence are practiced in the name of serving students' best interests: labeling and tracking of students, focusing on developing students' intellectual power at the expense of emotional and spiritual growth, rewarding students' obedience rather than their critical thinking, demanding nationalism and glorifying war, to just list a few. But they are impositional rather than educational. And they exist both in Chinese and American schools and colleges in different forms. If we locate peace education under such an impositional mode of pedagogy and in such an institutional system, the message of peace is already lost before it reaches students' ears. Educational systems, teaching contents, and pedagogical relationships all need to undergo radical transformation if we are to enact a peace education which locates wholeness, integrity, complexity, embodiment, and freedom at the center of educational practices. Peace education involves intellectual, emotional, social, aesthetic, and spiritual cultivation of personhood situated in history and society to promote a culture of nonviolence.

On a cautious note, achieving inner peace and world peace in the contemporary age cannot fully come from furthering any one tradition but lies in a dynamic interaction of different perspectives and positions. That is why both Confucianism and Daoism are discussed; historically Chinese culture, philosophy, and politics have benefitted from the interaction between both—sometimes in resonance but most of the time in conflict—in responding to the needs of particular contexts. Moreover, both traditions have their limitations, and Neo-Confucianism and Neo-Daoism have emerged in contemporary contexts to address those limitations and learn from the strength of other traditions. Neither of them can be the key to unlocking the complexity of contemporary transnational, cross-cultural, globalized society; even the complementary combination of the two may not be adequate. Dialoguing with Western thought and other Asian philosophies is a work that must be done, but cannot be covered in this essay. Advocacy of nonviolence and peace is part of the best worldwide tradition that we need to regenerate (Smith-Christopher, 1998; Wang, in press). It transcends national or cultural boundaries. We need to look more closely at the inter-space created by the mobile world in which we live now in order to create multiple pathways of nonviolence and peace education. In other words, "a third space" (Wang, 2004) holding transnational hybrid movements and inter-civilizational dialogues offers new promise in a new age. But in the context of Western education, which knows little about Confucianism and Daoism, we need to learn more from both in order to participate in both local and global dynamics of peace and peace education.

Note

1 See the autobiography of Leymah Gbowee, *Mighty be Our Powers*, a leader of the Liberian peace movement, for how peace among women activists became impossible after the war ended without achieving personal peace inside; the end of the war did not necessarily mean the beginning of peace.

References

Brantmeier, E. J., & Lin, J. (2008). Introduction: Towards forgiving a positive, transformative paradigm for peace education. In J. Lin, E. J. Brantmeier & C. Bruhn (Eds.), *Transforming education for peace* (pp. xiii–xviii). Information Age Publishing.

Chang, C. Y. (1963). *Creativity and Daoism: A study of Chinese philosophy, art, and poetry*. Harper Colophon Books.

Cline, E. M. (2004). Two interpretations of "de" in the Daodejing. *Journal of Chinese Philosophy*, 31(2), 219–233. https://doi.org/10.1111/j.1540-6253.2004.00151.x

Danesh, H. B. (2010). Unity-based peace education. In G. Salomon & E. Cairns (Eds.), *Handbook on peace education* (pp. 253–268). Psychology Press.

de Bary, W. T. (1998). *Asian values and human rights: A Confucian communitarian perspective*. Harvard University Press.

Ding, H. Z. (2004). 从尘世的超越到精神的逍遥 [From the transcendence of the secular world to the spiritual freedom]. 中国哲学 [*Chinese Philosophy*], 3, 28–35.

Fingarette, H. (1979). The problem of the self in the "Analects." *Philosophy East and West*, 29(2), 129–140.

Fung, Y. L. (1976). *A short history of Chinese philosophy*. The Free Press. (Original work published 1948)

Gu, L., & Guan, T. (1994). 老子十日谈 [*Talking about Laozi in ten days*]. 安徽文艺出版社 [Anhui Literature & Art Publishing House].

The great learning. (1992). In C. D. Liu Chongde & Z. Y. Luo (Eds.), B. J. Yang (Trans.), 四书 [*The four books*] (pp. 2–21). 湖南出版社 [Hunan Publishing House].

Li, R. L., & Ji, N. L. (2001). 修身, 齐家, 治国, 平天下新论: 中国传统整体主义价值观的历史理性与现代价值 [*Self-cultivation, managing family, governing the nation, and bring peace to the world*]. 天津社会科学院出版社 [Tianjin Social Science Institute Press].

Lin, J. (2006). *Love, peace, and wisdom in education*. Rowman & Littlefield Education.

Lin, J. (2008). Constructing a global ethic of universal love and reconciliation. In Lin, J., Brantmeier, E. J., & C. Bruhn (Eds.), *Transforming education for peace* (pp. 301–315). Information Age Publishing.

Lin, J., Brantmeier, E. J., & Bruhn, C. (Eds.). (2008). *Transforming education for peace*. Information Age Publishing.

Loy, D. (1985). Wei-wu-wei: Nondual action. *Philosophy East and West, 35*(1), 73–87.

Mair, V. H. (1994). Introduction. In Zhuangzi, *Wandering on the way: Early Taoist tales and parables of Chuang Tzu* (pp. xvii–xliii). University of Hawai'i Press.

Salomon, G., & Cairns, E. (Eds.). (2010). *Handbook on peace education*. Psychology Press.

Smith-Christopher, D. L. (Ed.). (1998). *Subverting hatred*. Orbis Books.

Sun, Y. K., Lu, J. H., & Liu, M. F. (2004). 道家与中国哲学 [*Daoism and Chinese philosophy*]. 人民出版社 [People Publishing House].

Tu, W. M. (1985). *Confucian thought: Selfhood as creative transformation*. State University of New York Press.

Wang, C. C. (2002). 和而不同: 比较教育的跨文化对话 [*Harmony in difference: Cross-cultural dialogues in comparative education*]. 首都师范大学出版社 [Capital Normal University Press].

Wang, H. (2004). *The call from the stranger on a journey home: Curriculum in a third space*. Peter Lang.

Wang, H. (2008). The strength of the feminine, lyrics of Chinese women's self, and the power of education. In C. Eppert & H. Y. Wang (Eds.), *Cross-cultural studies in curriculum* (pp. 313–333). Lawrence Erlbaum.

Wang, H. (in press). A nonviolent perspective on internationalizing curriculum studies. In W. F. Pinar (Ed.), *The international handbook of curriculum research* (2nd ed.). Routledge.

Zhu, X. P. (2009). 论当代道家哲学研究的新境域 [New realms in contemporary Taoist philosophical studies]. 江西社会科学 [*Jiangxi Social Sciences*], 6, 50–56.

Zhuangzi. (1994). *Wandering on the way: Early Taoist Tales and Parables of Chuang Tzu* (V. H. Mair, Trans.). University of Hawai'i Press.

· 5 ·

A NONVIOLENT PERSPECTIVE ON INTERNATIONALIZING CURRICULUM STUDIES (2014)[1]

> I have not the shadow of a doubt that any man or woman can achieve what I have, if he or she would make the same effort and cultivate the same hope and faith.
>
> —Mahatma Gandhi

Nonviolence as a political movement has dramatically drawn worldwide attention in recent years. Curiously though, compared to the proliferation of such discussions in political and social realms, there is a relative silence on the role of nonviolence in the realm of education, except on those occasions when tragedies occur (e.g., see the special issue of *Harvard Educational Review*, Fall 2007). Perhaps this silence is due to the narrow definition of nonviolence as peaceful uprising against social injustice, dictatorship, and colonization. Perhaps it is due to the nature of schooling which, in many nations, is incompatible with the message of nonviolence (Galtung, 2008). Perhaps the silence is due to misunderstanding nonviolence as soft and passive. Perhaps, I also

---

1 This chapter is reprinted with permission of Taylor & Francis Group LLC; permission conveyed through Copyright Clearance Center, Inc. Wang, H. (2014). A nonviolent perspective on internationalizing curriculum studies. In W. F. Pinar (Ed.), *The international handbook of curriculum research* (2nd ed.) (pp. 69–76). New York: Routledge.

think, it is due to our own implication in the logic of control that renders nonviolence unthinkable and unimaginable. Whatever the reasons may be, it is time for the field of curriculum studies to embrace nonviolence as an educational vision. It is long overdue. The recent internationalization of curriculum studies through the intellectual and organizational work of the International Association for the Advancement of Curriculum Studies (IAACS) and its various national affiliates provides a creative site for cultivating such a possibility. But it is a possibility that can only be realized by laboring in the field nonviolently.

Since the notion of nonviolence is underdeveloped in the field of education, I will start this essay with conceptual issues; then I will discuss three approaches to nonviolence education, and finally, further address the nonviolent relational dynamics of the local, the national, and the international. This work draws upon not only international wisdom traditions but also international nonviolence activism to envision nonviolence as a guiding principle for internationalizing curriculum studies.

What Is Nonviolence?

Both as an idea and a way of co/living, nonviolence has existed throughout human history in many different traditions (Lynd & Lynd, 2006; Smith-Christopher, 2007; Zinn, 2002). As an English translation of the Sanskrit word, *Ahimsa*, however, nonviolence is less than a century old (Nagler, 2004). An important principle in Indian traditions including Hinduism, Jainism, and Buddhism, *Ahimsa* means doing no harm and being kind to all living beings. *Ahimsa* is the absence of violence in word, thought, and deed, and its basis is the unity of all life. Michael Nagler (2004) argues that the English translation of *Ahimsa*, due to the negation of *himsa* (which means desiring or intending to harm), conveys a negative sense of the term "nonviolence." As a result, the positive quality of nonviolence is somewhat obscured in its English translation. However, "unlike the English situation, in Sanskrit abstract nouns often name a fundamental positive quality indirectly, by negating its opposite" (p. 44). Sunanda Y. Shastri and Yajneshwar S. Shastri (2007) affirm that "*Ahimsa* is a positive doctrine of love, friendship, and equality among all living beings of the universe" (p. 59). Here we can see that nonviolence is a way of living everyday life, not merely a response or reaction to violence or war in dramatic situations.

Arguing that nonviolence is fundamentally a positive force, Nagler (2010) further defines it as:

> a powerful method for harmonizing relationships with people, and other forms of life, for the establishment of justice and the ultimate well-being of all parties. It draws its power from awareness of the profound truth that all cultures, modern science, and common experience bear witness: that all life is an interconnected whole—is one.

Based upon a sense of interconnectedness, nonviolence evokes the compassionate and affiliating aspects of humanity to not only transform negative energies or dissolve violence but also enact mutually beneficial relational dynamics for the well-being of all members in a community, including nonhuman life. This sense of affirming fellowship and shared life can be found in many philosophical, religious, and ethical traditions such as the Christian principle of "love your enemy," the African notion of *ubuntu* in its relational ontology (Tutu, 1999), the Chinese notion of *Tao* in the interdependent movement of opposite forces (Wang, 2004; Zhu, 2009), or various indigenous peacemaking traditions in North America (Smith-Christopher, 2007).

Affirming the human capacity for nonviolence does not deny the existence of psychic and social violence in multiple dimensions across different scales. Just as many a spiritual tradition has a core principle of nonviolence, there is always a contested interpretation of the same tradition through violence as well (Smith-Christopher, 2007). Much of psychoanalysis is based upon the notion of psychic aggression as part of humanity. Current social, cultural, and ecological disasters are testimonies to various forms of violence. Precisely because we have co-existing narratives of violence and nonviolence, the aspect that is actualized in reality more fully will depend on which course—nonviolence or violence—we choose to follow. If we intentionally cultivate nonviolence to its full potential, the world will become more nonviolent and loving.

The root cause of violence is dualism (of mind and body) and the sense of separateness (of self and other) (Bai & Cohen, 2008; Shastri & Shastri, 2007). Control of and domination over *the other* (whether this other is individual, group, nation, or an ecological other) as the result of such a dualistic split feeds the cycle of violence. Here violence does not merely refer to physical violence but includes many realms, such as intellectual, emotional, spiritual, social, and cultural violence (Wang, 2010), and includes both individual and structural violence. To treat the root of violence, to dissolve its fundamental mechanism, and to work *through* the knot of violence take nothing less than nonviolence. In the case of gendered violence, for example, Allan G. Johnson (2005) argues, "there is no way around or over [patriarchy]—the only way out is through" (p. 232). We cannot ignore the social reality of patriarchy, neither can we use another mode of domination to destroy it, but we must work *through* it. To undo the mechanism of violence in its domination, we must confront and transcend the psychic and social dualism in such a way that the cycle of control and domination can be broken. Racism, sexism, classism, homophobia, colonization, imperialism, and other forms of violence are all caught in such a cycle. Only nonviolent pathways can work *through* violence to unravel the knot and carve out lines of interconnections.

As a positive force, nonviolence is *both* active *and* receptive. One of the misconceptions about nonviolence is that it is too soft and passive. So entrenched in the logic of control and aggression, especially in the United States, we often associate the evocation of nonviolence with being soft, despite the long-standing American tradition of nonviolence in feminist, civil rights, and other social movements (Cooney & Michalowski, 1987; Howlett & Lieberman, 2008). A person, a group, or a nation is *either* tough *or* soft, and there is no other alternative. But there *are* alternatives: nonviolence activism (Sharp, 2005; Stiehm, 2006; Zinn, 2002) is based upon compassion.

Nonviolence is not soft but radical in its denouncement of all forms of violence: Even though political leaders repeatedly evoked the ideals of democracy, justice, freedom, or even peace to lead armies into war, none of them could use the ideal of nonviolence as an excuse. Nonviolence does not accept sacrificing others' interests in order to serve one's own interest in any disguised way. And its active nature blends with its receptive quality to form a particular mode of strength capable of enduring attacks from inside and outside. Without the capacity for receptiveness, there is no capacity for compassion. In our dualistic world, we split active and passive, or aggressive and receptive, as if the two poles cannot be compatible. But reception is an action, and it takes more effort for such a response than for an impulsive aggressive reaction. By combining activeness with receptiveness, nonviolence shows us a different path, a more sustainable and humane way.

Nonviolence can be enacted not only from bottom to top, but also from top to bottom as a way of governing. The modern use of the term "nonviolence" has mainly referred to grassroots political uprisings against authority, such as Indian independence and American civil rights movements. But Nagler (2004) points out that nonviolent governing has existed. His examples include the Emperor Ashoka, who based his rule on Buddhist nonviolent principles (pp. 111–117), or William Penn's governance of the Delaware Indian tribe by nonviolent principles (also see Lynd & Lynd, 1995, pp. 1–3). My example is Taoism in China, which historically played the role of restoring the economy and society when a new dynasty was established, such as the successful restoration policy of the Han Dynasty leading to peace and prosperity in its initial periods (Cai, 2002).

Such a vertically downward motion has significant implications for establishing nonviolent pedagogical relationships and educational communities. Only if the teacher as the authority practices and embodies nonviolent principles, despite institutional constraints (e.g., the hierarchical system of schooling in most countries), can it become possible to educate about, for, and through nonviolence. Ultimately every member of a community becomes an important site for enacting nonviolent dynamics. Nonviolence is situated in the web of relationships, not only vertically, but also horizontally, between and among different individuals and groups. When it becomes the major orientation of a community in all directions, nonviolence can be fully practiced and have rippling effects.

Nonviolence is "a feminist issue" (Pinar, 2009, p. 68). Jane Addams' intellectual and life history, both in establishing Hull House to engage a democratic, communal life and in leading peace movements at national and international levels, demonstrates this fact (Knight, 2005, 2010). It was women who joined together during the First World War across enemy camps, ignoring the battlelines of the war, to work together for peace and to pressure their respective governments to negotiate, leading to the establishment of the Women's International League for Peace and Freedom. As its president, Jane Addams called for creating new channels to establish a "new internationalism" (Knight, 2010, p. 202) for peace. Addams' effort was not an isolated act, as Ian Harris (2008) points out: "many leading peace educators in the early twentieth century were women" (p. 17).

A twenty-first-century example is the Liberian Women's peace movement, which in 2003 ended a bloody civil war of more than a decade's duration (Disney & Riticker, 2008; Gbowee, 2011). Their nonviolent protests, organized efforts, and persistent involvement in democratic elections not only ended the civil war but also elected the first female president in Africa in 2005. These nonviolent activists understood that peace is not a discrete event, but a process of daily engagement in democratic life. In this case, motherhood subverted patriarchal warfare through women uniting together across class and religious differences to work for peace. The notion of maternity here is not the traditional notion of isolated reproduction and caregiving in a nuclear family, but a communal notion of motherhood working for social change. Danielle Poe (2010) gives another example of a mother, Naar-Obed, who participated in nonviolent activism and was held in prison, away from her two-year-old daughter (who was cared for by her partner and the community).

Women's influence has also been reflected in the formation of philosophical thought. According to Xiaopeng Zhu (2009), in contrast to Confucianism which followed the hierarchal and patriarchal society of three ancient Chinese dynasties, especially the Zhou, Taoism went back even further, before the Zhou Dynasty, to reach into matrilineal culture. If so, it would not be surprising that *Tao Te Ching* emphasizes the power of the feminine and maternal, not only incorporated into Chinese literary and philosophical traditions but also directly embodied in a long history of women intellectuals' works (Wang, 2008).

The gendered implications of nonviolence require a separate essay, but I can point out here that the interconnectedness and compassionate aspects of femininity (existing in men as well) should be embraced by both women and men in order to create a more loving society. Mohandas K. Gandhi's grandson Arun Gandhi (2003) credited three women for influencing his grandfather's commitment to nonviolence: his mother, Putliba, who taught M. K. Gandhi "inner discipline that comes through spiritual awareness" (p. 28), a baby-sitter, Rambha, who taught him how to overcome fear, and his wife, Kastur, who taught him about nonviolent responses in her own relationships with him. While Gandhi fought for independence from British rule, he also fought against the oppression of women and "untouchables," insisting that any source of oppression cannot be tolerated.

Nonviolence is *both* internal *and* external, and it is fundamentally an educational project. In fact, many philosophical, cultural, and spiritual traditions emphasize the internal search for peace and nonviolence as the bridge to collective efforts to transform the world. As Christopher Key Chapple (2007) explains Jainism, its emphasis is on personal discipline and strict observance of the nonviolence ethic, and public engagement is secondary. In Islam, according to Rabia Terri Harris (2007), the word " jihad," quite contrary to the Western public understanding of it as "holy war," means struggle or effort, including "the Greater Struggle—the inward effort" of confronting ourselves and "the Lesser Struggle—the outward effort of confronting social injustice" (p. 108). The emphasis, again, is on the effort to transform oneself first. In Confucianism, Taoism, and Buddhism, inner peace is the basis for outer peace.

The important role of education is made evident in such an emphasis on personal transformation as the basis for social transformation. Education here is defined in a broad sense as cultivating nonviolent orientations from within and transforming internal negative energies, not in the narrow sense of schooling, although school curriculum should be part of the project. (Unfortunately, school curriculum mostly focuses on warfare and other forms of violence versus peace and nonviolence: see Gemstone Peace Education Team's work, 2008). If we read the biographies or autobiographies of nonviolence and peace activists—Jane Addams (Knight, 2005, 2010), Nelson Mandela (1994/2003), Martin Luther King, Jr. (1998), Mahatma Gandhi (1927 & 1929/1993), Leymah Gbowee (2011), the leader of Liberian women's peace movement—we can see that all have gone through an internal journey before and during their engagement with political activism. For instance, both Jane Addams and Leymah Gbowee had to undo gendered violence imposed upon their lives in different historical periods and in different forms. Their inward journeys were painful at times, yet illuminating of an upward movement of the human spirit. It is this type of education that we should advocate in our educational work both in and outside of schools.

While unlearning is an important part of learning to shed the effects of violence both internally and externally, could we also teach our children and youth nonviolent principles? What might happen if the content, purpose, and means of education were united through nonviolence? If we participate in internationalizing curriculum studies, is not nonviolence education an inspiring vision for which we can work together? An educational project of nonviolence involves intellectual, emotional, social, and spiritual cultivation of personhood situated in history and culture, and the message of nonviolence should be embodied in the heart of curriculum studies.

By defining the notion of nonviolence, I hope that by now it is clear *why* I advocate nonviolence in internationalizing curriculum studies. Simultaneously incorporating the ideals of democracy, justice, or equality, *and* going beyond their individualistic basis (see Ted Aoki's [2005] analysis of these ideals as rooted in the individual), nonviolence constitutes an inherent mechanism for working through violence for a better life for all members of this world and this planet. Not negating the importance of those ideals which come largely from Western political and social history and have become the shared heritage across the globe, I see nonviolence as a thread that weaves through many non-Western and Western countries and cultures and thus may heal the divide between East and West, North and South, or the first, second, or third world. It belongs to the vital, life-affirmative, and best part of each culture and may have the potentiality to unite us across differences to co-create more compassionate and creative expressions of humanity.

Different Approaches to Nonviolence Education

Nonviolence education is closely related to peace education. Humans have taught each other how to solve conflicts without violence throughout history, but peace studies as a formal program was historically rooted in international studies and initiated after World War II (Hakvoort, 2010; Harris, 2008). To a great degree, peace education is about establishing nonviolent international, cross-cultural, and multicultural relationships in the midst of conflicts (Bajaj, 2008; Lin et al., 2008; Iram et al., 2006; Salomon & Cairns, 2010a). As scholars suggest (Galtung, 2008), peace education has lagged behind peace research and peace movements, but it has developed rapidly for the past several decades.

There are many definitions of peace education but, as Gavriel Salomon and Ed Cairns (2010b) point out, the underlying idea is that "peace education is to negate violence and conflict and to promote a culture of peace to counter a culture of war" (p. 4). Peace education involves cultivating knowledge, skills, and attitudes that can lead to peace rather than to violence through a formal curriculum or community-based activities (Gemstone Peace Education Team, 2008; Hakvoort, 2010). Education for and about peace is its primary message. Originally dealing with the causes of war and its prevention, peace education has recently evolved to embrace new paradigms that locate unity (Danesh, 2010) or harmony (Brantmeier & Lin, 2008) as the center of attention and shift the focus from negation to creation. As Edward J. Brantmeier and Jing Lin (2008) argue,

> Peace is to be understood as both a process and result of balance and harmony that is negotiated and renegotiated over time. It inherently transcends duality and dichotomy. In other words, peace is not "lack of" this or "absence of" that, but a balance, harmony, and interplay of opposites that constitute a living, ongoing interdependent dynamic. (p. xv)

This definition of peace is compatible with the conception of nonviolence rooted in nonduality. Within peace studies literature, nonviolence is often perceived as a means to achieve the end of peace; nonviolence education is considered one aspect of peace education (de Rivera, 2010). But I approach nonviolence, a non-dualistic cultivation of interconnectedness and creativity, as *fundamental*, not merely instrumental, to all education. I think that the content, means, and purpose of education should be united through nonviolence, and that the message of nonviolence must permeate all dimensions of education to fully play out its potential. Moreover, I prefer "nonviolence," rather than "peace" due to its clear-cut position against all forms of violence, which includes "negative peace," which Martin Luther King, Jr. (1961/1986, p. 50) defined as repressive acceptance of racial oppression. Furthermore, I think nonviolence has a broader meaning and significance for education while peace is usually perceived as an opposite to war.

Nonviolence-oriented education requires a radical approach of curriculum transformation. We usually perceive violence as physical aggression, but violence is much more than physical, and many practices at schools are impositional rather than educational, such as labeling and tracking of students, concentrating on students' intellectual development at the expense of emotional growth, constraining their freedom to explore through standardization, teaching narrow-minded ethnocentric nationalism, and glorifying war, to list just a few. To contest such imposition and to challenge its basis in dualism, the educational system, teaching contents, and pedagogical relationships all need to undergo transformation to locate wholeness, integrity, complexity, embodiment, and freedom at the center of educational practices. When the integrative power of nonviolence plays out in multiple dimensions of education, differences do not lead to violence but to expansion of horizons of students to adopt new lenses, form new relationality, and acquire new knowledge. Even if conflicts emerge, they can be resolved peacefully, as evident in the three approaches to nonviolence education that I review next.

Human Rights

At the beginning of the United Nations' International Decade for a Culture of Peace and Non-Violence for the Children of the World, the UNESCO published Jean-Marie Muller's (2002) "Non-Violence in Education."[1] This philosophical text represents a particular approach that many conflict resolution education and human rights education efforts adopt, initiated by various international organizations.

Based upon the Universal Declaration of Human Rights in 1948, teaching the ethics of non-violence to children and students is based upon "respect for and the dignity of each and every human being" (p. 8). Associating nonviolence with democracy and human rights, Muller (2002) further claims that "all anti-democratic ideologies are associated with the ideology of violence" (p. 9). Defining the notion of violence and non-violence, he suggests that nature and culture are not opposite to each other, and human nature is not a given but interacts with culture, and that the important issue is "which part of ourselves we decide to *cultivate*, both individually and collectively" (p. 60; emphasis in original).

The question of what to cultivate is essentially related to the question of education. Educators need to teach children how to think critically, how to embrace democratic values, and how to find alternative ways to solving conflicts constructively. In dealing with bullying and violence at school, Muller emphasizes the role of mediation and bystander intervention. When everyone participates in breaking the cycle of violence, bullying and violence are less likely to happen, or when they happen, they can be resolved in educative ways. Muller also argues that the history of non-violence is absent from school textbooks and official speeches but must be taught if we want to create a culture of nonviolence to replace a culture of violence.

This assertion of everyone's rights and following nonviolent and constructive ways of dealing with conflicts is an individual-oriented approach. While creating a culture of non-violence emphasizes the role of a community, the community is perceived more or less as the sum of individual persons. This orientation comes predominately from the principles of Western philosophy, even though Muller also explicitly draws upon Gandhi's principles. Gandhian nonviolence is based upon the notion of the unity of life, in which relational dynamics are essential, characterizing the second approach, as I discuss next.

Relationality

While Indian educational history embodying the principle of *Ahimsa* has existed for a long time, modern schooling in India has been Westernized. However, Takuya Kaneda (2008) identifies four modern educators—spiritual leaders—who set up residential schools compatible with traditional teachings of *Ahimsa* but different from the mainstream schools in the twentieth century. I briefly review the nonviolent principles of their educational efforts.

Ravindranath Tagore's (1861–1941) experimental school, Santiniketan, was located in a peaceful environment away from busy city life in order for students to experience oneness with nature. Tagore emphasized the role of meditation and aesthetic sensitivity with a school life filled with creative artwork such as poetry, painting, music, dance, drama, and literature. For Tagore, "the true principle of art is the principle of unity" (quoted in Kaneda, 2008, p. 178). Sri Aurobindo (1872–1950) thinks that "nurturing inner peace is an essential part of an integral education" (Kaneda, 2008, p. 180). His integral education is fivefold, including physical, vital, mental, psychic, and spiritual education. The role of silence and stillness for achieving a peaceful mind is emphasized, and the growth of inner peace is the goal of education.

Jiddu Krishnamurti (1895–1986) emphasized the importance of the individual's inward transformation, argued for "the necessity to be aware of violence within our minds" (p. 182), and called for going beyond nationalism, organized religions, and identity politics, which led to conflicts and violence (also see Kumar, 2013). In Rishi Valley School, simple lifestyles, optional yoga classes, farm work, and community service (Kaneda, 2008; Piirto, 2008) all contribute to students' well-being. Sri Sri Ravi Shankar (1956–), a contemporary leader, has conducted various educational endeavors to help children and teens to "effectively handle stress and negative emotions such as fear and anger and to live harmoniously with others" (Kaneda, 2008, p. 184). He advocates educating children holistically through the interconnectedness of body and mind. He believes that the natural tendency of our consciousness is "essentially to be at peace" (p. 185).

From these modern and contemporary examples, we can see that the underlying message is the nonduality of body, mind, and spirit and the wholeness of life. When such nonduality is at the center of education, the unifying force of life—nonviolence—permeates students' intellectual, emotional, social, and spiritual life. Here personal cultivation goes hand in hand with going beyond a separate sense of the individual self to be in communion with others and with nature, through stillness, meditation, yoga practices, and aesthetic activities. While such an orientation happens in alternative school settings, these leaders don't present "systematic curriculum structures to embody their educational visions" (Kaneda, 2008, p. 188) but adopt various forms as beneficial for integrating body and mind, and self and other. In other words, the principle of nonduality can be implemented in regular schools if the vision of nonviolence is shared by teachers, staff, and administrators. Many reform efforts across the globe focusing on educating "the whole child" are compatible with such an orientation.

Community

Based upon the nonviolent principles of Gandhi and Martin Luther King, Jr., community-based efforts through youth outreach programs, extracurricular activities, or internet-mediated global nonviolence youth alliances have been a mode of nonviolence education in the United States and international settings. Although they don't receive the mainstream attention, their influences have been spreading and profound. These efforts involve public lectures by nonviolence and peace leaders, film discussions, art exhibitions or concerts, workshops about nonviolent principles and practices, and other forms of public education. Sometimes students can obtain school credit for taking such workshops, and teachers also can participate in the professional development workshops to learn the lessons of nonviolence and how to incorporate them into the curriculum.

Different projects have used different creative strategies. For instance, the Teens on Target program in Oakland first trains high school students on violence prevention, and then lets them teach middle school students, with the hope that the message of non-violence will have more influence when it comes from peers (Federis, 2012). Another example is the nonviolence education and training provided by the Martin Luther King, Jr.'s Center for Nonviolent Social Change. The King Center has been developing its K-12 school curriculum, "which strives to not only describe Dr. King's life and accomplishments, but to impart his timeless teachings of nonviolence and service" (see http://www.thekingcenter.org). Educators around the world can learn how to weave the message of justice, peace, and nonviolence into their daily teaching through its online resources. Some centers or institutes, such as the Metta Center for Nonviolence (www.mettacenter.org) oriented by Gandhian nonviolent principles, use webcast courses to reach a wider audience.

Such community-based efforts are not new, but have had a long history. The women's settlement movement, such as Hull House in the Progressive era, is a good example. The educational function of Hull House was to create a democratic, communal life in a poor neighborhood through classes, activities, and services for immigrants. Through many years of dedicated work, Jane Addams was able to "perceive the connections between different kinds of oppression" (Knight, 2010, p. 96), including the links between social injustice in the domestic realm and warfare in the international realm. Thus she advocated "newer ideals of peace" (Addams, 1906/2007) which reject a "peaceful" society based upon class and gendered oppression or conquest of other nations, but favor a dynamic notion of peace as "the unfolding of worldwide processes making for the nurture of human life" (p. 131). Her peace activism at various levels was guided by this vision. The community-based education at Hull House still has much to offer for nonviolence education.

Today, very few U.S. school programs adopt the language of nonviolence, although individual teachers sometimes choose to integrate teachings about Gandhi or King's nonviolent resistance movements in their curriculum (Coghlan, 2000; Fishman, 2003; Gill, 2000). Educational activities that are not school-based can become powerful sites for spreading the message of nonviolence, and the collaboration between community and school can infuse positive energy into schooling.

These three approaches intersect between and among one another, and nonviolence education activism usually blends different approaches. While the starting point might be different, be it individual, relationality, or community, the issue is how to deal with differences nonviolently to promote the welfare of all students. Respect for others as individuals must be combined with the effort to transcend ego boundaries; otherwise such a respect can easily retreat into self-defense. We need to combine all approaches to fully realize the potential of nonviolence not only in dissolving violence but also in fostering an open-minded and loving community which does not lead to violence in the first place. Histories, principles, and practices of nonviolence must be taught; educational violence at schools must be deconstructed; and a shared vision of a nonviolent world must be fostered. Only through a systematic re-envisioning of education can nonviolence education be fully implemented. But we can start from different beginnings, small or big, and proactively infuse nonviolent principles into different dimensions of education.

Nonviolent Relationality and Internationalizing Curriculum Studies

Because curriculum is the heart of education, connecting macro and micro levels, nonviolence needs to be at the center of curriculum studies to influence the educational network. If we cultivate a "new internationalism," as Addams challenged us to do, then nonviolently mobilizing organic relationships *within* and *across* the local, the national, and the international becomes important. To envision nonviolent relationality as the central thread of internationalizing curriculum studies, I discuss the issue of power, identity, and difference in their relationships at various interactive levels of the local and the global as follows.

In the first edition of this handbook, William F. Pinar (2003) discusses the importance of focusing on education and curriculum, rather than international political tensions, for the internationalization of curriculum studies. If we have scholars acting as if diplomatic representatives of their own countries, the intellectual and educational possibility will be lost in power struggles. Actually, in political and social movements, the egocentric pursuit of political authority and control, either for an individual or for a group, can hardly lead to any success. Gandhi (1942/2007) specifically points out that the nonviolence movement is "not a program of seizure of power" but "a program of transformation of relationships" (p. 40). In the Liberian women's peace movement in 2003, they adopted the strategy of not criticizing the political policies of the dictatorship—even though there were more than plenty to criticize—but demanding of peace unyieldingly and wholeheartedly (Disney & Riticker, 2008; Gbowee, 2011).

Paradoxically, the key to winning social and political victories in nonviolence movements is to abandon the politics of power struggle, and instead to mobilize every participant in the *powerful* process of transforming the nature of relationships from dominating/being dominated to organic interconnectedness. If we cannot go beyond the confinement of national, group, or individual self-interest, there is no possibility of achieving "heart unity" with others who are distant or/and different from us. Here it is essential not only to dwell in *inter*national space, but also to move toward *trans*national space.

The inter-space and trans-space are both important for creating nonviolent dynamics of the local, the national, and the global through transforming relationships. The term "international" acknowledges the "in-between" fluid spaces where multiplicity and differences are neither excluded nor self-contained. Moreover, internationalization as a concept supports the decentering of both the national and the global through a focus on interaction and relationship that lead to the transformation of both locality and globalness. To borrow the language of chaos and complexity theory (Doll, 2012), the newness of the global comes from a dynamic interaction of local parts. Also as Peter Hershock (2009) argues, it is a fallacy to assume that "whatever is good for each and every one of us (individually) will be good for all of us (communally or ecologically)" (p. 156), since what is good for the local may become detrimental to the ecological or the global. Therefore the global as a whole is more than the addition of the national or the local, but emerges from interactive dynamics and is marked by organic relationality.

Noel Gough (2003) suggests that "internationalizing curriculum inquiry might best be understood as a process of creating transnational spaces in which scholars from different localities collaborate in reframing and decentering their own knowledge traditions and negotiate trust in each other's contributions to their collective work" (p. 68). The very usage of "trans-" indicates both an intense experiencing of the boundary and an effort to go beyond that boundary. Such transnational spaces not only sustain hybrid movements but also support embodied work to negotiate collaborative trust. Nonviolence education must be an embodied process. Sherry B. Shapiro (2002) asserts that it is the joy and suffering of the human body that extends "beyond the boundaries of nationality, race, ethnicity, gender, social class, or sexual or religious preference—all the ways of marking ourselves off from others" (p. 149). Peace and nonviolence education need to sensitize us to the collective body, and pedagogically we need to begin with the body as the connector between the public and the private, and between social identity and a wider shared experience.

In such dynamics of international and transnational movements, identity is destabilized, power struggles are displaced into fluid modes of relationships, and nonviolent relationality across differences becomes multidimensional—both horizontal (among the local) and vertical (between the local and the global), and both top-down (from the global to the individual body) and bottom-up (from the local to the international)—to form a network of nonviolence. Instead of intensifying the fragmentation (due to dualism) that marks the fragility of the modern life we share, the nonviolent modes of relationality we choose to establish can contribute to the integrative potential of the network.

For the dynamics of intergroup relationships within the nation, I use the American field of curriculum studies as an example due to my familiarity with it. Pinar (2013) identifies "power, identity, and discourse" as the key concepts of the reconceptualized curriculum field in the USA, but he suggests that these concepts have become assumptions—due to their success—and the newly taken-for-granted, with tendencies toward totalization and reductionism. Now the assumption that "power predominates, that identity is central, and that discourse is determinative (e.g. our research provides only narratives, never truth)—are widely shared" (p. 8). Accepted as given, they have become "abstractions split off from the concrete complexity of the historical moment" (p. 8) and exhausted in self-referentiality. Ironically, the central emphasis of identity leads to the casualty of individual agency and subjective specificity.

As both an observer and participant of the American field of curriculum studies who came from China in 1996, I also would like to add that another causality: organic relationality. The complexity and richness in the singularity of each individual or group co-exists with the complicated and organic relationality of humanity and life, and when one side of the coin is undermined, the other side deteriorates as well. While Pinar (2013) discusses the proliferation of "uncertainty" and "dispersion" in poststructural discourses and their effects, I also think the distance between self and other stretched by the poststructural discourses of otherness and the unknown Other may lead to the difficulty of not being able to bring self and other back into the fabric of relationality (Wang, 2013). In addressing "difference-centered politics of recognition and respect," drawing upon the Buddhist philosophy, Peter Hershock (2009) argues for "a concerted shift from considerations of how much we are the *same* or *different from* each [sic] another to how we might best *differ for* one another" (p. 160; emphasis in original).

In a non-dualistic, nonviolent view, subject and object, body and mind, and self and other exist interdependently. Hershock's perception of differences as essential for mutual contribution and shared welfare, as something positive that should not be erased or elevated, but as a part of a relationship network, is a challenge not only to the liberal notion of the individual as autonomous, but also to the identity politics of static diversity or the postmodern radicalization of singularity. The nonviolent relational dynamics of "differing for" rather than "differing from" are particularly imperative under the context of a profoundly shared sense of crisis in American public education. While particular differences such as racial or gendered differences must be discussed, the discussions need to orient toward changing our ways of relating to others and addressing the root cause of social violence, rather than fixing on any particular social identity. Nonviolence cannot exist without social justice, but social justice for one group at the expense of the welfare of others does not do justice to the shared human struggle for the common good of all.

Confronting the crisis in American public education, I suggest that challenging the violence of the conservative forces and working through the depressive position of educators in relation to the external attack from non-education sectors, we are called to form nonviolent relationships among different social groups and their affiliated scholarly camps. Identity-based struggles, when contextualized in the interconnected web of life, have played a progressive role in the field. However, without contextualizing and complicating one's own investment in a broader project of education for all, without taking a step back from one's own particular subjective positioning to see a bigger picture, any *fixation* upon one group's struggle—along or within the lines of either race, gender, class, sexuality, nation, or other social factors—at the expense of the collective good arrests democracy as an unfulfilled dream.

If we can initiate and participate in nonviolent dynamics of "differing for" an educationally informed, compassionate community across local and national borders, we are also challenging the international domination of American politics, along with its domestically repressive educational "reform" demand for raising test scores and maintaining global control. This suggestion is certainly not about subsuming diversity into uniformity, as any network has room for breaks and fragmentations. The organic relationality of nonviolence welcomes differences and does not avoid conflicts because it has the ability to stretch, transform, and rebuild.

Moving from the national to the international level, the dualism of "us" versus "them" has played a violent role in global relationships, and the possibility of moving beyond such a fixed boundary depends upon our capacity for refusing to dehumanize the other, both the friendly other and the hostile other. Through the psychoanalytic notion of "the stranger to ourselves," Julia Kristeva (1993) invites us "to recognize ourselves as strange in order better to appreciate the foreigners outside us instead of striving to bend them to the norms of our own repression" (p. 29). If we are aware of our subconscious rather than repressing it, aliens are no longer a threat to us. Kristeva believes that a transnational or international position is situated at the crossing of boundaries, which simultaneously affirms and transcends national borders. The idea of nation "at the same time affirmed as a space of freedom and dissolved in its own identity" (p. 32) affirms both the protective function of identification and the necessity of border-crossing. Situated at the fluid border, "nations without nationalism" support nonviolent relationality.

At the boundary of conflicts, international—or intergroups which are often related to international—education for peace and nonviolence has focused particularly on bringing citizens, teachers, students, and youth together from opposite sides in conflict situations, such as Palestinian and Israeli teachers (Bar-On & Adwan, 2006), dialogues and multilogues between Indians and Pakistanis in cyberspace (Naseem, 2008), German-Jewish life-story workshops

(Bar-On, 2010), promoting peace in Northern Ireland (Gallagher, 2010), and Americans and Muslims in international hosting programs (Radomski, 2008). Sometimes tensions are related not only to national/ethnic conflicts but also to religious conflicts in intercultural contexts. The assumption of bringing people from opposite camps together is to engage them in dialogues and trust-building for challenging biases and prejudices and promoting empathy for others' pain.

While different modes of curriculum are adopted for these projects, I highlight one case here. A project of developing a joint school textbook through the efforts of peace educators working with both Palestinian and Israeli teachers was initiated in 2001 in the midst of violence between these two countries. Because developing a joint narrative of their histories that can be accepted by both sides is impossible, the project adopts the strategy of presenting "at least two competing narratives to account for their past, present, and future" (Bar-On & Adwan, 2006, p. 310) and both narratives are presented in the joint curriculum so that students on each side can learn the two storylines of the history rather than only the familiar storyline of their own country. The team working on this project includes two co-founders of Peace Research in the Middle East—Sami Adwan and Dan Bar-On—two history professors, six Palestinian history and geography teachers, six Jewish-Israeli history teachers, and six international delegates, as well as one Jewish-Israeli observer. The collaborative nature of this project is reflected in the choices of team members, and teachers first worked together to develop narratives around certain historical milestones and then implemented this curriculum in their teaching. The workshops that teachers participated in, sometimes interrupted by violent episodes between the two countries, not only involved the activities of developing narratives but also involved sharing their own stories. The role of emotional work, essential to peacebuilding efforts (Yablon, 2006), is evident in this case, and nonviolence is a whole-being experience which involves the intellect/emotion/soul and the conscious/subconscious/unconscious.

In 2003, the curriculum that had been developed in Hebrew, Arabic, and English was carried out in teachers' classrooms. According to teachers' feedback, Bar-On and Adwan (2006) report:

> In general there was a surprise effect by presenting the two narratives, a surprise that created interest and curiosity. We could feel a general feeling of ownership and accomplishment of the teachers from both sides, in spite of the deteriorating external situation. They felt that they are creating something new for the future, which no one tried to do before. (p. 316)

This team of teachers and researchers ran various personal risks to carry out this program: curfews, border checkpoints, fear of shootings or suicide bombing. I think their courage to organize themselves to educate against the grain for nonviolence is not only inspiring for the future but also transformative of the present. Although Bar-On and Adwan (2006) perceived this project as in the "intermediate phase" that would lead to a joint narrative in the future when peace is reached between the two countries, I find the juxtaposition of two conflicting narratives generally applicable for international, intercultural, and transnational projects which are not necessarily situated in hostility and war. Juxtaposition without final solution (Miller, 2005) in North American curriculum studies has become an acceptable way of allowing ruptures and differences to both mutually challenge each other and bring out the unknown potential from each other. Juxtaposition can be an effective strategy of nonviolence education.

As we can see here, the simultaneity of the local, the national, and the international dynamics is important for orienting curriculum studies toward nonviolence education. The case discussed above, even though involving a limited number of participants (a dozen educators and hundreds of students), mobilizes all levels of interaction toward nonviolent relationality, against the official curriculum of violence. Participants were dealing with religious, cultural, national, and ethnic conflicts all at the same time, but they persevered and were able to negotiate out of the conflicts a space that recognizes differences and opens their students' eyes to another view of the shared world. Not just in wartime, but in time of peace, such a spirit of nonviolent sharing across differences is also important. Whatever starting point we can begin with, teaching against the grain for nonviolence, as difficult and at times dangerous as it is, can spread its influence throughout the network because nonviolence speaks to the humane aspect of life.

Ultimately, violence and nonviolence are felt by the individual body, and the fundamental task of education is personal cultivation. When we discuss global issues, it is relatively easy to forget the embodiment of international, transnational, and global in each particular person, but that is the site for education, curriculum, and pedagogy. One of the differences between education and social movements is that nonviolence movements need mass action to have an effect on society but education can work on the site of an individual student through an individual educator's efforts. Such an effect of education is necessarily long term, through the interplay between the personal and the global. While mobilizing and transforming the social occurs through destabilizing the personal, personal transformation is possible only through participating in societal reform and global change (Ye, 2005). In today's world, the international is not an abstract concept but is embedded in the daily fabric of our lives in both the "real" and virtual world. If we work together to find diverse ways of engaging personal cultivation for, about, and through nonviolence at various levels of education, we can carve out pathways from the difficulty of the present moment—competition-oriented national educational reform—toward new possibilities.

In the first edition of this handbook, David Geoffrey Smith (2003) critiques the neoliberalism embedded in the tide of globalization, but he further calls for engaging "a new kind of global dialogue regarding sustainable human futures" and for forming "a new kind of imaginal understanding within human consciousness" (p. 35). Responding to such a call, I suggest that the grassroots movements and organizational efforts of nonviolence education locally, nationally, and internationally provide such a vision for internationalizing curriculum studies. Martin Luther King, Jr. (1960/1986) stated half a century ago: "The choice today is no longer between violence and nonviolence. It is either nonviolence or nonexistence" (p. 39). This call is more urgent today. As educators, are we willing to take on the challenge?

Note

1 "Non-violence" is the term that Muller uses in his writing. The connotations of "non-violence" and "nonviolence" have a certain difference with the former emphasizing more on the negation of violence and the latter on the integrative potential of nonviolence. I use both terms in this chapter, following respective uses of different authors/activists, which often indicate their (different) orientations.

References

Addams, J. (2007). *Newer ideals of peace*. University of Illinois Press. (Original work published 1906)
Aoki, T. T. (2005). *Curriculum in a new key* (W. F. Pinar & R. L. Irwin, Eds.). Lawrence Erlbaum.
Bai, H., & Cohen, A. (2008). Breathing qi (ch'i), following Dao (Tao). In C. Eppert & H. Wang (Eds.), *Cross-cultural studies in curriculum* (pp. 35–54). Lawrence Erlbaum.
Bajaj, M. (Ed.). (2008). *Encyclopedia of peace education*. Information Age Publishing.
Bar-On, D. (2010). Storytelling and multiple narratives in conflict situations. In G. Salomon & E. Cairns (Eds.), *Handbook on peace education* (pp. 199–212). Psychology Press.

Bar-On, D., & Adwan, S. (2006). The PRIME shared history project. In Y. Iram, H. Wahrman, & Z. Gross (Eds.), *Educating toward a culture of peace* (pp. 309–323). Information Age Publishing.

Brantmeier, E. J., & Lin, J. (2008). Introduction. In J. Lin, E. J. Brantmeier, & C. Bruhn (Eds.), *Transforming education for peace* (pp. xiii–xviii). Information Age Publishing.

Cai, D. (2002). A Taoist approach to peace through its naturalistic principle. *Journal of Anhui University, 26*(5), 1–9.

Chapple, C. K. (2007). Jainism and nonviolence. In D. L. Smith-Christopher (Ed.), *Subverting hatred* (pp. 1–13). Orbis Books.

Coghlan, R. (2000). The teaching of anti-violence strategies within the English curriculum. *English Journal, 89*(5), 84–89.

Cooney, R., & Michalowski, H. (1987). *The power of the people.* New Society Publishers.

Danesh, H. B. (2010). Unity-based peace education. In G. Salomon & E. Cairns (Eds.), *Handbook on peace education* (pp. 253–268). Psychology Press.

de Rivera, J. (2010). Teaching about the culture of peace as an approach to peace education. In G. Salomon & E. Cairns (Eds.), *Handbook on peace education* (pp. 187–197). Psychology Press.

Disney, A. (Producer), & Riticker, G. (Director). (2008). *Pray the devil back to hell* [Film]. ro*co Films Educational.

Doll, Jr., W. E. (2012). *Pragmatism, post-modernism, and complexity theory* (D. Trueit, Ed.). Routledge.

Federis, M. (2012). *Oakland teens learn, teach nonviolence*. Retrieved July 30, 2012, from https://www.rschoolgroup.org/oakland-teens-learn-teach-nonviolence/

Fishman, S. (2003). Ghandi in the pre-school. *Journal of Education, 184*(2), 1–5.

Gallagher, T. (2010). Building a shared future from a divided past. In G. Salomon & E. Cairns (Eds.), *Handbook on peace education* (pp. 241–251). Psychology Press.

Galtung, J. (2008). Form and content of peace education. In M. Bajaj (Ed.), *Encyclopedia of peace education* (pp. 49–58). Information Age Publishing.

Gandhi, A. (2003). *Legacy of love.* North Bay Books.

Gandhi, M. K. (1993). *An autobiography* (M. Desai, Trans.). Beacon Press. (Original work published 1927 & 1929 in two volumes)

Gandhi, M. K. (2007). *Gandhi on non-violence* (T. Merton, Ed.). New Directions. (Original work published 1942)

Gbowee, L. (2011). *Mighty be our powers.* Beast Books.

Gemstone Peace Education Team. (2008). Peace education aimed at children everywhere in the world. In J. Lin, E. J. Brantmeier, & C. Bruhn (Eds.), *Transforming education for peace* (pp. 93–111). Information Age Publishing.

Gill, D. (2000). Giving peace a chance. *English Journal, 89*(5), 74–77.

Gough, N. (2003). Thinking globally in environmental education. In W. F. Pinar (Ed.), *International handbook of curriculum research* (pp. 53–72). Lawrence Erlbaum.

Hakvoort, I. (2010). Peace education in regions of tranquility. In G. Salomon & E. Cairns (Eds.), *Handbook on peace education* (pp. 287–301). Psychology Press.

Harris, I. (2008). History of peace of education. In M. Bajaj (Ed.), *Encyclopedia of peace education* (pp. 15–24). Information Age Publishing.

Harris, R. T. (2007). Nonviolence in Islam. In D. L. Smith-Christopher (Ed.), *Subverting hatred* (pp. 107–127). Orbis Books.

Hershock, P. (2009). Ethics in an era of reflexive modernization. In J. Powers & C. S. Prebish (Eds.), *Destroying Mara forever* (pp. 151–164). Snow Lion.

Howlett, C. F., & Lieberman, R. (2008). *A history of the American peace movement from Colonial times to the present.* Edwin Mellen Press.

Iram, Y., Wahrman, H., & Gross, Z. (Eds.). (2006). *Educating toward a culture of peace.* Information Age Publishing.

Johnson, A. G. (2005). *The gender knot* (2nd ed.). Temple University Press.

Kaneda, T. (2008). Shanti, peacefulness of mind. In C. Eppert & H. Wang (Eds.), *Cross-cultural studies in education* (pp. 171–192). Lawrence Erlbaum.

King, Jr., M. L. (1986). Pilgrimage to nonviolence. In J. M. Washington (Ed.), *A Testament of hope* (pp. 35–40). HarperOne. (Original work published 1960)

King, Jr., M. L. (1986). Love, law, and civil disobedience. In J. M. Washington (Ed.), *A Testament of hope* (pp. 43–53). HarperOne. (Original work published 1961)

King, Jr., M. L. (1998). *The autobiography of Martin Luther King, Jr.* (C. Carson, Ed.). IPM.

Knight, L. W. (2005). *Citizen: Jane Addams and the struggle for democracy.* W. W. Norton.

Knight, L. W. (2010). *Jane Addams.* W. W. Norton.

Kristeva, J. (1993). *Nation without nationalism* (L. S. Roudiez, Trans.). Columbia University Press.

Kumar, A. (2013). *Curriculum as meditative inquiry.* Palgrave Macmillan.

Lin, J., Brantmeier, E. J., & Bruhn, C. (Eds.). (2008). *Transforming education for peace.* Information Age Publishing.

Lynd, S., & Lynd, A. (Eds.). (2006). *Nonviolence in America.* Orbis Books.

Mandela, N. (2003). *Long walk to freedom.* Abacus. (Original work published 1994)

Miller, J. (2005). *Sounds of silence breaking.* Peter Lang.

Muller, J. (2002). *Non-violence and education.* UNESCO.

Nagler, M. N. (2004). *The search for a nonviolent future.* Inner Ocean Publishing.

Nagler, M. N. (2010). *Nonviolence today.* Retrieved August 6, 2012, from http://www.youtube.com/watch?v=gavOJG4IxpQ

Naseem, M. A. (2008). Peace-educational value of the World Wide Web. In J. Lin, E. J. Brantmeier, & C. Bruhn (Eds.), *Transforming education for peace* (pp. 185–202). Information Age Publishing.

Piirto, J. (2008). Krishnamurti and me. In C. Eppert & H. Wang (Eds.), *Cross-cultural studies in education* (pp. 247–266). Lawrence Erlbaum.

Pinar, W. F. (2003). Introduction. In W. F. Pinar (Ed.), *International handbook of curriculum research* (pp. 1–31). Lawrence Erlbaum.

Pinar, W. F. (2009). *The worldliness of a cosmopolitan education.* Routledge.

Pinar, W. F. (2013). *Curriculum studies in the United States.* Palgrave Macmillan.

Poe, D. (2010). Woman, mother, and nonviolent activism. In Andrew Fitz-Gibbon (Ed.), *Positive peace* (pp. 119–132). Rodopi.

Radomski, C. (2008). Building peace in the family. In J. Lin, E. J. Brantmeier, & C. Bruhn (Eds.). *Transforming education for peace* (pp. 23–44). Information Age Publishing.

Salomon, G., & Cairns, E. (Eds.). (2010a). *Handbook on peace education*. Psychology Press.

Salomon, G., & Cairns, E. (2010b). Peace education. In G. Salomon & E. Cairns (Eds.), *Handbook on peace education* (pp. 1–7). Psychology Press.

Shapiro, S. B. (2002). The commonality of the body. In G. Salomon & B. Nevo (Eds.), *Peace education* (pp. 143–154). Lawrence Erlbaum.

Sharp, G. (2005). *Waging nonviolent struggle*. Extending Horizons Books.

Shastri, S. Y., & Shastri, Y. S. (2007). *Ahimsa* and the unity of all things. In D. L. Smith-Christopher (Ed.), *Subverting hatred* (pp. 57–75). Orbis Books.

Smith, D. G. (2003). Curriculum and teaching facing globalization. In W. F. Pinar (Ed.), *International handbook of curriculum research* (pp. 35–51). Lawrence Erlbaum.

Smith-Christopher, D. L. (Ed.). (2007). *Subverting hatred*. Orbis Books.

Stiehm, J. H. (2006). *Champions for peace*. Rowman & Littlefield.

Tutu, D. (1999). *No future without forgiveness*. Doubleday.

Wang, H. (2004). *The call from the stranger on a journey home*. Peter Lang.

Wang, H. (2008). The strength of the feminine, lyrics of Chinese women's subjectivity, and the power of education. In C. Eppert & H. Wang (Eds.), *Cross-cultural studies in education* (pp. 313–333). Lawrence Erlbaum.

Wang, H. (2010). A zero space of nonviolence. *Journal of Curriculum Theorizing, 26*(1), 1–8.

Wang, H. (2013). A nonviolent approach to social justice education. *Educational Studies, 49*(6), 485–503.

Yablon, Y. B. (2006). The role of emotions in peace-building activities. In Y. Iram, H. Wahrman, & Z. Gross, (Eds.), *Educating toward a culture of peace* (pp. 207–222). Information Age Publishing.

Ye, L. (2005). Social development in the 21st century and elementary and secondary educational reform in China. *Journal of the Chinese Society of Education, 11*, 2–7.

Zhu, X. (2009). New realms in contemporary Taoist philosophical studies. *Jiangxi Social Sciences, 6*, 50–56.

Zinn, H. (2002). *The power of nonviolence*. Beacon Press.

6

UNTEACHABLE MOMENTS AND PEDAGOGICAL RELATIONSHIPS (2016)[1]

Educators cherish teachable moments, moments when an unplanned incident provides the teacher an opportunity to improvise a creative response to benefit students' learning. But unteachable moments are seldom discussed, when an unplanned incident leads to the collapse of the pedagogical relationship, in which the teacher cannot immediately overcome students' resistance. Such disruptions in the classroom are often indicators of the teacher's pedagogical failure to make meaningful connections between teaching and learning. However, precisely at such a moment, we as educators confront the challenge of making sense from loss to open up new possibilities. Julia Kristeva's (2000, 2002) theory of intimate revolt is particularly informative for how to come to terms with these difficult moments and reach pedagogical wisdom and compassion. In this article, I argue that on such occasions nonviolent relationality informed by intimate revolt is particularly called upon to unravel the knot of difficulty.

This paper uses the Kristevian notion of intimate revolt to theorize how breakdowns of meanings can be transformed toward (delayed) breakthroughs

---

[1] This chapter is reprinted with permission of the publisher (Taylor & Francis Ltd, http://www.tandfonline.com). Wang, H. (2016). Unteachable moments and pedagogical relationships. *Curriculum Inquiry*, 46(5), 455–472.

in teaching and learning. Using a moment of such a breakdown in my own teaching, I first define what I mean by an unteachable moment. Second, I re-read this moment through Kristeva's theory and its intersection with nonviolence. Third, I propose three important aspects as essential for creating transformative pedagogical relationships in which intimacy in revolt and nonviolent relationality become possible.

What Is an Unteachable Moment?

The concept of "teachable moments" in education has multiple meanings. It first refers to good timing so that learning can occur according to students' developmental stage (Havinghurst, 1952; Hyun & Marshall, 2003). It also refers to times when students are immersed in learning and are experiencing teaching as internally satisfactory and enjoyable (Hyun & Marshall, 2003; Woodhouse, 2011). It is often understood as a disruption or distraction inside or outside of the classroom that the teacher takes advantage of by sidetracking the original teaching plan and improvising an educational response to turn the disruption into something educative. While a teachable moment is mediated by the content of teaching and learning, teachable moments do not exist without certain dynamics between teacher and student. Jim Garrison (1997) defines teachable moments as "the times when spaces open for the student and teacher to interact in a synchronistic and dynamic rhythm" in which "imagination, emotion, and intuition" play a key role (p. 122). In such a pedagogical relationship, tension and dissonance may exist (Liddell, 2012), but the interaction between the teacher and the students brings the best potential of both as learning occurs and meanings are made. The role of the teacher in creating such a moment is crucial.

In contrast, by unteachable moment I refer to those moments when pedagogical relationships break down in a particular incident. It can be related to the content of teaching; for instance, "difficult knowledge" (Britzsman, 1998) in social justice education often has an unsettling effect, with the potential to provoke disruptive responses. But the "unteachable" aspect I refer to is not (merely) about content that is difficult to teach; relationships involving the subjectivity and intersubjectivity of teacher and student can collapse in teaching any subject matter. In this essay, I define an unteachable moment as a time when a pedagogical relationship falls apart, often triggered by a critical incident in which the clash between teacher and student makes it impossible to immediately restore the link between the two. An unteachable moment necessarily involves students' negative responses to teaching or their refusal to engage in meaningful learning, but since the teacher is the authority in the classroom and plays a crucial role, the teacher's role is the primary focus of this paper.

Teachable and unteachable moments are not dualistic opposites since unteachable moments can become teachable moments in the long term. The difference lies in the timing. In a teachable moment, the teacher's immediate improvisation of a productive response turns things around quickly; in an unteachable moment, however, the immediate repair does not occur. The teacher's reflective and critical understanding happens afterward and may benefit those students who experience such a moment only if the teacher/student relationship continues. Such a delay characterizes an unteachable moment even if it later leads to pedagogical insights. On the other hand, unteachable moments also may remain unteachable, either because the instructor perceives students as resistant learners and disregards their negative responses, or because the instructor does not engage in her own inner work to reach new understandings.

The purpose of this essay is to discuss how to make sense of and learn from unteachable moments so that better pedagogical dynamics can be established. I choose the word "unteachable" not to refer to any person or any topic as unteachable, nor to the inability of educators to teach (or students to learn), but rather to refer to the particular nature of relationality that polarizes teacher and student to the degree that what the teacher teaches cannot reach students, who are resisting learning at the moment. An unteachable moment calls for the teacher's critical self-consciousness in order for her to transcend difficulty.

Here I offer a story from my own experience to illuminate an unteachable moment: What follows is my own account of a teaching experience that can help to illuminate how I conceptualize the notion of unteachable moment:

> The fall semester of 2003 was the beginning of my third year of university teaching. I was teaching a multicultural education class. More than a month into the class, I had already sensed emotional resistance from the students who had to deal with issues of race and racism. One day we watched the video, *Understanding Race* (Dougherty, 1999), and I asked the students to respond to the video. They were silent except for one male student—the only male student in the class, as a matter of fact—who was ready to speak. He had already spoken several times in a row, and I wanted to encourage other students to speak first. I said, "Could you let others speak first?"

Silence was not a big problem for me, as it could invite contemplation, although it could be uncomfortable for my American students. After a few minutes, abruptly the one male student stood up and walked out of the classroom. What a protest! I phoned him after the class. He said angrily, "If you don't apologize to me in the class, I will go to the Dean and sue you. I am not paying my tuition for this!" I replied, "Well, we certainly can talk about this in the class; if you are still unhappy after that, I don't know what else I can do." I was angry too, and took what he said as a threat. What was most hurtful for me, however, happened when we discussed this incident in the class the next week. Except for a couple of students who mumbled about the delicate line between guiding the class and letting the class go, overwhelmingly everybody said that what I had done was wrong, that I should have let him speak, and that they did not know what to say, so they were grateful that he was the one who wanted to speak. So I felt that the whole class was against me!

The male student had come to the next class late, so I told him that his classmates were sympathetic with him and disagreed with me in my intervention. Holding my own emotions at bay, I spoke in a calm voice and then moved the class towards the topic of that day's teaching. Internally I wondered why I had become the target of students' displaced anger against learning difficult knowledge even though I was much less aggressive than my White woman colleague who taught the same class. Was my "alien" status under question? Was the popular image of a Chinese woman as docile and passive locking me into the position of playing "nice" even as an authority figure? Whatever the reasons might be, the gap between the instructor and students remained for the rest of the class despite my subsequent best efforts to bridge the distance.

This story recounts an unteachable moment related to a highly controversial issue, although such moments also exist in teaching other subject matter (Doll, 1996). Different from teachable moments, when teachers are able to improvise when encountering what is unexpected and to transform it into something productive at the site of the disruption, unteachable moments happen when teachers are unable to contain what is breaking down within themselves and with their students. In my case, the mutual distance and even resentment between teacher and student did not dissolve after that moment, and walking into that class for the rest of the semester was uncomfortable for me as I sensed difficulty in my relationships with the students each time I faced them. I was unable to fully transform the negativity I experienced during that class.

However, if we don't dismiss such unteachable moments, we can achieve deeper insights into the complexity of pedagogical relationships, which in turn can transform our daily educational work. Pedagogical insights into such occasions, when reached, are "delayed understandings" (Pitt, 2003) developed through a process of coming to terms with the undercurrents of shutdown moments. This incident has stayed in my memory. While I was aware that my teaching posed a challenge to students, it took me years to understand how the impact of the students' collective resistance against my pedagogical authority coincided with my struggles with the loss of my own motherland—albeit voluntary—by living in a foreign land. Since this loss stayed at the subconscious level and was covered by my conscious embrace of my Chinese cultural identity at that time, it remained difficult to work through. However, my internal dialogue about whether students' responses were related to my cultural and gendered identity already revealed the traces of the kind of unmourned loss that surfaced during that moment of intensity.

At the same time, the denial of such a loss on my part also made me fail to understand that when students' identity and subjectivity are destabilized, they also might suffer a sense of loss. For instance, in a previous class session they had encountered the Tulsa Race Riot of 1921, a tragedy that had happened in their home state. The intensity of students' emotions—not yet worked through—must have carried over, leading to the breaking point when my pedagogical intervention tipped them over the edge. What had happened before the moment had everything to do with what happened at the moment. Only through sustained long-term critical reflection afterward did I begin to understand the situation more deeply and reach new understandings. Such delayed understandings in working through loss to engage inter/subjective re/formation have transformed my pedagogy as I have learned to work *with* students and create generative pedagogical conditions for their own subjective work. For me, that unteachable moment eventually became a teachable moment.

Although at that moment I could not repair the broken link, I did not use my institutional authority as the teacher to overrule the students' resistance, but opened up the uncomfortable conversation and listened to the students' own responses to the situation. In holding on to the difficulty (Fowler, 2006), rather than simply dismissing students' collective resistance, I suspended my judgment so that the educational potential of the pedagogical gap between the instructor and students could be kept alive for generating new possibilities in the long run (Pitt, 2003). Working through breakdown moments to reach breakthroughs of meaning is a process of working through loss. In such a process, the teacher must be willing to sustain her engagement in an uncomfortable space.

Mary Aswell Doll (1996) recounts a classroom moment drawn from her experience teaching college students that I would call "unteachable." She describes a particularly popular male student who constantly challenged her in class. She had put up with him for half a semester, but then a moment came when she finally blew up and released her anger, "slamming the book onto the desk and railing. I railed about his continual challenge, his non-attentiveness, his mockery of my lessons" (p. 124). The class was shut down and students were silent. In reflection, Mary Doll says, "My virginal upbringing had militated against anger, such that I was unused to expressing negative feelings. When I did show anger, I was out of control, out of bounds, and almost out of a job" (p. 126). I learned from her story that when accumulated anger builds up within us as women teachers without a productive outlet, sooner or later our bodies revolt in unexpected and extreme ways, despite our will to control them. When our gendered upbringing prevents us from expressing anger and commands us to present "a nice, good girl image" (Miller, 2005) even as teachers, there is little space left for us to maintain "the right distance" between the teacher and the student for pedagogical purposes—not too close nor too distant (Taubman, 1990). We might either be seduced into students' projected image of ourselves as good, unthreatening mothers, or resort to institutional authority to uphold our endangered position when being challenged.

Yet we don't have to be trapped in this either/or dilemma if we can look into the eyes of unteachable moments, if we can go deeper and get in touch with what we are not consciously aware of. Experiencing anger, resentment, or frustration in a teaching situation can be a natural response on the part of the teacher, especially when students obstruct pedagogical efforts. Trying to repress anger and putting on a nice mask do not lead to authentic relationships between teacher and students. The issue is not about pushing difficult emotions away but about acknowledging and transforming these emotions into educationally productive directions in which students are encouraged to do their own emotional work. For the teacher, not doing violence to the self goes hand in hand with forming educative relationships with students.

If an unteachable moment is an important source of learning about ourselves as well as learning from others, then how can we as teachers engage in a process of working through loss to create meaningful pedagogical relationships? Here Julia Kristeva's notion of intimate revolt, and its intersection with nonviolence studies, can provide great insight.

Intimate Revolt, Nonviolence, and Unteachable Moments

A breakdown moment involves some sort of "revolt." Usually, revolt suggests rebellion against authority and institutional norms as demonstrated in the male student's departure from the class and then other students' support of him. However, there is another form of revolt—intimate revolt in Kristeva's (1974/1984, 1996, 2000) terms, which informs pedagogical efforts to bridge loss and meaning, bring "intimacy" to students' critical questioning, and develop nonviolent relationality in classroom dynamics.

Oedipal Revolt and Intimate Revolt

The Kristevian revolt is embedded in the semiotic and symbolic dynamics of language and subjectivity. Kristeva (1974/1984, 1996, 2000) proposes that both language and the human psyche are composed of two inseparable dimensions: the semiotic and the symbolic. Kristeva (1974/1984) considers "the *semiotic* as a psychosomatic modality of the signifying process" (p. 28), which indicates the imprint of the body in language, such as the tones, rhythms, and gestures of language. The semiotic is characterized by mobility and instability, and in psychoanalytic terms, it is "instinctual impulses, affects" (Kristeva, 2002, p. 19), the repressed and unconscious otherness related to the maternal body. The symbolic refers to the stable structure, grammar, or "syntax and all linguistic categories" (Kristeva, 1974/1984, p. 29) of language. In psychoanalytic terms, the symbolic corresponds to conscious judgment linked to the paternal law and social order. While the semiotic has the potential to challenge the symbolic order, the symbolic regulates the fluidity of the semiotic. These two dimensions are heterogeneous to each other but they cannot exist without each other: "they are two aspects that are always combined in a sort of dialectic of mutual contribution" (Kristeva, 1993, p. 91). Thus, their interaction becomes essential for the articulation of meaning and the formation of subjectivity.

Revolt happens as a result of the dynamics between the semiotic and the symbolic. Kristeva (1974/1984, 2002) distinguishes two forms of revolt: The first is the oedipal revolt, when the paternal and social laws are transgressed, and the second is the intimate revolt, when the symbolic incorporates the semiotic flow to transform social order. While oedipal revolt challenges conventions through breaking away from the rigid and stern paternal, intimate revolt works in a different way. Kristeva (2000, 2002) rearticulates the notion of revolt as a return to the archaic loving father to bring more complex and less immediately transgressive forms of revolt. First Kristeva (2000) traces the Latin root of revolt, *volvere*, to the connotations of "curve," "entourage," "turn," and "return" (p. 1) without the political meaning of rebellion. Going back to the original meaning of return and circular movement in revolt,

Kristeva (1987) brings to the foreground the "archaic, imaginary paternity" (p. 46). She follows Freud's notion of the "father in individual prehistory" (p. 26), which incorporates both the paternal and maternal functions. The imaginary father supports the signifying process while still playing the role of bringing the infant to the symbolic order with the mediation of the maternal as desiring and nurturing meanings. When revolt is formulated in this way, the edge of transgression is softened, but the role of ongoing questioning essential to meaning-making is kept alive.

Second, Kristeva (2002) examines the Latin root of intimacy as *intimus*, which means "the most interior" (p. 43), and argues that the liveliest aspect of the intimate "resides precisely in the heterogeneity of the two sensorial/symbolic, affect/thought registers" (p. 49). Intimate revolt as the return to the archaic blends the functions of both love and differentiation in an ongoing process of regenerating thought through sensation and inscribing the unspeakable in new words. As a form of working through, intimacy bridges affects and words, deconstructs the established ideology, and gives birth to new meanings where meanings have been lost. By going beyond the political meaning of protest, Kristeva positions intimate revolt not as a decisive rejection or negation but as an interminable "retrospective questioning" (Kristeva, 2002, p. 6) that generates the capacity for renewal. Such a questioning is not only directed toward symbolic order but also puts subjectivity on trial. Questioning the limit does not mean overthrowing it but rather negotiating more variety and flexibility and carving out more space for transformation and creativity for both the self and the social.

From an Unteachable Moment to Intimacy

Unteachable moments occur when the semiotic is most dynamic, erupting through the smooth surface of the symbolic. In my example, at first glance, the students' rebellion can be seen through the lens of the oedipal revolt in which their emotional discomfort in learning difficult knowledge transgressed the convention of students' respect for educational authority. Institutionally, I represented the authority figure and embodied the paternal law against which they rebelled, even though I am a woman. In some important ways, my teaching intensified the heterogeneous tension between the semiotic and the symbolic on the part of the students.

However, at a deeper level, although I did not realize it at that time, a sense of breaking with the social and political conventions of racial and gendered representation that my students were emotionally and socially familiar with had already been implied in my pedagogy before that moment. While a film visually conveys emotion, emotionally laden materials do not automatically lead to enlightenment but may provoke the most stubborn resistance. In social justice education, students often have to work on the limits of their subjectivity in order to critically examine the mainstream ideology. The Kristevian pedagogical question is how to make such questioning "intimate." In that class, through readings and activities, students had already encountered the implicit threat of losing their identity. Growing up in Oklahoma, including some who were born in Tulsa, my students were shocked to learn about the Tulsa Race Riot of 1921. Not knowing the dark history of their own home made them angry, frustrated, and sad, as they explicitly expressed these feelings in the class. The questioning of their own ignorance was also the questioning of their identity and subjectivity. In that situation, the pedagogical support for students to mourn such a loss and work through the pain must be present to facilitate students' meaning-making process. But I had stopped short of introducing intimacy into the classroom to let difficult learning occur.

This break was also complicated by my unrecognized loss. My revolt against racial and gendered injustice in the United States was linked to my psychic investment in holding on to the lost object of my native country, a loss that I did not acknowledge and thus could not work through. As Aparna Mishra Tarc (2013) points out, "The teacher's careful redirection of students' emotion might support students to new thinking about themselves, the world and others" (p. 384). Moreover, the capacity to appropriately redirect is based upon the teacher's capacity to contain her own emotions and affects and form generative pedagogical relationships. The ability to contain my affects and emotions was depended on my own willingness and ability to come to terms with my own loss which, unfortunately, I did not recognize, and thus I could not redirect students' strong emotions in more productive directions. Kristeva (2000) speaks about the necessity to attend to one's own otherness, because "by gaining access to my other-being, I gain access to the other-being of the other" (p. 67). Only through this effort to gain access to my other-being can I attempt to encourage students to get in touch with their own other-beings, including racial, gendered, sexual, class, and religious "other-beings." And "getting in touch" already suggests that it may not be a direct access or a direct teaching. Students have to *experience* such a link in their own ways.

Reading that unteachable moment now, I can see that my (subconscious) oedipal revolt clashed with the students' (subconscious) oedipal revolt. I have learned the importance of bringing intimacy to social justice education in order to move away from such positioning. Rearticulating words at the site of symbolic failure in an ongoing process of questioning, I have learned from that unteachable moment the necessity of cultivating our capacity for thinking with compassion and making *sense* of the world on the bridge between loss and meaning. I have rigorously searched for ways to build productive connections between feelings and understanding in the classroom, to give students more freedom to find their own balance, and to allow students to linger in their comfort zone if necessary so that new knowledge and new awareness can emerge in their own temporal rhythm. Experiencing new knowledge on their own terms, students are less likely to approach the edge of oedipal revolt; if revolt still happens, we need to make pedagogical use of it. In proposing intimate revolt, Kristeva does not necessarily negate oedipal revolt and its role, but proposes another possibility that is more sustainable of ongoing questioning for renewal.

After more than a decade teaching social justice issues in teacher education, I can trace a complicated trajectory of moving away from the transgressive mode to the renewal of intimate questioning in my pedagogy. I have shifted my pedagogical approaches and taken more detours from direct confrontations with social norms so that students' own meaning-making does not pressure them to break away from what they have deeply cherished but instead to build bridges for new modes of expression that incorporate the old. Furthermore, issues that have emerged from teaching difficult knowledge and my continuous working through difficult emotions within myself have also led me to reclaim nonviolent relationality from both personal and collective history for pedagogical use (Wang, 2013, 2014; Wang & Olson, 2009). Over the years, the coming together of intimate revolt and nonviolence has had profound influence on my subjectivity and pedagogical relationships with students.

The Loving Third and Nonviolence

I read the Kristevian imaginary father, the "father-mother conglomerate" (Kristeva, 1987, p. 40), as non-oedipal, non-dualistic interdependence that gives birth to meaning-making and forms the psychic capacity to love. Yet the term "father" is misleading here, as it implies privileging the paternal, coinciding with our patriarchal society. Because of this coincidence, Kelly Oliver (2002) prefers to read Kristeva's imaginary father as "the third term, which mediates the mother-child relationship from the beginning" (p. 53). She further claims it as the loving third, as "a conduit between drives/affects and words/symbols" (p. 55) that provides positive support for subjectivity. If I read the return of intimate revolt as a return to the archaic loving third (that incorporates both the semiotic and the symbolic), it seems to me that psychic nonviolence in individual prehistory is ontologically prior to psychic violence. As Oliver (2002) argues, the "violent break from the maternal" (p. 53) to establish identity and meaning in the traditional psychoanalysis model is not necessary. If nonviolence is inherent in humanity and is prior to individual psychic aggression, psychic rebirth is not merely for reparation but also for reconnecting with the always-already-existing interdependence. While creative individuality is suggested by the questioning spirit of revolt, intimacy as the bridge between body/semiotic and mind/symbolic requires a third possibility beyond both dependence and independence: interdependence.

Nonviolence is not Kristeva's language. However, Kristeva (1974/1984, 2002) valorizes the role of the maternal in initiating the child into language and subjectivity and emphasizes the incorporation of the semiotic, maternal function in psychic and social transformation. In foregrounding the imaginary father's function of love and the maternal function of desiring meanings, Kristeva (1987) goes beyond the traditional (male) psychoanalysis model. Kristeva (2002) also suggests that achieving intimacy in revolt involves exhausting psychic aggression, first through getting in touch with it and then through word-representations to enable tender relationships with others. Containing and sublimating psychic aggression in productive activities requires social support, as Oliver (2002) argues, and the teacher is part of such support. Kristeva's (2000) intimate revolt suggests the need for transforming the excess and violence associated with political revolution into more intimate and less violent forms of questioning. This direction toward less violence and more intimacy comes close to nonviolence defined as dissolving violence through both resisting injustice and promoting interconnections.

Based upon the fundamental awareness that "all life is an interconnected whole—is one" (Nagler, 2010, n.p.), Michael Nagler (2010) defines nonviolence as a positive principle of promoting unity between body and mind within the self and compassionate relationships between the self and the other. Nagler (2004, 2010) also discusses nonviolence as the conversion of a negative drive through embracing the interconnectedness of life. Nonviolence extends both hands at the same time: resisting all forms of violence, including intellectual, emotional, and psychic violence, and proactively developing nonviolent relationality to affirm human fellowship and organic relationships with nature. Following both directions requires inner work. Working from within to understand the complexity of one's own psyche in order to work through difficult emotions and refuse to project one's own repressed desires onto others is the site where psychoanalysis and nonviolence converge (Pinar, 1994; Tayler, 2009). Engaging nonviolence within the self and engaging nonviolence with the other go hand in hand.

Certainly there are tensions between psychoanalysis and nonviolence studies, because the former assumes inherent psychic aggression (along with love) while the latter assumes inherent interconnectedness (along with negative energy). I argue that both aggression and compassion exist in the psyche and in society, and they are not a binary but on a continuum. Recognizing the existence of psychic aggression in both the self and the other is important for further "exhausting" it to form compassionate relationships while compassion also springs from interconnectedness and works on aggression to dissolve it. The tension between psychoanalysis and nonviolence is generative. In the process of coming to terms with loss, I have learned to approach such tensions dynamically, pedagogically adopting the double gestures of not only working through psychic and social aggression but also embracing the vital life energy of interconnectedness. While I cannot fully discuss the relationship between psychoanalysis and nonviolence in this article, it is sufficient to say here that these two gestures, if embraced simultaneously, can mutually enable each other. Containing and sublimating psychic aggression can be done through integrative work in nonviolence while nonviolence can be achieved by the psychic working through of repression and projection.

Intimacy, Nonviolence, and Pedagogical Positioning

In social justice education, acknowledging the role of anger, guilt, shame, and fear in encountering the other is important (Shim, 2012; Todd, 2001; Wang, 2008). The denial of difficult emotions can lead to devastating results when these unacknowledged feelings are projected onto others who are socially or culturally marginalized. Working through these negative energies becomes essential: How does one transform guilt or shame into social responsibility (Howard, 2006)? Can anger be converted into the action of searching for creative solutions that all parties can accept for a just cause (Nagler, 2004)? What makes it possible to dissolve fear into a commitment to establishing nonviolent relationality? Here is where knowledge of the psychic life must be coupled with nonviolence work, because understanding an emotion does not necessarily lead to its dissolution. Efforts must be made to integrate the body and the mind in various ways in order to create the conditions for working through difficult emotions through embracing interconnectedness. Nonviolence provides a basis of interconnectedness for this psychic working through.

Over time, I have learned that nonviolent relationality has to be developed through many activities that connect body and mind and connect self and other. Responsibility cannot be demanded, but must be cultivated from within; just action cannot be imposed, but must be initiated by the doer; positive relationships cannot be required, but must be developed within a community. In short, when students' whole beings are touched, they are more likely to participate in the process of making new meanings, which also means that as a teacher educator I have to work on my whole being. The teacher educator's revolt against social injustice needs its semiotic grounding within herself in order to move students to question and generate meanings through working from their inner worlds.

Introducing intimacy in revolt and nonviolence to social justice education, the teacher educator, metaphorically, can be informed by the position of the Kristevian loving third to support students' playful, rather than fearful, entrance into transformative education. Bridging between affects and words, the teacher educator has a unique role in guiding students to make *sense* of the text and the world through investing meanings with sensory experience. The importance of the paternal in Kristeva's third term also corresponds to the position of the teacher educator as the mentor. Without giving up her pedagogical authority, but being willing to suspend her judgment, the teacher educator works with students in such a way that their sense-making activities lead to their feeling of ownership of the new knowledge. Intimate revolt "gives the individual a sense of inclusion in meaning-making and belonging to the social that supports creative activities and the sublimation of drives" (Oliver, 2005, p. 79). Feeling included and that they belong to the class community, students are much more likely to open themselves up to difficult knowledge.

When that unteachable moment broke out in my class, students did not feel a sense of inclusion and belonging in the pedagogical space of the classroom. There was a contradiction in my students' rebellion, as it simultaneously upheld the stable racial representation and opposed the paternal authority that is embodied in the figure of the teacher. As the instructor, I transgressed the paternal law because my teaching challenged the social and cultural status quo of a predominantly White campus. However, as an authority who demanded that students learn what they did not want to learn, I was also a paternal figure who did not adequately incorporate the maternal function, subject to students' transgression. Understanding the complexity of pedagogical positioning in such a situation has gradually led me to follow the circular and complicated movements of intimate revolt and nonviolence in order to engage self-questioning and social questioning together with students in various sustainable ways.

Importantly, I must point out that just as I was not informed of my own sense of loss at that particular moment, I still walk into the classroom now unaware of other affects that I bring to my teaching. This effort of self-understanding on the part of the teacher educator never ends and must be renewed on a daily basis through ongoing questioning. I don't assume that a reflective teacher educator is necessarily more enlightened than students since there is always a third participant—the unconscious—in the pedagogical relationship (Ellsworth, 1997). The teacher educator cannot control the outcome of students' learning even if the best efforts are made, and there is no guarantee that unteachable moments will not happen again. But I believe that the teacher educator has a pedagogical responsibility for both critical self-understanding and creating educative conditions that support students in reaching enlightenment, growth, and self-understanding on their own terms and in their own time. As a part of such conditions, teacher educators' pedagogical companionship with care, watchfulness, and thoughtfulness is essential (Aoki, 2005). This companionship is unconditional and provides an opportunity for students to engage difficult knowledge, but without requiring to "convert." Transformation has to happen from within.

Ongoing Renewal of Pedagogical Relationships

Since that unteachable moment, I have learned that the nonviolent dynamics of building relationships between and among teacher educator, student, text, and context in a community of learners are the key to bringing intimacy to revolt against social violence. Such a dynamic does not shy away from the necessity of challenging the taken-for-granted because questioning is an essential part of intimate revolt; however, providing consistent pedagogical support to students in their difficult journey is necessary.

Approaching pedagogical relationships through the lens of intimacy and nonviolence, I think several aspects need our attention as teacher educators: staying with difficulty and working from within; shifting relational dynamics; and playful engagement beyond categorical thinking. These elements are essential for leading the class to search for meanings in an interminable, ongoing process of individual and communal sense-making, a process of achieving intimacy in revolt. While my unteachable moment happened in the context of social justice pedagogy, the lessons that I have learned from it are applicable to other teaching situations. Social justice pedagogy deals with the issue of how to approach difference and form a relationship with the other who is unfamiliar, and as such it embodies the difficulty of teaching and learning in an intensified way. However, as Sharon Todd (2001) points out, all learning must confront the other, or the stranger in Dwayne Huebner's (1999) terms, which is not only a person, but may also be a text, or the world in general. Addressing the tension of encountering the other provides fertile soil for cultivating pedagogical awareness, understanding, and insights into relationality.

While these lessons are helpful in dealing with unteachable moments, they are also beneficial for creating positive pedagogical conditions to balance the dynamics between the semiotic and the symbolic so that unteachable moments do not happen or happen less often. It is this positive site that I particularly address in this section, focusing on the renewal of pedagogical relationships as an ongoing process of forming nonviolent relationality to support intimacy in questioning and transformation, with or without unteachable moments.

Staying with Difficulty

Intimacy in revolt is achieved by holding the heterogeneous tension between the semiotic and the symbolic to generate new thoughts and meanings. The original difficulty in teaching, to let students learn, is beyond the teacher yet dependent upon her capacity to enable learning (Fowler, 2006). In this sense, teaching is already full of difficulty, indeterminacy, and uncertainty (Ellsworth, 1997; Pitt, 2003); but it is in this unsettling space that teaching hosts generative possibilities. When unteachable moments happen, the gap left by the breakdown of pedagogical relationality is filled with emotional intensity, which invites us to go deeper into the internal dynamics of the relational world for more pedagogical understanding. We have to be able to hold on to the moment, sometimes without knowing what it means, until light is shed into the complexity and depth of pedagogical relationships. Kristeva (2002) uses the term "stagnation" (p. 36) to characterize the endurance of working through in intimate revolt that eventually results in accepting loss and generating new thoughts and relationships.

In the case of my students' rebellion, I listened to students while holding my emotions; in this effort to suspend my response, I made my best attempt at that time to channel the semiotic energies within myself to enable later insights. And these years—still ongoing—of processing my own feelings and working through the difficulties of teaching difficult knowledge have kept inspiring new pedagogical insights. Being able to stay with difficulty rather than dismissing it has been beneficial for me in carving out my own learning curves. At that moment, the challenge for students to re-examine their own identities, or in other words, to confront the loss of their previous self, was thrown back to hit my own (subconscious) sense of losing cultural and teaching identity. If I was not willing to endure the pain of loss and build bridges between loss and meaning, how could I expect the students to do the same? In other words, staying with difficulty requires the teacher educator to encounter and work through loss just as she expects students to do. According to Kristeva's theory, the revolt of the semiotic to destabilize the symbolic needs to be contained by the presence of the loving third for regenerating thinking with compassion. The double difficulty for the teacher educator is that she has to hold this position not only for her students but also for herself. The latter requires her to find her own supportive network.

Dismissing difficulty or blaming others for relational problems often happens in teaching. It is not uncommon for the teacher educator to blame students for not being able to meet pedagogical expectations while students blame the teacher educator for not making learning meaningful. Blaming the other for the relational difficulty, however, usually locks both parties into defensive mechanisms that perpetuate a vicious cycle. For teacher educators, getting in touch with our own other-being within is crucial for learning "how to find the smallest window of opening for relational connection" (Fowler, 2006, p. 179) even when unteachable moments happen. We as teacher educators need to look into our interior world and understand how our responses to students are implicated in the relational complexity we have with ourselves, which has also been influenced by our own parents and teachers in specific social and cultural contexts (Shim, 2012, 2014). If there is a third essential participant, the unconscious, then this participant has a passion for ignorance rather than knowledge (Ellsworth, 1997). In encountering students' passion for ignorance, we must attend to our own passion for ignorance in order to build relational bridges (Gaztambide-Fernández, 2012).

There are different ways of getting in touch with the semiotic so that its interplay with the symbolic can be intimate rather than rebellious. Dream work is one of them. Jeremy Taylor's (2009) discussion of the role of dream work in uncovering the hidden biases on the part of social activists is particularly informative of how the subconscious functions in pedagogical work. In the 1970s, when Taylor was running workshops on overcoming racism for social activist volunteers who had failed to reach local communities, he discovered that staying at the conscious level did not lead to any new understanding but led only to antagonism and accusations. In desperation, he asked participants in the workshop to stop talking about ideas and to share dreams instead, especially dreams that had overt racial overtones. Little did he know that such a shift would become a turning point that eventually transformed those volunteers into effective communicators and collaborators who worked with community members to combat racism. According to Taylor (2009):

> when we started to share those scary, repugnant dreams of being attacked and menaced by dark, sinister, hostile, and dangerous people of other races, we began to lift the repression of aspects of our own unconscious personalities *that had previously been denied and therefore projected onto people of other races in waking life.* (p. 96; emphasis in original)

Only by owning the problematic aspects of ourselves—not repressing them within and thus projecting them onto others—can we have a better and more compassionate relationship with others (Shim, 2014). Taylor (2009) names such work the work of "nonviolence" (p. 108).

While dream work is not something that most teacher educators can do, projects of transforming individual consciousness can be used effectively in pedagogical settings for going deeper into the self to integrate different elements. For example, the method of *currere* focuses on the individual's experiencing of education to reach awakening and transform subjectivity (Miller, 2005; Pinar, 1994; Pinar & Grumet, 1976). Engaging imaginative literature and aesthetic experience, as Maxine Greene (1995) advocates, enables us to travel to unfamiliar worlds to encounter surprises and newness. Using mindful and meditative activities that lead to experiencing the interconnection between body and mind and between self and other is also beneficial for cultivating intimacy and calming the mind at a much deeper level (Bolliger & Wang, 2013; Wang, 2014). All these activities can nurture both the teacher educator's and the students' capacity for enduring difficulty and imagining openings. It is important that the teacher educator practices what she asks students to do. Our ability to dwell in difficulty in order to reach new insights may pull us back from approaching the edge of falling apart in the next situation. Even if an unteachable moment occurs again, we know that we can emerge from it with more insights. As our students are prospective or practicing teachers, they also need to learn how to stay with difficulty so that they can help their students negotiate a space for learning and understanding.

Shifting Relational Dynamics

If staying with difficulty is more about the teacher educators working through their own difficult emotions, then shifting relational dynamics is more about enabling students to work through difficulty and cultivate the courage to step into the unknown to expand themselves. When students have nurtured the capacity for living with uncertainty and accepting loss, they may be able to accomplish subjective and psychic rebirth.

James Jupp and Patrick Slattery, Jr. (2010) argue against the dichotomy between critical pedagogues and resistant students implicated in conversion pedagogy. Some studies of students' resistance to learning difficult knowledge in teacher education portray mainstream students as not being receptive to social justice education and needing to be transformed (Wang & Olson, 2009). In my early years of teaching, I was implicated in such a position. However, such an approach tends to polarize teacher/student relationships and pit one against the other. Shifting relational dynamics toward a mutually enhancing relationship requires moving away from such a dichotomy.

The dualism between critical pedagogues and resistant students implies not only teacher educators' lack of trust in the students' capacity to work through difficulty to reach new understandings on the students' own terms, but also the teacher educators' lack of awareness that their own perspectives are also fluid, temporal, and subject to change. Nonviolent relationality, on the other hand, not only acknowledges the inherent potentiality of both teacher educators and students to confront the psychic and social violence that tears apart the web of life but also suggests that the cultivation of social justice awareness and understanding cannot be accomplished by pedagogical imposition. With a profound faith in students' transformative potential, the teacher educator can provide *both* support *and* challenge for students' psychic rebirth while transforming her own perspectives. The function of the loving third that encourages *questioning* while grounding questioning in students' *desire* for new knowledge becomes especially informative here. Interrupting social norms and students' psychic investment in them must be coupled with returning students' own potentiality, situated in the interconnectedness of life, back to them through detours and curved movements, rather than imposing what is perceived as a better or more progressive ideal from without.

Such attentiveness to bringing the unacknowledged potential into existence may not be pleasant initially but is genuinely educative. Kristeva (2002) speaks about analytic benevolence not as "softness or insouciance but [as] rigor" (pp. 21–22) that grafts meanings to unspeakable desires. Such rigor lies in the capacity of intimate revolt to enable both independence and connections. In a pedagogical setting, Kristeva (1996) discusses the teacher's need to reflect the unknown in the students back to them. Such a return of the unknown semiotic is not a direct return of inaccessible knowledge, which may only reinforce the student's passion for ignorance, but is a return with a different lens through which to look at the same situation in a different way. Students can learn from this process how to ask themselves questions in a new direction and thus integrate into the self the element previously perceived as alien. Here questioning is not only about institutional constraints but also about the self, which leads to both psychic and social renewal. It is a return that encourages students to engage on their own terms, under the teacher educator's guidance, rather than looking for the teacher educator's own ideas.

While confronting pain in working through difficult emotions cannot be avoided, the question in pedagogical relationships is how to go from there to making compassionate connections that compel students to take responsibility by themselves *willingly* rather than taking on an *imposed* obligation. Creating pedagogical conditions in which students make sense out of loss and feel called to contribute to social change involves not only creating a "holding environment in which students are supported and encouraged to reveal what they do not know" (Shim, 2014, p. 123), but also cultivating the teacher educator's receptivity "to hear[ing] and listen[ing] for the meanings that students work out for themselves" (Todd, 2001, p. 439). If loss is a part of learning (Garrison, 1997), as teachers we can never take loss lightly; neither can we abandon the pedagogical responsibility to accompany our students in their difficult journey. Pedagogical companionship has the effect of holding students in the very moment of loss to make it possible for them to work through difficulty later.

Encountering differences can be evocative and inspiring, not merely painful. If the unknown of the self is no longer threatening but inviting, encountering differences can bring the joy of adventuring into the unknown to expand one's own horizons. One way of helping students to work through difficulty is to shift their lens to see difference as an opportunity for integrating newness into the self. As teacher educators, we need to create such conditions of invitation in the classroom so that difference becomes life-affirming. A number of students, after they take on such a difficult yet expansive journey, comment on how their unlearning and learning enabled by difficult knowledge has changed their lives as educators (see students' writings in Wang & Olson, 2009). Such a sense of growth and willingness to explore new ideas and new modes of relationship cannot be built without an essential awareness that life is interconnected and that one's well-being is tied to others' well-being. The emphasis on interconnectedness in nonviolence is a necessary part of enabling intimate revolt in social justice pedagogy.

Understanding the emotional complexity of the teacher-student relationship, the teacher educator also needs to pay attention to network effects, in which the selection and mixture of texts, students' peer support, and local community resources can all play a supportive role. The interaction between and among the teacher educator, the student, the text, and the context shapes the nature of the relational dynamics in the classroom. In shifting relational dynamics from an oppositional mentality to communal questioning, the teacher educator needs to select a unique combination of texts addressing students' needs in their contexts and to provide conditions for students to build together a mutually enriching community that welcomes the stranger.

Matching texts with students involves touching different layers of learning, such as both the personal and the social dimensions, but it does not mean simply catering to students' backgrounds; difference must be included. Discussing controversial issues can lead to confrontations and debates that suppress some students' voices, so it is important to set up discussion guidelines and use strategies to include everyone's perspectives in class discussions (Wang, 2008). Antagonism between teacher educators and students or among students can happen from time to time despite the best pedagogical efforts, and when it happens, humanizing the situation and creating a receptive space for class members to get to know one another as persons is essential for going beyond conflicts. Relational dynamics are often complex and beyond the teacher educator's control, yet conditions can be created to facilitate the flow of the class in order to invite intimate revolt and enact nonviolent relationality in an ongoing process of renewal.

Playful Engagement

Intimate revolt suggests the necessity of play, playing with limits to make passages between the semiotic and the symbolic; the notion of nonviolence also suggests play that goes beyond categorical thinking (Wang, 2014). Educator Leah Fowler (2006) speaks of the importance of play, of playing with "educational conventions, with expectations (of those teachers and students and the knowledge they produce between them), with language, with multiple interpretations, with stories, with each other within the chaos of (daily) life" (pp. 135–136). In dealing with diversity issues in education, identity is sometimes treated as if it were fixed, stable, and fit into a neat box. Competency-based multicultural education approaches often assume that if students in teacher education understand the essential characteristics of an ethnic group, they can effectively teach "ethnic children." However, categorical thinking and categorical teaching can be disastrous (Wang, 2014). Intimate revolt provides a radical openness to ongoing transformation because the process of questioning does not intend to establish a new stable order, and any reification of new values is immediately suspect.

In my early years of teaching, I struggled with how to go beyond categorical thinking yet still teach the social and political realities of "race" and "gender." That rebellious student's response in that unteachable moment seemed to indicate that my initial efforts had not achieved a balance between the symbolic meanings of a social category and the semiotic flow underlying lived experiences. I have learned that teacher educators' and students' engagements with ideas, with texts in context, and with each other need to go beyond categorization while acknowledging the role of difference. As Elizabeth Ellsworth (1997) argues, teaching about and across social and cultural difference has to confront "how the meanings and uses of difference constantly overrun the categories available for analyzing them" (p. 11). We need to find ways to discuss racism and sexism and their effects on our everyday lives without resorting to categorical thinking.

If teaching and learning difficult knowledge is beyond categories, then engagements with difference can be playful and nonjudgmental. Play is not just about enacting hands-on activities in the classroom as it is often perceived, but it is also about being playful with subject matter, ideas, and relations (Doll, 2012). I would add that playing with subjectivity and intersubjectivity leads to a "psychical suppleness" (Kristeva, 2002, p. 237) that allows silent voices to emerge and the missing link to be remade. When playing with tensions rather than fighting over conflicts, people can come together to see a bigger picture of interconnectedness. If I had learned the art of play in teaching, I would have developed productive relationships with students that can contain that unteachable moment (if not prevent it from happening).

In that incident, I questioned whether my own international and gendered backgrounds put me into a disadvantaged position in pedagogical relationships. Although they have played a role at times, since biases and stereotypes do negatively impact minority faculty's pedagogical authority (Guillory, 2011), over the years I have shifted my attention from the effects of the teacher's identity to the effects of the teacher's capacity to shift relational dynamics in the class. The difference between the teacher and the student always exists socially, culturally, intellectually, and individually, so the key is not to be bound by the category of difference but to play with such a pedagogical gap in order to generate more possibilities for both teacher educators and students. What really matters is the nature of relationality; whether or not pedagogical relationships can promote compassionate affiliation, curb aggressive control, or lift repressive mechanisms. If the teacher educator is more playful and does not take herself or her thoughts and beliefs too seriously, students have more room to move around and make their own discoveries beyond categorical thinking. As I have become committed to nonviolence education over the past few years, I often remind myself of the necessity to not reify nonviolence into a fixed ideal but to allow critical questioning of it. A pedagogy of intimate revolt and nonviolence must leave room for self-questioning to keep the process of renewal and rebirth ongoing in daily teaching practice.

In narrating and understanding unteachable moments, my intention is to illuminate how the Kristevian notion of intimacy in revolt, through a lens of nonviolence, opens up more possibilities for a pedagogy that takes on the responsibility of challenging the conventional while at the same time connecting to students' semiotic flow in order to enable their critical questioning. The rebellious posture of oedipal revolt needs to be brought back into a connection with the archaic loving third for a more sustainable transformation of both individuals and society. Intimate revolts inspire educators' pedagogical courage to transform moments of breakdown into generative sites for new awareness and more willingness to bridge sensory experience and new thought in teaching. Such transformation is a process that does not end with the ending of a class because teaching and un/learning is an ongoing process of sense-making. A pedagogical relationship of nonviolence in teacher education evokes both teacher educators' and students' working from within to engage in self-transformation and (future) pedagogical transformation through intimate revolt.

References

Aoki, T. T. (2005). Layers of teaching. In W. F. Pinar & R. L. Irwin (Eds.), *Curriculum in a new key* (pp. 187–199). Lawrence Erlbaum.
Bolliger, L., & Wang, H. (2013). Pedagogy of nonviolence. *Journal of Curriculum and Pedagogy, 10*(2), 112–114.
Britzman, D. P. (1998). *Lost subjects, contested objects*. State University of New York Press.
Doll, M. A. (1996). *To the lighthouse and back*. Peter Lang.
Doll, Jr., W. E. (2012). *Pragmatism, post-modernism, and complexity theory* (D. Trueit, Ed.). Routledge.
Dougherty, L. (1999). *Understanding race*. Films for the Humanities.
Ellsworth, E. (1997). *Teaching positions*. Teachers College Press.
Fowler, L. (2006). *Curriculum of difficulty*. Peter Lang.
Garrison, J. (1997). *Dewey and eros*. Teachers College Press.
Gaztambide-Fernández, R. (2012). Our passion for ignorance. *Curriculum Inquiry, 42*(4), 445–453.
Greene, M. (1995). *Releasing the imagination*. Jossey-Bass.
Guillory, N. (2011). What is a hip hop feminist doing in teacher education? *Journal of Curriculum Theorizing, 27*(3), 20–32.
Havinghurst, R. J. (1952). *Human development and education*. David McKay.
Howard, G. R. (2006). *We can't teach what we don't know* (2nd ed.). Teachers College Press.
Huebner, D. (1999). *The lure of the transcendent* (V. Hillis, Ed.). Lawrence Erlbaum.
Hyun, E., & Marshall, J. D. (2003). Teachable-moment-oriented curriculum practice in early childhood education. *Journal of Curriculum Studies, 35*(1), 111–127.
Jupp, J., & Slattery, Jr., P. G. (2010). Committed White male teachers and identifications. *Curriculum Inquiry, 40*, 454–474.
Kristeva, J. (1984). Revolution in poetic language (M. Waller, Trans.). Columbia University Press. (Original work published 1974)
Kristeva, J. (1987). *Tales of love* (L. S. Roudiez, Trans.). Columbia University Press.
Kristeva, J. (1993). Foreign body. *Transition, 2*, 172–183.
Kristeva, J. (1996). *Julia Kristeva: Interviews* (R. M. Guberman, Ed.). Columbia University Press.
Kristeva, J. (2000). *The sense and non-sense of revolt* (J. Herman, Trans.). Columbia University Press.
Kristeva, J. (2002). *Intimate revolt* (J. Herman, Trans.). Columbia University Press.
Liddell, D. L. (2012). Identifying and working through teachable moments. *New Directions in Student Services, 139*, 17–26.
Miller, J. (2005). *Sounds of silence breaking*. Peter Lang.
Nagler, M. N. (2004). *The search for a nonviolent future*. Inner Ocean Publishing.

Nagler, M. N. (2010). *Nonviolence today*. YouTube. Retrieved August 6, 2012, from http://www.youtube.com/watch?v=gavOJG4IxpQ

Oliver, K. (2002). Psychic space and social melancholy. In K. Oliver & S. Edwin (Eds.), *Between the psyche and the social* (pp. 49–65). Rowman & Littlefield.

Oliver, K. (2005). Revolt and forgiveness. In T. Chanter & E. P. Ziarek (Eds.), *Revolt, affect, collectivity* (pp. 77–92). State University of New York Press.

Pinar, W. F. (1994). *Autobiography, politics, and sexuality*. Peter Lang.

Pinar, W. F., & Grumet, M. R. (1976). *Toward a poor curriculum*. Kendall/Hunt.

Pitt, A. (2003). *The play of the personal*. Peter Lang.

Shim, J. M. (2012). Exploring how teachers' emotions interact with intercultural texts. *Curriculum Inquiry, 42*(4), 472–496.

Shim, J. M. (2014). Multicultural education as an emotional situation. *Journal of Curriculum Studies, 46*(1), 116–137.

Tarc, A. M. (2013). "I just have to tell you." *Pedagogy, Culture & Society, 21*(3), 383–402.

Taubman, P. (1990). Achieving the right distance. *Educational Theory, 40*(1), 121–133.

Taylor, J. (2009). *The wisdom of your dreams*. Jeremy P. Tarcher/Penguin.

Todd, S. (2001). "Bringing more than I contain": Ethics, curriculum and the pedagogical demand for altered egos. *Journal of Curriculum Studies, 33*(4), 431–450.

Wang, H. (2008). "Red eyes": Engaging emotions in multicultural education. *Multicultural Perspectives, 10*(1), 10–16.

Wang, H. (2013). A nonviolent approach to social justice education. *Educational Studies, 49*(6), 485–503.

Wang, H. (2014). *Nonviolence and education*. Routledge.

Wang, H., & Olson, N. (Eds.). (2009). *A journey to unlearn and learn in multicultural education*. Peter Lang.

Woodhouse, H. (2011). Storytelling in university education. *Journal of Educational Thought, 45*(3), 211–238.

· 7 ·

AN INTEGRATIVE PSYCHIC LIFE, NONVIOLENT RELATIONS, AND CURRICULUM DYNAMICS IN TEACHER EDUCATION (2019)[1]

This paper draws upon both Carl Jung's theory of the psyche and nonviolence philosophy to re-examine curriculum dynamics in the context of teacher education. The Jungian theory is about individualized pathways of integrating the conscious and the unconscious, while nonviolence theory is about integrating the body and the mind within the self and developing compassionate relationships with others. For the past decade I have elaborated the meanings of nonviolence philosophy for curriculum studies in various contexts, and intentionally chosen the word "nonviolence" over "non-violence" to emphasize its positive capacity for individual and social integration. While the primary focus of analytical psychology is the individual person, Jung situates the individual in the collective unconscious, so an individual's integration of the psychic life is connected to both the personal and human history. Although the connections between nonviolent relations and Jung's theory of the psyche might not be obvious at first glance since they follow different directions, I think there are several important intersections—in direct or complementary ways—that can transform the inner and relational dynamics in curriculum.

---

1 This chapter is reprinted with permission of the publisher, Springer Nature. Wang, H. (2019). An integrative psychic life, nonviolent relations, and curriculum dynamics in teacher education. *Studies in Philosophy and Education*, 38, 377–395.

These intersections are sites for teacher education to create conditions for individual growth and social transformation (Pinar, 2012; Wang, 2018, 2019).

It might be helpful to note here that there is a distinction between the psychotherapeutic room, in which changing individual personality is the goal, and the classroom setting, in which integrative education is for students' intellectual and personal growth. In this paper, incorporating Jungian principles in education is not about direct applications, but about using philosophical orientations of Jungian theory for understanding the internal dynamics of curriculum as lived experience. The informative role of psychoanalysis and analytic psychology in the field of education and teacher education has long been discussed (Britzsman, 1998; Kincheloe & Pinar, 1991; Mayes, 2005, 2007; Shim, 2018; Taubman, 2012; Wang, 2004); however, few deal with its intersections with nonviolence theory. The focus of this paper is on the intersections between Jungian and nonviolence theory, rather than on analytic psychology alone, and its argument is that these intersections are educationally informative.

Recently, school violence and mass shootings have frequently made the headlines in the United States. The public outrage often focuses on the means of violence rather than its psychic and cultural roots, which must be treated along with critically handling means. To treat the roots of violence and its damaging impact on the younger generations, educators should embrace nonviolence as an educational project of cultivating the unity of the self and loving relations with others—not only as an antidote to violence but also as a source of positive energy. Nonviolent relationships with others, however, cannot be built without a nonviolent relationship with the self, as Carl Jung (1966) points out: "Relationship to the self is at once relationship to our fellow man [sic],[1] and no one can be related to the latter until he is related to himself" (p. 233).

Violence is not new to our age. As Heesoon Bai and Avraham Cohen (2008) argue, the dualistic split between the body and the mind and between the self and the other is the source of violence both historically and contemporarily. In this sense, the current mainstream focus in American education on intellectual excellence and competitiveness and in teacher education on an instrumental mentality to achieve rational mastery and control serves only to reinforce rather than dissolve the mechanism of psychic and social violence. In this paper, I will focus on teacher education, although it is intimately related to K-12 education. If teachers are not educated to understand and practice nonviolent integration with themselves and in their teaching, curriculum dynamics at K-12 schools can hardly be mobilized to contest the controlling mechanism; nor can they contribute to building a loving community. Certainly, there is no simple relationship between K-12 education and teacher education. There are certain differences between educating children and educating adults, and it is beyond the scope of this paper to discuss both levels (see Mayes, 2005, 2007 and Lindsey & Wang, 2013 for implications for school-based education), so I focus on the intersections between Jungian theory and nonviolence studies and their important implications for teacher education.

This paper argues for foregrounding the role of nonviolence through an integrative psychic life in teacher education to enact curriculum dynamics beneficial for personal and social transformation that bridges the divide and promotes compassionate relationships. Focusing on the integrative power of the psyche—Jung (1953) also terms it "the transcendent function" (p. 80)—and of nonviolence (Nagler, 2004), we can heal the wounds of psychic and social violence while simultaneously spreading the positive energy of "heart unity" (Gandhi, 1947, p. 228) both within the self and with others in a mutually flourishing community (Hershock, 2012). With this focus on integration and nonviolence, engaging curriculum dynamics becomes *an everyday practice* of education in an ongoing process of positively cultivating integrated personhood and compassionate relations (Wang, 2019). The purpose of this paper is not to present a model of intervention to counteract violence, but to illuminate one possible less-traveled pathway on which educators and students can embark for individual and social reconstruction to create a better world together.

Laboring in American teacher education for many years, having taught both Jungian theory and nonviolence philosophy to pre-service and in-service teachers, I choose the context of teacher education to elaborate three important intersections between an integrative psychic life and nonviolent relations for enacting transformative curriculum dynamics: the thread of interconnectedness, shadow awareness and nonviolent relationality, and complementary modes of psychic and nonviolent integration. After a discussion of these aspects and their curriculum implications, the final section highlights some possibilities for integrative and nonviolent curriculum dynamics with the inclusion of a few teaching examples.

The Undercurrent of Interconnectedness

The thread of interconnectedness runs through both Jung's theory of the psyche and nonviolence theory, although both recognize the individual as the site for initiating transformation (Jung, 1968a; Nagler, 2004). The notion of the unconscious in Jungian analytical psychology, different from classical Freudian psychoanalysis, is not only individual but also collective, where archetypal energy is most dynamic. As Jung (1956) argues, "The essence of conscious processes is adaptation, which takes place in a series of particulars. The unconscious, on the other hand, is universal: it not only binds individuals together into a nation or race, but unites them with the men of the past and with their psychology" (p. 177). If archetypes are universal while the contents of archetypes can be culturally specific, then interconnection underlies humanity across cultures, and between humans and other beings. The integrative psychic life is about assimilating the personal and collective unconscious into consciousness in order to become the Self beyond the ego, a unifying symbol of the psyche.

Nonviolence theory is based upon a strong sense of interconnectedness among all beings. Originating in Indian philosophy, the Sanskrit term for nonviolence, *Ahimsa*, means doing no harm and being kind to all living beings as "a positive doctrine of love, friendship, and equality" (Shastri & Shastri, 2007). This sense of nonviolence both as negating violence and affirming love extends across cultures. Martin Luther King, Jr., (1986) approaches nonviolence as the ethic of love, "a creative force in this universe that works to bring the disconnected aspects of reality into a harmonious whole" (p. 20). The feeling of being part of the whole is echoed in the African notion of *ubuntu*, which affirms the individual person's humanity through other persons because "we belong in a bundle of life" (Tutu, 1999, p. 31).

However, there is a certain difference between Jung's theory and nonviolence theory. The Jungian theory of the psyche positions the collective unconscious that connects humanity as the undercurrent of human life, generally inaccessible unless the individual engages in the difficult labor of integrating its contents through the process of individuation. Western ego-consciousness, as Jung (1968a) points out, tends to "swallow up" or "suppress" the interconnectedness as unconscious (p. 288), even though neither tendency is beneficial for the individual's well-being. For Jung (1956), the psyche existed before the existence of individual consciousness, and through making contact with the source, the individual can "regain something of that mysterious and irresistible power which comes from the feeling of being part of the whole" (p. 178). In other words, individuality can be enriched and energized by assimilating the collective energy. However, the collective unconscious also has the power to overwhelm—or "devour"—the individual who is not aware of its influence. In that sense, interconnectedness of the whole is double-edged, and its positive potential can be realized through psychic energy that unites the conscious and the unconscious.

By contrast, nonviolence theory is built upon the conscious awareness of interconnectedness as the foundation of human life, an awareness which requires the individual to move beyond the appearance of separate existence. In other words, interconnectedness is in general approached as positive, although the relational dynamics of nonviolence already imply contesting any collective tendency toward suppressing individuals. Drawing upon Buddhism, Peter Hershock (2012) argues for a relational ontology in which separate entities exist as aspects of relational dynamics in which diversity plays a positive role. He also points out that realizing patterns of interdependence "necessarily entails both a *critique of self* and a *critique of culture*" (p. 41; italics in original), going beyond modern dualism. In a non-dualistic view, commonality and difference, the subject and the object, and the self and the other exist interdependently. Nonviolence transforms the nature of interpersonal, intergroup, and international relationships from ego-centered power struggles to a mutual flourishing of humanity and community. As I noted above, Jung privileges individuation, so there is a difference here. In other words, nonviolence theory has a more optimistic view of human nature, interpersonal relationship, and community than does Jungian theory. However, interconnectedness as the fundamental thread of life is a shared foundation.

Situating curriculum dynamics in psychic, intellectual, spiritual, and cosmic interconnectedness, teacher educators have a double task: First, to shift the focus from individualism to the Jungian individuality that incorporates the collective; and second, to highlight the organic relationality that makes nonviolent relationships possible. Because of the individualistic cultural orientation in the United States and in the West in general, students often find it difficult to imagine nonviolent relations beyond their immediate circle (Wang, 2013). From the challenges of teaching nonviolence, I realize that starting with re-imagining the individual as embodied and relational often has a more receptive response from students than starting with the notion of interconnectedness. The Jungian notion of individuality provides a bridge to students' further move into understanding the meanings of organic relationality. On the other hand, the unity of life must also be experienced and critically reflected on to unfold the integrative dynamics of curriculum. Students' exposure to a radically different approach sometimes evokes heightened awareness, when they are moved to step outside of their comfort zone, as examples I discuss later show.

The Individual and the Social

In Freudian theory, more often than not, the individual is picked against society since civilization is perceived as having an inherent repressive mechanism (Freud, 1961). However, in Jung's (1953) theory, morality is a function of the human soul, so it is perceived as inherent in humanity: "Morality is not imposed from outside; we have it in ourselves from the start—not the law, but our moral nature without which the collective life of human society would be impossible" (p. 27). This view of human nature builds a bridge to the notion of nonviolence as ethical relationships. Jung approaches individuality as a unique "fulfilment of the collective qualities of the human being" (pp. 173–174) because the collective unconscious is the foundation of an individual's psychic life. But Jung also warns repeatedly against the danger of individuals' being carried away in mass culture's pursuit of uniformity, or the shadow-side of archetypes, which leads to personal and collective disaster. In this sense, the individual and the collective are intricately interrelated and mutually embedded rather than separate, but the self cannot be submerged into the social without losing its creative capacity.

Nonviolence supports relational dynamics that spread integrative power to individuals who can hold tensions within and to communities that are hospitable to difference. Such an integration is first of all the aspiration of an individual who reaches a higher level of existence by getting in touch with the interconnected life, which hosts difference. At the social level, to heal the divide between the self and the other, Nagler (2004) discusses the role of imagination:

> If I don't have the imagination to realize that you and I are one, despite our physical separateness and the differences in our outlooks on life, what's to prevent me from using violence if I think you're getting in my way? (p. 42)

Social imagination, aesthetic experience, spiritual quests for transcending divisions are needed for going beyond dualism and creating a meaningful community (Greene, 1995). Gandhi (1947) speaks about unbreakable heart unity in the context of religious conflicts in a communal life. Heart unity is the thread in nonviolent relations across contestation, conflicts, and fragmentation.

It is at the level of the productive and positive energy of nonviolence that violence can be questioned and dissolved from its root when the power of psychic and cosmic interconnectedness is embraced. While classical psychoanalysis seems to position aggression and violence as primary and non-violence as secondary (Todd, 2001), the intersections between Jungian psychic life and nonviolent relations question such an assertion; our ancestral and individual histories have made human fellowship a necessity for an individual's existence and our species' survival. Between the individual and the social, I argue, the strongest link is not the psychoanalytic reparation but the inherent human need for an affiliated way of life. Clifford Mayes (2007) also points out that "Jung believed that the archetypally feminine is epistemologically prior to the archetypally masculine" (p. 127), so knowing through intuition and relations has primacy over knowing through logic and differentiation.

In teacher education, dynamic relationships between the individual and the social need to be explored and experienced. The social imagination of interconnectedness can be activated through experientially-based pedagogy, autobiographical writings about relationships, literary and poetic expressions, and community engagement projects. For example, I assign students a writing project on "relationships and me" to trace the intergenerational influence of parent/mentor on them and theirs on their students. They write journals on their own for the first part of the class and then engage in critical reflection on their experiences. While autobiographical reflection always runs the risk of reinforcing the focus on the individual, when social experience and imagination of beyond the self is the focus of such a reflection, students are more likely—there is no guarantee, of course—to step outside of rigid boundaries, discover missing links, and transcend the usual sense of separation.

On the other hand, sudden awakenings to the integrative power of organic relationality can also shock many students into new awareness. In my teaching experience, both Desmond Tutu's (1999) book on the Truth and Reconciliation Commission's work in South Africa and the Liberian women's peace movement depicted in the documentary, *Pray the Devil Back to Hell* (Disney & Riticker, 2008), had dramatic effects on students. Because the notion of *ubuntu* was alien to them and the women's collective power was unimaginably stronger than masculine domination, students were captivated by experiencing an unfamiliar life energy. The pull of cultural difference became an opening to alterative possibilities. Here the self is not lost in the social—students questioned the social conventions of violence and their own complicity in it—but the horizon of their consciousness was expanded when they encountered the unexpected possibilities.

Spirituality of Interconnectedness

Both the integrative psychic life and nonviolent relationality have a strong spiritual dimension. The term that Carl Jung uses to describe coming to terms with the unconscious, "the transcendent function" that unites opposites, already carries a spiritual implication. For Jung (1960), the unconscious is half instinctual and half spiritual. He points out, "The collective unconscious contains the whole spiritual heritage of mankind's evolution, born anew in the brain structure of every individual" (p. 158). Here the spiritual is broader than formal religions. Jung rebels against religious dogmas, but he interweaves the images and symbols of ancient mythologies in various cultures, indigenous spiritual traditions, and modern monotheism.

Jung (1960) points out that spirituality is paradoxical. He argues, "Just as the archetype is partly a spiritual factor, and partly like a hidden meaning immanent in the instincts, so the spirit, as I have shown, is two-faced and paradoxical: a great help and an equally great danger" (p. 222). Thus, the human capacity for finding balance through the paradoxical condition of spirituality becomes important. Integrating the conscious and the unconscious requires becoming aware of archetypal energy, making an effort to realize its constructive potential while not losing oneself in the flood of the collective unconscious. In this sense, embracing the spirituality of interconnectedness is an upward journey through transcending the self.

Nonviolence leaders are often spiritual leaders: Mahatma Gandhi, Martin Luther King, Jr., Jane Addams, and Desmond Tutu, to list a few. King (1986) speaks about "the love of God operating in the human heart" (p. 19) in nonviolent resistance. Here he does not speak of love as sentimental but as *agape*:

> It means understanding, redeeming good will for all men [sic]. It is an overflowing love which seeks nothing in return. It is the love of God working in the lives of men.... Here we rise to the position of loving the person who does the evil deed while hating the deed that the person does. (pp. 140–141)

Such a universal sense of love that supports nonviolent resistance against social oppression is not dependent on personal liking or disliking, but is based on a spiritual unity that redeems all people. The African notion of *ubuntu* is also a spiritual philosophy in which "the individual is implicated in the whole" and "the self bears witness to a transcendent, transphenomenal capacity for human good, no matter how complicated and ethically complex that 'good' might be(come)" (Swanson, 2009, p. 11). While there are debates about the contemporary applicability of *ubuntu* for democratic education (Letseka, 2012), as a philosophy of life, its spiritual dimension of transcending ontological separateness has profound educational implications. A strong sense of spirituality—without religious imposition—is necessary for rising above fragmentation and hatred, for nurturing nonviolent relations and creating the beloved community.

In this transformative and transcendent spiritual quest, making connections and seeking meanings and purposes bridges between a dynamic psychic life and nonviolent relations. Michael Nagler (2004) associates the prevalence of violence with a crisis of meaning and lack of purpose in life. He argues that, in engaging nonviolence work, "real meaning comes when we get connected in some way to a purpose higher than ourselves and beyond ourselves" (p. 155). Jung (1960) also argues that "the question of meaning and purpose" (p. 75) is important for one's engagement with the transcendent function of integrating the unconscious. He points out,

> The achievement of a synthesis of conscious and unconscious contents, and the conscious realization of the archetype's effects upon the conscious contents, represents the climax of a concentrated spiritual and psychic effort, in so far as this is undertaken consciously and of set purpose. (pp. 210–211)

Beyond the individual yet within the individual, the spiritual dimension of life supports a meaningful and purposeful engagement in education. Teacher educators need to tap into the collective energy to foster an environment that is a "sacred space" (Mayes, 2005, p. 36) where students have the freedom to communally explore emergent ideas and complex relationships. Such interactions bring out synergetic energy to shift curriculum and classroom dynamics toward a higher level of purpose. A sense of flow can emerge to connect students with texts and among themselves in such a spiritual—beyond the religious—space.

Shadow Work and Nonviolent Relations

Shadow and archetypal awareness is important for both psychic integration and nonviolent relationality. According to Jung (1953), "By shadow I mean the 'negative' side of the personality, the sum of all those unpleasant qualities we like to hide, together with the insufficiently developed functions and the contents of the personal unconscious" (p. 66). Here the shadow contains multiple aspects: the dark aspect that one wants to hide; the potential talents or dispositions that family or society disapproved of; and the underdeveloped functions that need more attention. To become conscious of these aspects and integrate the shadow, one needs multiple types of nonviolence work: withdrawing shadow projections; uncovering the potential; and developing weaker functions to achieve balance. These aspects are connected to archetypal energy of anima and animus in the collective unconscious, although this paper addresses only the shadow work. While nonviolence theory has a positive approach to the human psyche, acknowledging and working through the shadow is also necessary for forming compassionate relations. Not recognizing one's own shadow risks projecting it onto others and losing the possibility of building a dynamic community that is hospitable to difference.

Withdrawing Shadow Projections for Compassionate Relationships

The shadow in the individual person, if unrecognized, is projected onto others or the world, and such projections distort the reality of others or the world and cause misunderstandings and conflicts between the self and the other. Once recognized, projections can be detached and become integrated into the ego-personality to expand the horizon of consciousness. However, "no one can become conscious of the shadow without considerable moral effort" (Jung, 1968b, p. 8). It is an ethical issue for the individual to own up to the shadow so as not to thrust the perceived darkness onto others.[2]

Clearly the projection of the shadow has social and cultural implications. What we don't want to see in ourselves, we ascribe to others in a different social group with a lower status. In the contemporary setting, racial minorities, immigrants, refugees, or the poor can easily become the carrier of the shadow for psychic projections. Withdrawing these projections is a necessary step for self-understanding, respecting others for who and what they are, and confronting social prejudices. In this sense, detaching shadow projections and engaging nonviolent relations are intricately related.

Jeremy Taylor (2009) discusses using Jungian dream work for transforming social justice volunteers' unconscious racial attitudes in a community organizing project in 1969 in a small town in California. A number of White volunteers had come into the Black neighborhood but failed to establish any meaningful relationships with residents. He organized seminars on overcoming racism, but after attempting to reason and argue about issues as a group, he found that rational debates did not work. As a last resort, he invited participants to share dreams particularly related to dark figures. As they began to share nightmares, Taylor reports, the usual "cynicism and increasingly antagonistic debate" (p. 94) in previous meetings subsided and

> we began to lift the repression of aspects of our own unconscious personalities that *had previously been denied and therefore projected onto people of other races in waking life*. The nasty characters in those dreams were, as they always are, reflections of those problematic parts of *ourselves* that we had been unable to accept. (p. 96; italics in original)

The group became much better at recognizing the psychological roots of racism and began to be aware of their own racial stereotypes. After dream work, they were able to form better relationships with residents. Shadow projections break social connections and shadow integration through dream analysis heals the broken links. Accepting the complexity of the inner life makes it possible for one to suffer *with* others and develop compassionate relationships. At the collective level, the "national, cultural, and racial psyches—all of which naturally have their shadow sides" (Mayes, 2007, p. 105) and the collective shadow projections must be withdrawn in order to form nonviolent intergroup relations. Detaching the shadow projection from others is closely related to "nonviolent conversion" (Nagler, 2004) of negative thoughts and emotions, a notion that is discussed in the next section.

In teacher education, we must confront social violence such as racism, sexism, classism, and homophobia. However, rational debates and discussions about these deeply emotional issues—or in other words, collectively shared trauma—often cannot go very far, because students' psychic defensive mechanisms are quickly mobilized to block off different viewpoints. Part of the defense is related to their refusal to discover what is inside the self, those layers that evoke painful memories or difficult emotions. Building bridges to inner emotional complexity is necessary and yet often neglected in the classroom. The ability to recognize and integrate the shadow within the self is enabled by subjective reflection (Shim, 2018). Although we frequently discuss teacher reflection in teacher education, it often stays at the level of reflecting on events and what is going on in the classroom, and seldom goes deeper into the subjective happenings in the teachers' inner landscapes.

"The best way to educate others is for the educator himself to be educated" is Jung's (1954, p. 132) advice for educators. Anne Phelan (2015) also argues for the central role of teacher subjectivity in teacher education. Engaging students' inner work to understand the mechanism of psychic projections and cultivate compassionate relationships with others who are culturally different lays the foundation for connecting one's psychic life and nonviolent relationality. While dream work may not be applicable in the formal setting of teacher education, a variety of activities—engaging students' sensory experience and imaginative capacities through literature and film analysis, for example—can help students to work through difficult emotions, open up to difficult knowledge, and build relationships across differences and tensions. Teacher educators should be aware of their own psychic condition, not only for deepened self-understanding but also because they influence their students explicitly and implicitly through their presence.

Realizing the Shadow and Building a Community of Nonviolence

The shadow is not necessarily negative, and sometimes societal norms make an individual to devalue his or her potentiality. Jung (1960) talks about "the realization of the shadow" (p. 208) and how such a realization is not an intellectual activity but an emotional engagement with suffering and passion. The growing awareness of one's potentiality can be painful, as it involves unlocking the mechanism of exclusion, but it also taps into new possibilities. For instance, for a male school leader who had to sacrifice his artistic talents from a young age to become a culturally sanctioned authority figure, realizing that he gave up his potential to fit into the social and family expectations for manhood can be distressing. However, integrating the shadow can transform his consciousness and shift his attitude toward life and education in a new direction.

Raising shadow awareness is often in conflict with the social and culturally constructed images of identity, such as race, gender, class, or sexuality. The gendered image of the teacher—essentially female—as innocent, self-sacrificing, and caring does not have any psychic depth and pushes complicated emotions to the shadow side in woman teachers. But the shadow can come out unexpectedly. Mary Aswell Doll's (1996) story is a good example. Teaching in a local university, Doll had put up with a male student's aggression for more than half a semester: "I was my usual affable self, answering his challenges with ever-so-professional replies, setting up conference appointments which he missed and I dismissed" (p. 124)—until she exploded and slammed her book onto the desk and railed against him in front of the whole class. While the damaging effect of her repressed anger was evident, what had also become a shadow for her was the inner authority as an intellectually successful woman who could affirmatively counteract male aggression and yet not lose her caring attitude. After the incident, Doll realized the need to reclaim her pedagogical authority to curb aggression while recognizing her passion for infusing emotions into teaching. Navigating the complexity of their inner worlds, woman teachers need to lift the repression and realize their potential that has been excluded by gendered norms.

Jung is well known for formulating four major personality types—thinking, feeling, sensate, and intuitive. While everyone has elements from different types, a person tends to have a predominant orientation, and the correspondingly weaker areas become the inferior functions. As each type is not inherently better than other types, Jung advocates for paying more attention to the underdeveloped functions for balance, although doing so is not intended to compete with but to supplement the superior function. Realizing the shadow involves "the growing awareness of the inferior part of the personality" (Jung, 1960, p. 208) and if one's weakness is strengthened, one becomes fuller and more integrated.

Understanding one's own fears of the dark, the unpermitted, and the underdeveloped in order to recognize and integrate one's shadow is also a form of engaging nonviolence with the self. If the shadow within the self today can be the unrealized potential of the past or a new possibility for the future, then the shadow becomes a friend to support the self. Similarly, instead of projecting the shadow onto those who are rejected and unwelcome today in a community, those who are different can be perceived as bringing new opportunities for the benefit of the whole community. In this sense, at the intersection of realizing the shadow and establishing a community of nonviolence, accepting one's own difference within the self opens up a psychic space for accepting a social space composed of members who are diverse in thinking, feeling, and being.

A nondual approach to the relationships between the self and the other is essential for forming nonviolent social relations. Nonduality implies that the self and the other cannot be reduced into sameness and yet cannot be fully separated into two entities either. The dynamics of nonviolent relations do not rely on commonality, and differences must be recognized, incorporated, and transformed; thus, creating an integrative communal life is compatible with constructing an integrative individual psychic life in which tensions, conflicts, and oppositions are worked through. Such a community of nonviolence approaches the other not as a hostile enemy, but as a symbol of the potential growth of the self to enrich the collectively shared life together.

Teacher education needs to create conditions for students to experience such a community in the classroom, a community in which self-reflection, critical inquiry, and connections across differences are supported. Here difference cannot be erased or radicalized, but is an intimate part of the psyche and the community for realizing potentiality. Realizing the shadow within the self cannot be taught, but students sometimes volunteer to share their own stories when moved by other people's lives and class discussions. Sharing personal stories and struggles in the classroom contributes to nurturing mutual trust that in turn cultivates a community of learners. Nonviolent conversion of negative energy can happen in a classroom setting either quietly within the self or explicitly in interacting with others. Teacher educators can design curriculum in such a way that encourages students' inner work and critical inquiry. In such a community, agreement among members is not pursued, but ongoing opening to psychic and social difference is the condition for transforming curriculum dynamics, which requires teacher educators to have the capacity to hold tensions and contain uncertainty.

Multiple Modes of Psychic and Nonviolent Integration

Analytical psychology originated in the treatment of people who were experiencing difficulty in their lives; thus, many of its underlying principles are about how to remove obstacles for psychic integration, although it also reveals principles of the psyche that are generally applicable. In contrast, nonviolence originates in a strong sense of organic relationality and doing no harm to others in one's daily life. Here confronting difficulty and spreading positive energy go hand in hand: analytic psychology deals with negative psychic energy while affirming a transformative attitude; nonviolence relies on positive life energy while converting dualistic approaches so as to dissolve violence. Moreover, psychic integration and social integration interrelate: Psychic wholeness promotes compassionate relationships with others and nonviolent social relations are enabled by the individual's mindful experiencing of body/mind/spirit interconnectedness.

At the site of confronting the unconscious and cultivating nonviolent relations, what modes of integration can be used to mutually enhance the efforts to seek the wholeness of the psyche and create a community of nonviolence? What means can be used to bring into the light repressed or excluded memories, thoughts, or emotions? What can we rely on to achieve nonviolent conversion of pain, grief, fear, anger, anxiety as they emerge from our psychic and social lives? Understanding multiple modes of psychic and nonviolent integration can help teacher educators engage curriculum dynamics in such a way that defensive and aggressive mechanisms can be dissolved and nonviolent engagements can be inspired.

The archetypal image of wholeness is based upon integrating opposites to achieve dynamic balance. Free association, dream analysis, and active imagination are commonly used in psychotherapy to remove obstacles for recovering balance. While these methods can seldom be used directly in the classroom, Jung's emphasis on the role of imagination, art, myth, experiential understanding, and embodied engagement for psychic wholeness has important implications for education. Psychic integration and the inner work of nonviolence are intimately linked. Nonviolence is also a guiding principle for social movements, with a variety of nonviolent strategies that can inform educators of how to effectively use social action and service learning projects in education. In this section, I focus on multiple pathways of psychic and social integration that are particularly informative to teacher education.

Beyond the Intellect: Synthetic Method and the Integrative Power of Nonviolence

Moving beyond the intellect is called for by both analytical psychology and nonviolence studies. Jung (1966) discusses the change in attitude that is necessary for the transformation of the personality:

> An attitude that seeks to do justice to the unconscious as well as to one's fellow human beings cannot possibly rest on knowledge alone.... If books and the knowledge they impart are given exclusive value, man's emotional and affective life is bound to suffer. That is why the purely intellectual attitude must be abandoned. (pp. 278–279)

During Jung's long period of confrontation with the unconscious, from 1913 to 1930, he drew many images that came from his own dreams, highlighting the role of translating emotions and fantasies through image-drawing and symbol-making (Jung, 2009; Wehr, 1987). That period was also emotionally intense, and his imaginative expressions of what was beyond the intellect led to his creative formulation of the collective unconscious. Jung terms this method of integrating archetypal images through mandala drawings as a constructive or "synthetic" treatment of the unconscious, in contrast to the analytical, causal-reductive interpretation. Jung (1960) believes that "integrative unity" and "inner division" form a pair of opposites that seek balance through a dynamic process (p. 51). How this process unfolds is unique to each individual, with each one's different talents, but in general it requires the combination of and interplay between creative formulations and experiential understanding of the meaning.

The integrative power of nonviolence also goes beyond the intellect. Without heartfelt experiences of engaging nonviolent relationships with the self and the other, transcending dualism is difficult. Both the inner work and the outer work of nonviolence involve the experiencing of organic relationality. The inner work of nonviolence involves meditation practices and the conversion of negative energy. Here, *experiencing* difficult emotions such as anger, fear, or anxiety is a necessary step before approaching their conversion because holding down negative feelings can be a form of violence to the self, as Doll's story tells us. In meditation that heals the divide between body, mind, and spirit, accepting emotions as they emerge and then letting them go allows an individual to experience, rather than ignoring or suppressing, a wide range of feelings. Experiencing emotions without identifying with them cultivates a critical attitude that can hold anger and fear without acting upon them and eventually transforms them in constructive directions. Importantly, the unity of life underlies the possibility of the nonviolent conversion of hostile thoughts, negative emotions, and aggressive action.

Such conversion also involves mindful interactions with others to construct mutually beneficial relationships—the outer work of nonviolence. Finding alternative ways out of the usual "flight or fight" reactions to conflicts and forming creative nonviolent responses to antagonism call for practicing *agape* love, which invites humane interactions among people while addressing individual and social wrongdoings. In pursuing restorative social justice, we need to make an effort to recover the broken relationships in a community through curbing psychic and social aggression, evoking humane responses from all parties, and seeking heart unity among members, especially those who contest one another. Notably, the shared constructive work everyone in a community pursues together has a profound effect on evoking the integrative power of nonviolence, and this positive energy has both healing and creative power for human relations.

In today's competitive world, education is often deeply embedded in an intellectual attitude at the expense of emotional, social, and spiritual growth. When American schools are under pressure to perform and raise test scores, only those intellectual functions that can be measured get highlighted (Pinar, 2012; Taubman, 2009). By extension, teacher education emphasizes discipline-based intellectual capacities and focuses on discipline-based teaching methods. However, intellectual development without personal growth has disintegrative effects on the individual because the dissociation between intellect and emotions splits the human psyche and upholds the mechanism of rational control. The synthetic method and the nonviolent experiences that are essential to psychic and social integration remind us that teacher education must not neglect the role of the embodied, the aesthetic, the symbolic, and the contemplative as well as social engagement in students' development, not only in curriculum content but also in teacher education pedagogy. Interdisciplinary understanding and lived experience are essential for creating conditions to enable students' subjective integration and the relational dynamics of nonviolence.

The use of an integrative approach is demonstrated well in *currere*, which I have adopted in teacher education for more than a decade (see Wang, 2010 for details of specific methods). In William F. Pinar's (1975, 2012) formulation, oriented by Jungian analytical psychology, existentialism, and Buddhism, the practice of *currere*, with its focus on "the subjectivity of the socially engaged individuals" (2012, p. 43), helps students in teacher education make connections between academic knowledge and life history. It includes four steps: the memory work of understanding one's own educational experiences, the vision work of imagining what the future may unfold, the analysis of the past and the future in the context of the present situation, and the synthesis of repositioning oneself as a (prospective or in-service) teacher. Specific methods involve free association, meditative breathing exercises, creative visualization, and imaginative photographing of the past, the present, and the future. When introducing *currere* as a semester-long writing project, I encourage students to use diverse synthetic forms of expression such as poetry, photography, narratives, and creative juxtaposition in their final papers. While I provide guidance and nonjudgmental feedback during the process, students are in charge of their own learning and go as far as they are willing. I also invite students' voluntary sharing in partners and in class for intersubjective interactions.

As some students acknowledge (Jenkins, 2017), *currere* as a project of emptying oneself of psychic violence and forming more authentic relationships with the self is a form of engaging nonviolence. Such an engagement is an ongoing process and does not lead to any easy closure. Particularly when it involves experiencing difficult emotions, it is a complex process as one goes through "the pain of digging out all those miseries and struggles ... and experiencing them for a second time" (Yang, 2009, p. 26). Not getting stuck in the past is not only about one's individual past but also the collective past. "Productive remembering" (Strong-Wilson, 2013, p. 26) on the site of historical trauma is open-ended; it not only requires the person who is undertaking it to bear responsibility but also invites others to make sense of the past and care for the future. Nonviolent engagement with personal and collective pain is circular, not linear, but for those who are willing to do so, it opens up possibilities for psychic and social integration.

The Unity of Means-End in Psychic Integration and Nonviolent Relations

The means and the end of psychic integration and nonviolent relations are united. It is not a coincidence that the circle is an important part of the symbol of *ahimsa*—or contemporary symbols of nonviolence—and of the mandala images that Jung uses to symbolize the integrative psychic life. In a circle, means and end cannot be clearly identified or separately located, and circular movements unite means and end toward integration.

Achieving a more integrative personality in Jungian theory can be engaged through multiple means, such as audio-verbal, visual, or hands-on activities that bring the mind and the body together for creative formulations of what is difficult to express. By bridging psychic divisions, the aesthetic or embodied means that are beyond the intellect have a healing effect on the individual person. During the process, Jung also speaks about the importance of the individual person's increasing awareness on the person's own terms. In psychotherapy, he argues:

> Things cannot be forced, and wherever force seems to succeed it is generally regretted afterwards. Better always to be mindful of the limitations of one's knowledge and ability. Above all one needs forbearance and patience, for often time can do more than art. (Jung, 1966, p. 254)

The therapist cannot force or impose the "right" approach or interpretation but must let the patient take charge of becoming conscious of the unconscious. In other words, a nonviolent rather than authoritarian approach to the patient's insights and enlightenment is necessary. Such an approach requires that the therapist as an authority remain skeptical of his or her own expertise and patiently follow what emerges from the process. However, it does not mean non-intervening because becoming conscious requires critical questioning and reflecting to dig out what is hidden.

The unity of means-end is also paramount in nonviolence theory. Gandhi makes it clear that he is "an uncompromising opponent of violent methods even to serve the noblest of causes" (as cited in Easwaran, 1997, p. 3). Achieving India's independence from colonial control through peaceful means demonstrated the human capacity for freedom through "universal interdependence" (Gandhi, 1947, p. 299) rather than armed force. Martin Luther King, Jr. (1986) also insists that we must struggle "for moral ends through moral means" (p. 109). In social and political movements, nonviolent means include noncooperation with violence, collective strikes, peaceful protests, and participants' willingness to sacrifice and suffer for the cause. Struggling against the system of injustice while simultaneously evoking the humane aspects of all participants, including the perpetrators in that system, is a hallmark of nonviolence at the societal level.

In teacher education, neither psychotherapy nor nonviolent social protest is directly applicable to the classroom setting, but the importance of means-end unity is a shared educational concern that aims at psychic and social integration. Dissolving the mentality of domination in the classroom requires non-impositional pedagogical relationships and integrative teaching that relies on experiential understanding and emotional resonance. It also means giving students enough time and room to move around, explore, and reach new awareness on their own terms.

The unity of means-end informs teacher education pedagogy that allows students' processes of meaning-making to play out their own dynamics, temporality, and relationality. Psychic time is not linear but circular, and pedagogical patience and companionship as students work out issues through detours and curves facilitate the temporal flow of their growth to unravel knots of difficulty (Wang, 2016). While forcing change reinforces resistance, nonviolent pedagogical relationships do not force change but lead to eventual change by creating conditions in which students willingly engage in their own transformation. In refusing pedagogical imposition, the teacher educator must have faith in students' potential for transformation and transcendence and help students see their own abilities. When students reach a new awareness, their learning is grounded in their own desire for new knowledge even if it challenges their previous assumptions. At the same time, the teacher educator must take on the pedagogical responsibility of mentorship and support students in questioning and generating new meanings through integrative activities. In such a pedagogical relationship, it is important to create conditions in which students are both supported and challenged to examine the self and the world in a different way for psychic rebirth and social renewal.

Integrative Curriculum Dynamics in Teacher Education

While I have discussed the curriculum implications of psychic integration and nonviolent relations in previous sections, here I bring them together to formulate integrative curriculum dynamics toward nonviolence in teacher education. By definition, the unconscious cannot be fully known, and for Jung there is no flow of psychic energy without tensions between opposites, so achieving an integrative psychic life is an ongoing process that can never be completed. Forming nonviolent relations is also an ongoing process in which psychic and social violence is continually contested and compassionate relationships are established and renewed in daily practices. There is no final solution to completely eliminating violence in the human psyche and in society, but what emerges from the process keeps meanings and purposes alive.

I do not position this approach as a model for teacher educators to follow, and I am fully aware that self-integration and nonviolent relations are not inspirations shared by all. My teaching experiences have shown that some students in teacher education refuse to look inside the self, or do not believe that nonviolence works in a competitive society. But many students become inspired by or even passionate about stepping onto the less-traveled path between self-integration and nonviolence education, including some who were skeptical in the beginning. I choose to focus on the possibilities, rather than on the challenges and limitations of this approach, not only because I have addressed the difficulty in various publications previously (Wang, 2010, 2013, 2016), but also because the possibilities of engaging integration and nonviolence *should be more foregrounded* in teacher education to show what is *possible*. It is not my intention to demonstrate successful teaching, but to share my experiences as an invitation for more teacher educators to join in the effort to create educational conditions for integrative curriculum dynamics.

As achieving an integrative psychic life and building nonviolent relations are both dynamic processes, I take a dynamic approach to curriculum to re-examine the relationships within and between teacher educators, students, texts, and contexts, including in individual and social contexts. Conditions can be created for mobilizing teacher educators' relationships with texts, pedagogical relationships, students' relationships with texts, students' peer relationships, and a communal space of mutual growth toward integration and nonviolence. Here content and process, and means and ends are intertwined in a circular movement of spiraling downward and upward toward a more advanced level of understanding, awareness, and relationality. From many years of teaching in teacher education, I have learned that efforts to integrate body/mind, self/other, inner/outer work through curriculum materials, learning activities, and social interactions beneficial for students' whole-being experience can contribute to psychic integration and nonviolence work. Therefore, it is not about advocating any particular pedagogical strategies, but about introducing integrative orientations and shifting relational dynamics in teacher education. Here I discuss several important aspects of curriculum dynamics for psychic integration and nonviolent relations, including the selection of curriculum materials, engaging in self-education, pedagogical relationships of nonviolence, an integrated teaching approach, and a community of compassionate companionship.

In teacher education, the selection of curriculum materials is important because it orients the class into particular directions. As discipline-based curriculum development and teaching methods are predominant in both textbooks and students' ways of thinking, I intentionally introduce interdisciplinary readings related to Jungian theory and nonviolence studies to open windows to that unfamiliar world, adopting an embodied approach to teacher education that is beyond the intellect and beyond the mechanism of control and domination. The curriculum and educational implications of analytical psychology are particularly important in today's pursuit of standardizing and instrumental education (Gitz-Johansen, 2016)—a form of psychic, intellectual, and spiritual violence. As Pinar (2012) points out, "Without the agency of subjectivity, education evaporates, replaced by the conformity compelled by scripted curricula and standardized tests" (p. 43). Voices of nonviolence also must be heard in curriculum to present the possibilities for working through tensions peacefully, voices which are often excluded in the official curriculum (Wang, 2018; Brantmeier, 2009). These texts provide unique opportunities for students to explore new possibilities. When students first encounter these materials, they may find them difficult or even radical, but the message can sink in over time.

In selecting these materials, I also organically interweave their multiple lenses—the social and structural lens, the personal narrative lens, and cultural difference lens—so that the social, the individual, and the diverse views form an organic whole in which students are situated in their engagement with these materials. For instance, coming to terms with loss in one's individual history can be juxtaposed with confronting historical trauma, such as the Tulsa Race Massacre of 1921 or the Trail of Tears in Oklahoma (Wang & Olson, 2009). Multiple layers of emotional experiences have the power to move students to understand themselves better and cultivate compassion for others. The nonviolent conversion of difficult emotions requires confronting pain—personal or collective or both—and loosening the knot that ties one to a particular position and shifting one's viewpoint with the lens of relationality. Teaching social justice on a predominately White campus often requires dealing with a sense of guilt, shame, and despair in understanding the effect of racism in historical wrongdoings and everyday life. Here doing shadow work and transforming guilt into a sense of social responsibility through experience-based projects are necessary for enabling transformative action for cultural change.

In encountering the unfamiliar, students are initiated into the task of self-education. Although the methods of Jungian analysis cannot be used directly in teacher education, other forms of facilitating subjective reflection—such as *currere*—can be employed. The use of mindfulness for teachers has been flourishing (Jennings, 2015) and I have used mindful practices in teacher education. Reflectivity and mindfulness in combination can enable subjective and intersubjective transformation in complementary ways. Clifford Mayes (2007) goes further, proposing archetypal reflectivity in which pre-service teachers consider their calling as an archetypal hero/heroine's journey to achieve a higher vision of teaching. Here using literature or films rich in psychic and archetypal implications can effectively build bridges to facilitate students' awareness. For instance, I used the film, *The King's Speech*, which provides fertile materials for analyzing the Jungian notions of shadow and persona (Jung, 2016), anima, and the archetypal hero/heroine. What happened between the king-in-the-making, who had experienced speech difficulty, and the therapist, who treated this difficulty not as a technical but as an existential issue, unfolds the story of seeking psychic wholeness to take on social responsibility. As students analyzed the interactions, they were also drawn into in-depth reflection on their own inner struggles. The eruptions of strong emotions in the film were also informative for how to deal with difficulty through nonviolent pedagogical relationships. Classroom uses of these resources show that establishing nonviolent relations with others is mediated through subjective, intersubjective, and archetypal reflection to form a nonviolent relationship with the self.

To support students' self-education, teacher educators also need to engage in self-education (Shim, 2018) for meaningful pedagogical relationships to facilitate integrative classroom dynamics. With a deepened experiential understanding of the self, both teacher educators and students are in better positions to engage in the shadow work and form nonviolent relations. The teacher educator occupies a unique, mentoring position here to guide students in their process of making sense of the inner and outer world through engaging with texts in context. While the Jungian non-forcing position is more about fulfilling individuality through integrating yet not losing the self in the collective energy, nonviolent means is more about individuals embracing the integrative power of interconnectedness to transform hostile thoughts and difficult emotions. In combination, pedagogical relationships that support individual becoming and nonviolent relationality, through "pedagogical watchfulness" (Aoki, 2005, p. 195) and "pedagogical thoughtfulness" (p. 196), lead students to questioning conventions and generating new knowledge on their own terms and in their own time.

In creating conditions in which students engage in sense-making and meaning-making activities to reach new awareness and insights, the teacher educator's pedagogical approach must go beyond the intellect to incorporate the experiential, imaginative, mindful, social, intuitive, and spiritual dimensions of teaching and learning in the classroom. The intellect should not be abandoned, but intellectual activities must be embedded in and intertwined with literary, aesthetic, embodied, and social activities to engage students' creative, transformative, and transcendent journeys (Rowland, 2012). I used a nonviolent companionship project in which students were required to each choose a non-human companion and regularly spend time interacting with it. Often students started the project without knowing what to do or what to expect, but over time this opening to the other that was radically different led them to surprising discoveries. Through experiential understanding, they affirmed not only the role of interconnectedness but also respect for the differences of the other that is beyond their control (Wang, 2018). I also designed a mindful relationship project in which students were asked to mindfully interact with a person they knew but with whom they had experienced certain tensions or conflicts. This project required students to de-familiarize with what was already familiar to understand the inner worlds of the self and the other differently. It was a deeply emotional experience for students who were able to shift their positionality in engaging in their relationships with new awareness. For both projects, students informally shared their progress in the class, which not only enriched students' intersubjective reflection but also contributed to a class climate of mutual trust.

A class community of mutual trust, cooperation, and civility with hospitality to difference nurtures and is nurtured by an integrative psychic life and nonviolent relations. Such a community requires that class members have a capacity for deep listening, a playfulness with difference, the ability to stay with difficulty and tensions, mindful interactions with others, and containing and dissolving aggression. At the same time these capacities are developed in such a community, so they are mutually enhancing and interactively enabling. A class climate that supports the engagement of subjective reflectivity and nonviolent relations is co-created by aligning elements of curriculum dynamics around psychic and social integration. From my teaching experiences, I have found that sharing stories, reflecting on lived experiences, learning as whole persons, meeting the challenges of texts together, allowing emotional expression and containing its intensity, and providing pedagogical companionship in the classroom can all contribute to building a community. Importantly, meaningful interactions among classmates grappling with difficult texts, knowledge, and emotions are essential for leading to an integrative community in the midst of difference.

In short, after discussing three major intersecting threads between the Jungian integrative psychic life and nonviolent relations, I have proposed several important aspects of facilitating curriculum dynamics in teacher education: shifting the focus of curriculum materials and learning activities to interdisciplinary and lived experience with multiple perspectives; engaging self-education within both teacher educators and students while simultaneously forming pedagogical relationships of nonviolence; emphasizing the experiential, mindful, and spiritual approach; creating a culture and a community of subjective becoming and nonviolence. These aspects are interrelated and intertwine to form a dynamic process in a complex web that is ever-shifting depending on the internal and external contexts (Doll, 2012). Such circular curriculum movements carrying the integrative power of psychic life and nonviolent relations open up the horizon of teacher education toward subjective and cultural transformation.

Notes

1 In Jung's collected works, the term "man" refers to humanity. While his use of terms is limited by the historical time, his theory also has evoked feminist critiques and revisions. The scope of this paper does not permit including these important discussions; however, a feminist re-reading of Jung is necessary.
2 Shadow projection is related to transferential and counter-transferential relationships that have important implications for pedagogical relationships. Since it is a complicated issue, it is beyond the scope of this paper. Clifford Mayes (2005, 2007) discusses these relations both at the interpersonal and archetypal levels.

References

Aoki, T. T. (2005). *Curriculum in a new key* (W. F. Pinar & R. L. Irwin, Eds.). Lawrence Erlbaum.
Bai, H., & Cohen, A. (2008). Breathing qi (ch'i), following Dao (Tao). In C. Eppert & H. Wang (Eds.), *Cross-cultural studies in curriculum* (pp. 35–54). Lawrence Erlbaum.
Brantmeier, E. J. (2009). A peace education primer. *Journal of Conflict Management and Development, 3*(3), 36–50.
Britzman, D. P. (1998). *Lost subjects, contested objects.* State University of New York Press.
Disney, A. (Producer), & Riticker, G. (Director). (2008). *Pray the devil back to hell* [Film]. ro*co Films Educational.
Doll, M. A. (1996). *To the lighthouse and back.* Peter Lang.
Doll, Jr., W. E. (2012). *Pragmatism, post-modernism, and complexity theory* (D. Trueit, Ed.). Routledge.
Easwaran, E. (1997). *Gandhi the man* (3rd ed.). The Blue Mountains of Meditations.
Freud, S. (1961). *Civilization and its discontents* (J. Strachey, Trans. & Ed.). W. W. Norton.
Gandhi, M. K. (1947). *India of my dreams.* Navajivan Publishing House.
Gitz-Johansen, T. (2016). Jung in education. *Journal of Analytical Psychology, 61*(3), 383–384.
Greene, M. (1995). *Releasing the imagination.* Jossey-Bass.
Hershock, P. (2012). *Valuing diversity.* State University of New York Press.
Jenkins, H. (2017). Illuminated footprints of nonviolence. *Journal of Curriculum Theorizing, 31*(3), 67–80.
Jennings, P. A. (2015). *Mindfulness for teachers.* W. W. Norton.
Jung, C. G. (1953). *Two essays on analytical psychology* (R. F. C. Hull, Trans.). Princeton University Press.
Jung, C. G. (1954). *The development of personality* (R. F. C. Hull, Trans.). Princeton University Press.
Jung, C. G. (1956). *Symbols of transformation* (R. F. C. Hull, Trans.). Princeton University Press.
Jung, C. G. (1960). *The structure and dynamics of the psyche* (R. F. C. Hull, Trans.). Princeton University Press.
Jung, C. G. (1966). *The practice of psychotherapy* (R. F. C. Hull, Trans.). Princeton University Press.

Jung, C. G. (1968a). *The archetypes and the collective unconscious* (R. F. C. Hull, Trans.). Princeton University Press.
Jung, C. G. (1968b). *Aion* (R. F. C. Hull, Trans.). Princeton University Press.
Jung, J. (2009). *The red book* (S. Shamdasani, Ed.). W. W. Norton.
Jung, J. (2016). *The concept of care in curriculum studies*. Routledge.
Kincheloe, J. L., & Pinar, W. F. (Eds.). (1991). *Curriculum as social psychoanalysis*. State University of New York Press.
King, Jr., M. L. (1986). *A testament of hope* (J. M. Washington, Ed.). HarperOne.
Letseka, M. (2012). In defense of *ubuntu*. *Studies in Philosophy and Education, 31*, 47–60.
Mayes, C. (2005). *Jung and education*. Rowman & Littlefield Education.
Mayes, C. (2007). *Inside education*. Atwood.
Nagler, M. N. (2004). *The search for a nonviolent future*. Inner Ocean Publishing.
Phelan, A. (2015). *Curriculum theorizing and teacher education*. Routledge.
Pinar, W. F. (1994). The method of *currere*. In W. F. Pinar (Ed.), *Autobiography, politics and sexuality* (pp. 19–27). Peter Lang. (Original work published 1975)
Pinar, W. F. (2012). *What is curriculum theory?* (2nd ed.). Routledge.
Rowland, S. (2012). Jung and the soul of education. *Educational Philosophy and Theory, 44*(1), 6–17.
Shastri, S. Y., & Shastri, Y. S. (2007). *Ahimsa* and the unity of all things. In D. L. Smith-Christopher (Ed.), *Subverting hatred* (pp. 57–75). Orbis Books.
Shim, J. M. (2018). Working through resistance to resistance in anti-racist teacher education. *Journal of Philosophy of Education, 52*(2), 262–283.
Strong-Wilson, T. (2013). Waiting in the grey light. In T. Strong-Wilson, C. Mitchell, & S. Allnutt (Eds.), *Productive remembering and social agency* (pp. 17–27). Sense Publishers.
Swanson, D. M. (2009). Where have all the fishes gone? Living *Ubuntu* as an ethics of research and pedagogical engagement. In D. M. Caracciolo & Mungai, A. M. (Eds.), *In the spirit of Ubuntu* (pp. 3–22). Sense Publishers.
Taubman, P. M. (2009). *Teaching by numbers*. Routledge.
Taubman, P. M. (2012). *Disavowed knowledge*. Routledge.
Taylor, J. (2009). *The wisdom of your dreams*. Jeremy P. Tarcher/Penguin.
Todd, S. (2001). "Bringing more than I contain": Ethics, curriculum and the pedagogical demand for altered egos. *Journal of Curriculum Studies, 33*(4), 431–450.
Tutu, M. D. (1999). *No future without forgiveness*. Doubleday.
Wang, H. (2004). *The call from the stranger on a journey home: Curriculum in a third space*. Peter Lang.
Wang, H. (2010). The temporality of *currere*, change, and teacher education. *Pedagogies: An International Journal, 5*(4), 275–285.
Wang, H. (2013). A nonviolent approach to social justice education. *Educational Studies, 49*(6), 485–503.
Wang, H. (2016). Unteachable moments and pedagogical relationships. *Curriculum Inquiry, 46*(5), 455–472.
Wang, H. (2018). Nonviolence as teacher education: A qualitative study in challenges and possibilities. *Journal of Peace Education, 15*(2), 216–237.

Wang, H. (2019). Nonviolence as daily practice of education. In N. Ng-A-Fook, A. Ibrahim, B. Smith, & C. Hebert (Eds.), *Internationalizing curriculum studies* (pp. 193–206). Palgrave Macmillan.

Wang, H., & Olson, N. (Eds.). (2009). *A journey to unlearn and learn in multicultural education*. Peter Lang.

Wehr, G. (1987). *Jung: A biography*. Shambhala.

Yang, Y. (2009). Opening up intellectual and emotional gates. In H. Wang & Nadine Olson (Eds.), *A journey to unlearn and learn in multicultural education* (pp. 25–28). Peter Lang.

· 8 ·

NONVIOLENCE AS TEACHER EDUCATION: A QUALITATIVE STUDY IN CHALLENGES AND POSSIBILITIES (2018)[1]

Introduction

This paper grows out of seven years of teaching and scholarship in nonviolence education (Wang, 2013, 2014a, 2014b, 2016). During the process of teaching nonviolence and its meanings for education, I have found that when pre-service and in-service teachers first encounter the notion, most find it difficult to imagine nonviolence rooted in interconnectedness because of the individualistic and competitive orientation in the United States, even though there is a history of American nonviolence activism (Lynd & Lynd, 2006). It appears that it is more challenging to teach nonviolence than democracy, social justice, or multiculturalism. However, over time these challenges were turned into new possibilities for some students as they moved out of their comfort zones, deepened their understanding, and became passionate about nonviolence education. I became interested in diving deeper into students' own perspectives and their process of grappling with difficult knowledge in order to inform the pedagogy of teaching nonviolence in teacher education.

---

1   This chapter is reprinted with permission of the publisher (Taylor & Francis Ltd, http://www.tandfonline.com). Wang, H. (2018). Nonviolence as teacher education: A qualitative study in challenges and possibilities. *Journal of Peace Education*, 15(2), 216–237.

In today's world with occurrences of school violence and the current political divisiveness, teaching and learning nonviolence to get in touch with the unity of life, heal wounds, and create communities has become more imperative than ever.

Nonviolence is often perceived to be a political concept because of social and political movements such as those led by Gandhi and Martin Luther King, Jr. In rising above hatred and embracing compassion for the well-being of all during peaceful uprisings against political dictatorship and social injustice, nonviolence sends a powerful message of humanity. However, the philosophy of nonviolence rooted in nonduality and interconnections among all beings is much broader than a political means; it is existential and ontological. It is also a fundamentally educational project because nonviolence can be nurtured in word, thought, and action through both unlearning violence and cultivating compassion. As Michael Nagler (2004) argues, the fundamentally positive quality of nonviolence—"ahimsa," a Sanskrit word—in fostering human affiliation and fellowship is often obscured by the negative sense of non-violence in its English translation. Shastri and Shastri (2007) also point out, "*Ahimsa* is a positive doctrine of love, friendship, and equality among all living beings of the universe" (p. 59). In this positive sense of developing loving relationships lies the power of nonviolence to dissolve violence before it can emerge, disrupt violence when it appears, and shift relational dynamics toward a community of "sustainably shared flourishing" (Hershock, 2012, p. 19).

Nonviolence as an educational concept is defined in a broad sense as cultivating body/mind unity within an individual person and promoting compassionate relationships between the self and the other. In such cultivation, violence must be curbed—but nonviolence is also a positive force for individual and communal integration. Here my choice of the word "nonviolence" over "non-violence" is intentional, to focus on the proactive capacity of nonviolence in personal cultivation and community building rather than as a reaction to violence or war.

With the development of peace studies as an interdisciplinary field for decades, peace education has contributed a substantial literature on establishing humane multicultural and international relationships in the midst of war, conflict, and violence (Bajaj, 2008; Lin et al., 2008; Salomon & Cairns, 2010). However, as Bajaj (2010) suggests, there is a disconnection between peace education and Gandhian studies, and he calls for their mutual contributions to serve the purpose of peace, nonviolence, and social justice. For example, while "reflective individual analysis" (p. 49) is important in peace education, and the social and the communal is essential in Gandhi studies, they foreground different aspects of agency in enabling peace or nonviolence. Although they are situated in different social and cultural contexts, they can also be complementary. In nonviolence studies inspired by Gandhi's philosophy, the underlying thread is the unity of life, and each individual is embedded in this interconnectedness (Nagler, 2004). In the Western-oriented peace education framework, the individual person is foregrounded and non-violence is associated with human rights and conflict resolution (Muller, 2002). I believe that in nonviolence education, we need to foreground the individual and the relational in a productive relationship despite their potential tensions, and through dynamic interactions between the two, both the individual and the community can cultivate the inner strength and relational potentiality that are mutually beneficial for personal and communal flourishing.

In peace studies literature, nonviolence, when mentioned, is often presented as a means to the end of peace and more often than not, the term "non-violence" is used. There are exceptions, such as a critical pedagogy for nonviolence developed by Chubbuck and Zembylas (2011) at the intersection of critical peace education and nonviolence. This paper approaches nonviolence as fundamental, not merely instrumental, in all aspects of education including purpose, content, and method. For both teachers and students, nonviolence can be practiced daily to dissolve aggression and cultivate compassion for personal and social transformation. Although many curriculum and teaching resources in peace education have been developed and there are some studies on teaching the nonviolence of Gandhi and King in school curricula (Allen, 2007; Fishman, 2003; Gill, 2000), in general there is a lack of studies that focus on nonviolence education in teacher education, even though the teacher's capacity to engage nonviolence is important. This paper is based on such a study and promises to make a contribution to the field of peace education, particularly in how to negotiate the individual and the communal aspects of nonviolence education and approach nonviolence as a positively transformative force.

This study is situated in understanding how and why students in teacher education respond to nonviolence and nonviolence education in their particular ways and what pedagogical conditions can be created for shifting students' relational orientation toward integration and compassion. It is qualitative teacher research (with IRB permission and pseudonyms for all the students), based upon the analysis of three classes with nonviolence as both the topic and the teaching orientation. I taught these classes and am the teacher researcher for this study. Analyzing the students' understanding and their changes over time, reflectively examining the relationship between my teaching approaches and students' learning, and addressing the challenging aspects of class dynamics, as the teacher researcher I rethink the arrangement of teaching materials, strategies, and community building in the classroom in order to open up more possibilities. The paper proceeds as follows: the theoretical framework, the research setting and methodology, the major findings, and a discussion of implications.

Theoretical Framework

The theoretical framework of this study, compatible with the orientation of curriculum and pedagogical design in these classes, is based mainly upon nonviolence studies, but it also blends with principles of psychoanalysis and poststructural theory. Several key threads in the conceptions of nonviolence informed by Gandhi and Buddhism (Kaneda, 2008; Nagler, 2004) are used in this study. First, organic relationality that transcends dualism lies at the heart of nonviolence, and nonduality heals the divide between the body and the mind and the separation of the self and the other (Wang, 2014a). Second, nonviolent relationships with others are interdependent with the integration of the self. Meditation and mindfulness practices enable inner peace and compassionate relationships. Third, means and end are united through the principles of nonviolence.

Under the relational orientation of nonviolence studies, psychoanalytic work with its emphasis on the psychic working through of difficult memories and difficult emotions, adds depth to the inner work of nonviolent engagement with the self. One can learn to integrate the shadow of the self and refuse to project it onto the other so that the enriched and fuller self does not make an enemy out of the other (Mayes, 2005; Pinar, 2012; Shim, 2014). Here the psychosocial dynamics of the individual are necessarily tied to contextualized relational interactions with others.

Drawing upon poststructuralism, which values the alterity of the other, this framework also involves building nonviolent relationships with difference. Often commonality is viewed as the basis for building relationships, and conflicts and difference are perceived as needing to be smoothed out or erased by compromise. However, leading scholars in poststructural theory—Jacques Derrida, Emmanuel Levinas, and Julia Kristeva—argue that erasing difference into commonality is itself a form of violence. Assimilating the other into the self runs the risk of imposing one's own positions and perspectives. From a Buddhist point of view, Hershock (2012) argues for the necessity of diversity for a mutually enhanced community. Both poststructural insights and Buddhist wisdom inform this approach to difference as a positive site for nonviolent engagement.

In drawing upon these different theories, the individual and the relational aspects become the double foci of nonviolence education that unite purpose, curriculum, and teaching in a daily practice of transforming negative energies and forming positive relationships. Curriculum should highlight the contributions of nonviolence but, unfortunately, studies of history textbooks have shown that "students are learning very little about the history of peace, though they learn a great deal about wars and other forms of violence" (Gemstone Peace Education Team, 2008, p. 94). Stoskopt and Bermudez (2017) also argue that representations of nonviolent resistance have been silenced in four American history textbooks, which leaves students little access to nonviolent social change. In my classes, nonviolence was explicit curriculum, but a pedagogy of nonviolence in which the interactions between teacher and students and among students led to students' embrace of nonviolence was also enacted to match the content. When the content and means were united, the purpose of education for nonviolence could be served. My course design, including the choices of textbooks, the nature of the assignments, pedagogical relationships, and the fostering of relational dynamics are discussed in more detail later.

As a teacher researcher "living the question" (Shagoury & Power, 2012) of how to meet challenges and open possibilities for teaching nonviolence, I intertwine theory, practice, and research intimately in this study. Since nonviolence suggests a unity between thought and action, teacher research as a research methodology that integrates theory and practice matches the topic of this study.

Research Settings and Methodology

This study is based upon three graduate courses in teacher education. One class was a special topics class on nonviolence and education, taught as a one-month summer class in 2013 (this class is referred to as the nonviolence class). The second class was a summer class in 2014 focusing on gender issues (this class is referred to as the gender class). It included materials related to women's peace movements and gender aspects of nonviolence. The third class was a regular semester-long class in 2013 that focused on multicultural diversity issues (this class is referred to as the diversity class). It began with a book on nonviolence studies, followed by multicultural education books.

Out of 31 students from the three classes, 14 students volunteered to participate in the study; all the data were collected after classes ended to avoid potential conflicts of interest. There were only two male students in these classes but all participants were female. Students' online discussion postings, weekly questions about readings, writings, self-evaluation papers, and follow-up interviews are the major sources of data. Six participants came from the nonviolence class: Camellia, Teresa, Elaine, Cydney, Holly, and Ethel. Five participants came from the gender class: Darlene, Amanda, Laura, Helen, and Angela. Three participants came from the diversity class: Toni, Gloria, and May. Among the 14 students, 11 completed the follow-up interview. All the interview transcriptions were member-checked by participants. I kept research notes throughout the classes. For data analysis, students' writings, the interview transcriptions, and the researcher's journals as well as other materials were thematically coded. I first analyzed each individual student's perspectives and then synthesized the whole group's responses.

The pedagogical arrangements for introducing the topic of nonviolence in the three classes and students' familiarity with the topic were somewhat different. The nonviolence class was an elective, and most students were already interested in the topic and had taken classes with me before. *The Search for a Nonviolent Future* (Nagler, 2004), a book on nonviolence in education (Wang, 2014a), and *Transforming Education for Peace* (Lin et al., 2008) were required texts. The diversity class began with Nagler's (2004) book to introduce nonviolence as the orientation for addressing cultural differences. The class was required for some students and an elective for others. The gender class was an elective course, which started with the documentary film, *Pray the Devil Back to Hell* (Disney & Riticker, 2008). The film describes the women's peace movement in Liberia between 2003 and 2005, and the gendered aspects of nonviolence were also discussed later.

The discussion format and assignments I used for all three classes were similar. All students were required to have at least three questions related to the weekly class readings before the class and were expected to participate in class discussions. Class sessions were conducted in a conversational style that included pair sharing and small group activities. All students wrote a course goal in the beginning and a self-evaluation at the end. For writing assignments, the nonviolence class wrote a definition-of-nonviolence paper, a summary of the companionship project journal entries, and a final paper on nonviolence in action. The gender class wrote a film analysis paper and a relationality-and-my-life paper. The diversity class wrote a reflection paper on the Tulsa Race Riot of 1921 and a final paper on their overall perspective on multicultural education.

The Shift in Students' Understanding of Nonviolence

While nonviolence was a difficult concept to think about in the beginning for many participants, they began to reposition themselves to understand it in different ways throughout the semester and re-imagine education through the lens of nonviolence. Two participants already saw nonviolence as part of their life beliefs before the classes, although they had not intentionally made the connection with education. Thus, the class reinforced and enriched their understanding of what it means for education. Here I discuss several major shifts to address how and why students responded to nonviolence in an ongoing process of learning.

The Shift from a Narrow to a Broad Understanding

As students began to understand the notion of violence in a broad sense, they became aware of the deeper meanings of nonviolence. Before the class 9 out of 14 participants perceived violence mainly as doing physical harm. As they learned that violence can be psychological, emotional, structural, or cultural, they also approached nonviolence in a broad sense. As Cydney acknowledged, nonviolence is "inclusive of emotional and mental aspects of human beings, like taking care of the self and taking care of all living beings" (Interview). They also learned the role of the language in reinforcing violence or nonviolence (Nagler, 2004) and how language can be shifted in the educational context nonviolently, even as simply as replacing "bullets" with "dots" to refer to a list of things (Interview with Teresa).

Seeking heart unity, as Nagler (2004) phrases it, Cydney considered nonviolence as "an awakening to the interconnectedness to the universe and all that shares with us" (Final paper). This assertion of interconnectedness in nonviolence was echoed throughout participants' writings and interviews. It is an ontological and cosmological shift from the individual component to relational dynamics, a shift that requires students to question the mainstream individualism both in the culture and in education. As Hershock (2012) points out, we need to shift from "the ontological primacy of individual and independent existents" to the "primacy of relationality" (p. 11) so that relational transformation can happen for individuals and communities. It is encouraging to see that these participants could accomplish this shift in one semester.

While the concept of nonviolence was not taught in close alignment with religion, several participants explicitly discussed its spiritual dimension. Teresa wrote beautifully, "Nonviolence lies in cultivation of one's inner soul" (Definition paper). She believed that nonviolence was compatible with her Christian beliefs and cited the Bible to support nonviolence as Jesus' teaching. She further argued that "developing the inner soul is the only way to empower students to think and act nonviolently as they encounter daily life" (Definition paper). This connection she made between nonviolence and Christianity is important because *ahimsa* originates in Indian religions and might be perceived as non-Christian. However, studies show that nonviolence is an important message in the teachings of all major religions (Smith-Christopher, 2007), a shared spiritual and cultural resource. It is difficult to imagine interconnectedness without a certain sense of spirituality that transcends the individual ego, although it does not have to be religious in a conventional sense.

This shift from a narrow to a broad sense of nonviolence in its intellectual, emotional, cultural, and spiritual dimensions also pushed participants' understanding of nonviolence beyond the negation of violence. Laura observed, "Our society has coined peace with the notion that two parties have some sort of conflict and that conflict becomes resolved after a violent struggle or fight. It is amazing that I (and most kids) grew up believing that in most situations peace only comes after some form of violence" (Film analysis paper). Such an understanding of peace as the absence of war—or nonviolence as the absence of violence—is not uncommon, and peace studies as a field emerged from the need to deal with war, violence, and conflicts (Bajaj, 2010; Harris, 2008). However, if interconnectedness is the underlying thread of nonviolence, then nonviolence is an essentially positive force in cultivating peace within the individual person and in building a compassionate community. Education can play an essential role in cultivating and spreading this positive force.

The Shift from a Passive View to a Proactive View

Even though political movements of nonviolent resistance have demonstrated activist aspects of nonviolence, many Americans—with their particular polarized gendered image (Jhally, 1999) —still associate it with weakness and passivity. My students were no exception. Exploring the notion further, however, participants began to embrace nonviolence as an active energy that spreads a positive influence.

Reading Nagler's book and his critical analysis of the violence perpetuated by the media and power structures, Toni realized that "if you are not proactive to pursue something positive, you may be very likely to contribute to a culture of violence" (Interview). She took it as a call for action to promote constructive relationships. Teresa, Elaine, and Ethel would like to move beyond transforming classroom interactions to reach a broader audience through social activism such as community service for social justice and environmental activism. Holly became committed to an action-oriented pedagogy of nonviolence and asserted, "Contrary to many people's beliefs, nonviolence is not the absence of violence: Nonviolence is the action which persuades others to act humanely" (Definition paper). After the class, she further used Chubbuck's and Zembylas' (2011) approach to critical pedagogy for nonviolence in her master's final project to create a unit of study on nonviolence within the English language arts curriculum.

Participants from the gender class, influenced by the Liberian women's peace movement, in which motherhood across differences became a powerful connector, were mostly explicit about the proactive nature of nonviolence and associated it with maternal power. Darlene commented on the gendered aspect of nonviolence as activism. As a woman who had not fit into gender norms but had played a leadership role, she embraced the link between nonviolence and asserting women's power to change the world.

As a positive energy, nonviolence is not passive but proactive through receptiveness as it promotes mutually beneficial relational dynamics for the well-being of all members in a community. This attention to relational dynamics in activism steers it away from power struggles but appeals to the human desire for belonging and affiliation to achieve social and political change. Mohandas K. Gandhi (1942/2007) long ago commented that nonviolence is not a program for seizing power but "a program of transformation of relationship" (p. 40), which the Liberian women successfully implemented to achieve peace. Such a focus on relational transformation has important educational implications. Education is a relational field, and the dynamics of nonviolence between and among teacher, student, text, and context in educational institutions can play a proactive role in enacting grassroots change.

The Shift to Looking Inside and Engaging in Emotional Work

Many participants were surprised to realize that nonviolence is not just about others but also about the self. As Camellia came to understand, "It is something happening within, being able to look within, the examination of what is happening within, within my heart, within my center" (Interview). Such work from within necessarily involves emotional work, transforming anger, fear, guilt, loss, pain into positive relational orientations (Boler, 1999; Pinar, 1994). Such inner work also means unlearning social and cultural norms that enact violence in various forms.

In working with their own sense of loss and difficulty in relationships, participants unlearn what is imposed on them by family and society and get in touch with their own voices. In doing so, as Cydney explained, she became "more 'in tune' with my psychical and emotional self" and in turn with students' emotional needs (Interview). Listening to the body, listening to the inner self, she became more willing to deal with conflicts rather than avoiding them. However unlearning violence is not a linear, straightforward process. Angela discussed the abusive relationships in her childhood and their impact. She was worried that recent motherhood put constraints on her ability to refuse to "be a good girl" (Relationality paper). Janet Miller (2005) unpacks the impact of "being a good girl" on women's identity formation and discusses the difficult negotiation between societal expectations and women's own voices. Haunted by her traumatic past, Angela is still searching for her voice.

While exploring emotional aspects of learning and teaching, participants were surprised at the lack of language they had to describe emotions. Amanda commented on the class discussions about gender and the emotional expressions that are permitted or not permitted by societal norms. She realized that "we are so shut off to discussing emotions that we did not even have the vocabulary for the exercise" (Journal entry). If patriarchy not only produces knowledge and action but also feelings, she further asked, "Is it possible to unlearn a feeling?" (Weekly questions). Unraveling the knot of emotions at the intersection of the personal and the social is an important educative work for teachers, because without such understanding of and engagement in emotional work, how can they get in touch with students' complex inner landscapes?

Elaine commented that she did not realize that she was doing "violence to the self" by trying hard to please others and demanding that she herself be perfect (Interview). In working through those issues inside of her, to reconcile with her inner battle and to integrate the shadow, she found a deeper layer of compassion and commitment to converting difficult emotions into constructive outlets for educating her students. Such inner work, informed by psychoanalytic insights, is essential to teachers' subjective re-formation, but is usually neglected by teacher education that is preoccupied by "right" methods and techniques (Pinar, 2012).

Internal emotional work is also intimately related to collective action. Nagler (2004) pays particular attention to the transformation of fear and anger to enable nonviolent action. To overcome anger or fear, one needs to see a bigger picture in which the self and the other are intimately related. That requires stretching out two postures simultaneously: one is "no" to the action of violence; the other is being receptive to the other person's humanity (Slattery et al., 2005). Multiple participants from the gender class commented how those women in Liberia were able to transform their anger and fear into nonviolent collective resistance. Quoting Arun Gandhi (2003), "Overcoming fear both imagined and actual is essential for the practice of nonviolence" (p. 31), Laura pointed out that "as the men chose to overcome their fear in a violent way, women chose to overcome their fear in a positive way by advocating for peace and nonviolence" (Film analysis paper). Here we can see how the individual and the communal aspects of nonviolence are united in action and each aspect enables the other: The individuals' working through of anger and fear to integrate their internal shadow is supported by the communal project while the communal action cannot be possible until the individual cultivates courage by transforming difficult emotions.

From these three shifts, participants approached nonviolence as an educational project as they developed deeper understandings. Using the metaphor of the circle, Camellia argued that nonviolence is "the circular configuration of integrated, interpersonal power that can be the foundation of the educational constructive programme we have yet to build for all children" (Definition paper). And they became committed to working for this "yet to be" and transforming their educational practices. In and out of the classroom they were making efforts to bring orientations of nonviolence into their relationships with students, parents, and other teachers as well as institutions. However, not all participants were able to embody principles of nonviolence in teaching. Darlene felt that she practiced nonviolence in her life but did not practice it in teaching mathematics. Although the nature of the subject matter seemed to be an obstacle, interactions between the teacher and students are always relational, no matter what subject one teaches. This split between the inner and the relational raises questions for me about how to help students bring them together in teacher education.

Pedagogical Conditions for Students' Learning of Nonviolence

While the shifts in students' understandings were always an ongoing process, pedagogical conditions had to be created to facilitate such a process. The participants in this study had responded positively to my teaching of nonviolence, but what I have learned from them might not be applicable to all students. My research interest, however, lies not in establishing any cause-effect relationship but in understanding students' processes for meaning-making and what pedagogical arrangements would be beneficial. I have learned several lessons regarding how to create experiences both in and out of the classroom that enable students' learning of nonviolence: engaging students in practicing nonviolence to the self; creating experiential projects of nonviolent relationships with the other; transforming relational dynamics in the classroom; and not positioning violence/nonviolence as binary.

Engaging Students in Practicing Nonviolence to the Self

I used autobiographical journaling and writing and mindfulness practices in these classes as important modes of practicing nonviolence to the self. Using principles of *currere* in curriculum studies, a particular form of autobiographical writing based upon phenomenology, psychoanalysis, and Buddhism (Pinar, 1994), I designed writing projects to deepen students' self-understanding. For instance, in the gender class, I asked students to reflect on the role of gender in their own lives in a journal entry three times a week for two weeks. The journal entries were free writings that were not graded or even collected by the instructor but that could be used for class discussions and writing formal papers. Students also read Mary Aswell Doll's (1995) autobiography, which details how her relationship with her mother changed from mutual negation to authentic mutuality and how this change influenced her teaching. Further, students completed a writing assignment in which they, drew from their journal entries and readings, critically reflect on how their significant relationships influenced them and their teaching.

All participants in the gender class wrote about the impact of their mother-daughter relationships and all except one narrated their struggles to negotiate a space, struggles which were full of tears, pain, and loss as well as laughter and celebration. Becoming "enlightened" (Amanda, Self-evaluation writing) about their relationships with their parents, they began to understand more of their own parenting and teaching and further reposition their pedagogical relationships (Pinar, 1994; Wang, 2010). Such a healing process of coming to terms with difficulty was practicing nonviolence to the self because it helped participants unburden themselves from their past, find strength and forgiveness in their heart, and aspire to a more humane future together with their students

It is worth mentioning that some participants had already written a full-length *currere* (the 16-week semester-long project with weekly writings) before they took these classes (see Wang, 2010, for the educative effect of *currere* in teacher education). *Currere* uses the psychoanalytic technique of free association, which helps students to free themselves from the constraints of the present to experience their past as it was, to come to terms with difficult emotions, and to reveal their aspirations for the future. Elaine commented, "It was like I felt such a calming of haunting childhood and personal issues after I did *currere*" (Self-evaluation writing). It took time for her to process her complicated feelings as she affirmed the voice of nonviolence from within and became passionate about the role of nonviolence in healing the individual psyche and building relationships. Putting down the burden of the past, making an effort to accept and let go, participants' own experiences of working with intense emotions revealed to them the power of engaging in nonviolence to the self.

It is also interesting to notice that both negative and positive life experiences contributed to these participants' receptiveness to the message of nonviolence. Some participants were influenced by their parents' positive teaching of openness to difference or a peaceful attitude toward life, so nonviolence reinforced their existing approach to life and education but in a more systematic way. Others had difficult relationships in their families and had to make new meanings out of their life history through embracing nonviolence. Clearly the relationship between one's life history and one's openness to learning difficult knowledge is not simple, but if the past does not determine the present, education can play a crucial role in undoing the damage of the past, supporting students' self-education and reinforcing positive relationality.

Autobiographical work is not simple storytelling (Miller, 2005) but is a form of education to negotiate complicated passages among the past, the present, and the future for new awareness and new learning.

I also used mindfulness practices, to different degrees, in these three classes because meditations are central to cultivating inner peace (Nagler, 2004). In the nonviolence class, I rotated among three forms of practice according to the topic of the class session: a quiet form such as mindful breathing; an emotion-focused form such as meditating on anger, fear, or loving-kindness; and an active form such as mindful walking. While initially these practices were a surprise, participants learned to enjoy them. May commented on her quick-tempered disposition and said that "doing those meditations really slowed me down. It calms me down" (Interview). Elaine explained both the benefits and limits of practicing mindfulness in a group setting: "I am not really that comfortable with group meditation, because I have a certain level of alertness around other people.... But I love the moment when we all look up, [and] I see that we've all been on this journey together" (Interview). Students in the nonviolence class developed a strong sense of "togetherness" as they engaged in inner work communally, and when the individual and the social realms met in mutual support, class dynamics become a generative flow.

Mindfulness practices helped participants to process their emotions and become more aware of their relationships. Several participants said that the loving-kindness meditation was their favorite, as the loving words and imagery start with the self, move to a loving other, a neutral person, and finally a person that one has difficulty with. They experienced resistance in their bodies when they moved to thinking of the last person. They became more aware of bodily sensations associated with emotions and more committed to working on difficult relationships. Helen also introduced mindfulness into her teaching and led students to practice mindful breathing, mindful seeing, and mindful tasting (David, 2009) for five minutes in her classes. She found that mindfulness had positive effects on her middle school students who began to learn students centering themselves in study and in life. Moreover, a class climate that fostered learning and emotional growth was created by mindfulness.

In addition to positive effects, this study reveals that more pedagogical crafting of mindfulness practices can be considered. First, classroom seating arrangements can be rethought so that students can practice mindfulness with a sense of their own space. Second, more tangible forms that catch students' attention, such as mindful listening using a bell, can be attempted before introducing students to mindful breathing, which is difficult to sustain for first-time practitioners. In addition, the relationships between mindfulness and education need to be strengthened through demonstrations of how mindfulness can be used in the classroom setting (Jennings, 2015) and how it can also be an orientation that guides pedagogical interactions and is applicable to all school subjects.

Creating Experiential Relationships with the Other

In peace education literature, finding commonality is often perceived as the foundation for building connections, so difference is perceived as something to be overcome or resolved. However, I believe that difference must not be erased but must be engaged so that relationships built out of interconnectedness across differences are dynamic and enrich all involved. Such engagement with the other that builds connections without reducing difference into sameness is essential to cultivating nonviolent relationships. Experiential projects in these classes were designed to challenge students to make connections with others who are different, to build bridges that do not consume the other's unique existence, and in turn to come back to question their own taken-for-granted assumptions. Self-transformation happens through learning from the other, which can be cultural or cosmic. Here I give two examples: one is in social justice education and the other is about ecological relationships.

One particular project in the diversity class was about the Tulsa Race Riot of 1921. I asked students to understand what had happened "in their back yard" through watching a documentary film in class; visiting the Greenwood Cultural Center, which houses historical materials related to this tragedy; walking around the site near the Center; and studying the report from the Oklahoma Commission to Study the Tulsa Race Riot of 1921 and other readings in preparation for writing a paper. As my students are predominantly White, this was a difficult project of encountering historical trauma in which a flourishing African American neighborhood was destroyed overnight by a White mob and hundreds of African American people lost their lives.

Gloria particularly emphasized her emotional growth as a result of engaging in this project, growth that transformed pain and anger into social justice commitment. She commented that the best thing was to visit the site of the riots and imagine how heartbreaking it was for Black people to lose a booming Black Wall Street in an overnight massacre. This experiencing of the past on the very site of her home in addition to class discussions and study had given her a lens that she had not had, and the emergence of this new lens was enabled by her growth in working through intense feelings of shame, remorse, anger, and guilt. As a result of this project, she felt greater responsibility to combat racial stereotypes and injustice in everyday encounters both in life and at her school with a large Hispanic student population. I intended to position this radical engagement with the oppressed other through memory work not as seeking the commonality of humanity but as connecting with the other who is different. The relational orientation of this project, as Gloria's story shows, is enabled by working through difficult emotions within the self, and thus affirms the role of individuals (in cultural context) in shifting the nature of relationality toward repairing the broken links in a community.

I have already discussed this project elsewhere in a book where my students published their papers (for more details, see Wang & Olson, 2009). Here I discuss more the experiential effect of the companionship project on students' learning in the nonviolence class. The project was about forming a nonviolent relationship with a non-human companion. Students were required to choose a plant, a rock, a walking trail, a garden, or anything else that they were interested in, and then spend at least half an hour interacting with their companion three times a week for two weeks. At the end of each interaction, students wrote a journal entry and at the end of the project, wrote a summary of their journal entries. In this assignment, I particularly asked students not to choose a pet and encouraged them to choose something less familiar. In experiencing what is *other* than they are and what cannot speak to them directly through language, students were asked to step out of their comfort zone and become open to "the other heading" (Derrida, 1992) and receptive to what the other offered without assimilating it into their own framework. This radical openness to the other, however, was coupled with their effort to make connections through listening with their heart and seeing what is invisible. In the end, making connections across difference without reducing difference into sameness was demonstrated well in this project.

All students found it to be an amazing experience and discussed their choice and findings periodically in the class. They chose a wide variety of companions, from the wind to a rocking chair, from the sky to a bird nest, from a statue to a garden, and their initial skepticism quickly changed and they made surprising discoveries during the two weeks. Elaine, who focused on her garden, wrote: "I have tended it and it has tended my heart, opening me to the pursuit of nonviolence in my relationships with all living things and to the 'self'" (Companionship project paper). While the garden is a more familiar choice, the wind is more unusual. Ethel commented, "It surprised me how the wind started out as boring and in a very short time became highly profound. . . . I feel much more in tune with nature and humanity through this assignment and value the new interconnectedness I have formed with the wind" (Companionship project paper). From laboring in a garden to experiencing the wind, participants came in touch with the central thread of nonviolence: interconnectedness. The project opened up their imaginations about new possibilities of nonviolence in life and education.

Several participants named their companions; for example, Camellia named her bushes and Holly named the bird eggs, with the help of her daughter. This act of naming brought a sense of closeness to their non-human companions, often mediated through human relationships such as family members or distant others. However, in getting close to their companions, they also began to realize in a profound way that their companions' existence, while related to them, was beyond their control. Teresa enjoyed the companionship of a statue, Ivy, and did not realize the human expectations she projected on the relationship until the end of the project:

> The ivy girl gives to me in her own way, not in a human way but still in a relational one . . . . She is confirmation that no matter how much a person gives to a relationship, that person cannot force a connection or try to manipulate the relationship in a way that she wants. (Companionship project paper)

Accepting the other *as the other* led Teresa to further question what kinds of relationship an educator should form with students who may have different needs from the educator's expectations.

In general, this project enhanced my participants' sense of interconnectedness and helped them learn how to nonviolently engage the other, including the non-human other. In particular, they began to understand that the alterity of the other is a site for them to learn from through making connections, not something that needs to be removed. In forming generative relationships through differences, they enriched themselves.

Transforming Classroom Relational Dynamics

As nonviolence is about the unity of means and end, the pedagogy of nonviolence must be coupled with the purpose of education to transform classroom relational dynamics. In classroom dynamics, teacher, student, text, and context interact to form pedagogical relationships, peer interactions, and students' connections with texts, all meditated by personal, social, and cultural contexts.

Participants responded positively to my choice of textbooks in its blend of the personal and the structural analysis and its combination of theory, practice, and research in readings. They also appreciated the conversational style of class discussions, even though it was new to some of them. As Ethel pointed out, "[I used to want answers right away], but then I found out how nice it was to be able to think for myself" (Interview). Participants felt they had freedom to make connections with texts and with their classmates through both inner and outer engagement, and that the instructor left enough room for ambiguity and contradictions without judgment to foster a climate of nonviolence in the class.

However, my research journal clearly indicates a contrast between the nonviolence class and the diversity class. The nonviolence class had an excellent flow both the instructor and students enjoyed. The diversity class was contested, with many debates. Interestingly when I asked three participants who took both classes from me (two had taken the diversity class prior to my study), all of them said that I did not teach any differently in the two classes, but conflicting perspectives and strong personalities in the diversity class caused discomfort. In other words, the difference was less about my teaching style and more about students' readiness and peer relationships.

As Elaine observed about the nonviolence class, "It was the openness to the other that contributed to building a community in the class" (Interview). The openness that students in the nonviolence class had toward one another and toward difficult knowledge had led to a class climate of exploration (rather than debate) and of shared interest in learning something new (rather than refusal to learn). In such a generative flow of ideas and intersubjective connections, however, students still needed to balance being open and being vulnerable. Both Camellia and Ethel commented on the necessity of risking vulnerability for a transformative conversation. As Palmer and Zajonc (2010) point out, a transformative conversation requires participants to take "relational risks" (p. 137) in a community of trust. The nonviolence class achieved such a community while the diversity class did not.

The three participants who took both classes acknowledged that most students came into the diversity class expecting to learn how to teach minority students. For them diversity was about "other" kids. May further pointed out that the way that I taught nonviolence required students to critically reflect on themselves but that was not something they wanted to do. I started the class with the notion of nonviolence with the hope that students could shift relational dynamics and bring a compassionate orientation into examining different cultural groups. I failed at that attempt for most students and

I realized later that nonviolence is a more radical concept to grapple with than the notion of cultural diversity. The pedagogical gap between my intention and students' expectations contributed to students' resistance.

When the gap between students and the instructor is too great, learning may not happen. The challenges of teaching nonviolence in the diversity classes made me rethink the pedagogical arrangement. In my future attempts the intertwining of readings on diversity and nonviolence throughout the semester will be preferable over starting with nonviolence, which some students may perceive as irrelevant. Moreover, my embodiment of approaching differences as an organic part of life must be demonstrated through redirecting intense discussions toward constructive outlets. The intensity of discussions needs to be guided through the instructor's calming presence and ability to play with difference, which I must further develop for peacefully navigating debates toward meanings without consensus. In addition, exercises in deep and mindful listening and activities for building a class community should be conducted throughout the semester, especially in a class of contestation, so that different perspectives do not negatively impact interpersonal relationships and the class climate.

Positioning Violence/Nonviolence as Not Binary

As I discussed earlier, understanding violence in a broad way also helped students to understand nonviolence in a broad way. However, when the logic of violence seemed to be so permeating into the fabric of daily life, some students became defensive. As Toni said, "It was almost like that everything I was doing was different forms of violence" (Interview). Part of the contestation in the diversity class centered on whether violence or nonviolence worked, as if there were only two options. May commented, "You can use positive energy to transform [violence] but you cannot expect to remove all of it" (Interview). Participants pointed out that structural violence and institutional constraints made it difficult to implement nonviolence principles systemically. Holly discussed her experience in a school with metal detectors installed, backpack checks, and benchmark tests every six weeks. Struggling with these issues, she nevertheless asserted agency in rejecting "the power of testing to define me as a teacher or my students as people" (Weekly response). Most participants believed that an individual educator could play a role in facilitating mindful and nonviolent interactions at school despite the constraints, but that structural violence must be acknowledged (Chubbuck & Zembylas, 2011) in order to question the system of social violence and negotiate a critical space.

Learning from participants' struggles, I realize that violence and nonviolence should not have been approached as binary, especially since nonviolence is more than the negation of violence. Weigert (1999) points out it is better to see "violence-nonviolence as a continuum" (p. 16). In other words, nonviolence is not seen as completely empty of violence but becomes an ongoing process of converting negative energies and building compassionate relationships. Just as Dutta, Andzenge, and Walkling (2016) designed innovative, everyday peace projects for their students to help them develop skills and capacities for peacebuilding, nonviolence should be engaged in as a daily practice in which we can all participate, both individually and communally.

Nonviolence approached as a process is also compatible with the temporality of learning in which complex thinking takes time (Doll, 2012). Participants commented that it took time for them to learn nonviolence. When they encountered the notion of nonviolence the second time, they were able to learn more, while the first time they had to work with their resistance to the notion. Holly elaborated on why there was so much resistance:

> There is so much attention given to violence and so little attention given to nonviolence so that violence is normalized. We live our lives in metaphors. And there is so much metaphorical violence in the way we speak, the way we talk about education, and many things in our lives that it is so normalized that we assume that violence is natural. (Interview)

So it does take time to deconstruct the naturalness of violence, to realize that both violence and nonviolence can be learned, and to practice nonviolence in order to enhance its role in our lives as persons and educators. The temporality of unlearning violence and engaging nonviolence is a lived time, situated in the lived experience of body, emotions, place, and relationality, as this study has shown.

Nonviolence as Teacher Education: Implications

My experience of teaching nonviolence in teacher education demonstrates both the challenges and possibilities in approaching nonviolence as an educational project. The challenges lie in unpacking the stereotypes of nonviolence and restore its proactive and relational force and thus fundamentally question socially and culturally constructed orientation of individualism and dualism between the self and the other. It is a radical shift that takes time and experience to sink into students' views, but it opens up new possibilities for integrating both the individual and the community and has important implications for teacher education. Foregrounding the role of both relational dynamics and individual integration through students' learning experiences, this study shows possibilities of teaching and learning nonviolence in teacher education as an ongoing process of counteracting aggression and cultivating compassion in daily educational practice. Creating pedagogical conditions for students to learn requires shifting relational dynamics in the classroom including relationship with the self and relationship with the other, guided by nonviolent pedagogical relationships. In framing nonviolence as teacher education, educational purpose, means, process, content, and context are integrated for, about, and through nonviolence. Here I highlight several key aspects of what this study means for teacher education and teacher educators and also briefly indicate directions for future research.

First, the individual and the relational aspects of nonviolence need to be in dynamic interplay in order to transform teacher education. The design of the texts and learning activities in these classes combined the structural analysis and the autobiographical analysis with the intention to encourage students to critically re-examine emotions, languages, and actions at the intersection of the personal and the social. Through various contemplative and self-education practices (Gunnlaugson et al., 2014; Miller, 2014; Pinar, 1994), students learned to make the connections between the self and the communal as mutually influencing each other. The future research is needed for negotiating a meaningful connection between nonviolence as a way of life and teaching particular school subjects as well as for facilitating the mutual support of the individual and the social. Here drawing upon critical peace education can be beneficial. In these classes, although I asked students to do experience-based individual projects, further efforts can be made to combine social action projects in pairs or small groups with nonviolence education so that students directly experience introducing orientations of nonviolence into community and society.

Second, engaging nonviolent relationships with difference in teacher education is an important task for crafting pre-service and in-service teachers' experiences in a culturally and ecologically diverse society. While difference should not be erased, students' stories and experiences demonstrate the importance of making connections through difference. A balanced approach of neither removing nor radicalizing difference is the key here, as the companionship project shows that difference with nature can teach us important lessons about humanity while allowing nature to be nature. Human relationships influenced by history and culture are complicated as social diversity is laden with memories, emotions, and collective unconsciousness. In a nonviolent approach, social difference must be recognized and social injustice must be challenged. At the same time, such differences should not reinforce separation and fragmentation, or lead to the radical unknown that eludes connections; students can be invited to experience them as enrichment for an interconnected life in which everybody and everything are participants (Hershock, 2012; Wang, 2014a).

Related to the role of social difference, the gendered experiences of participants and the gendered differences of doing emotional work suggested in this study indicate the need for further research on gender and nonviolence education. Nonviolence can be considered a feminist project as historically and contemporarily women have played a key role in peace movements (Harris, 2008; Wang, 2014b) and have engaged daily caring relationships. Since all participants were female, a future study on the social and individual construction of femininity and masculinity and its role in engaging nonviolence work in teacher education will be informative.

Third, Brantmeier (2009) discusses peace as text, peace as subtext, and peace as context in doing peace work in schools and communities, which is applicable to teacher education. Nonviolence as teacher education infuses nonviolence into text, subtext, and context to transform content, process, method, and purpose of education. Nonviolence as text highlights the importance of curriculum in constructing versions of reality that opens up more spaces for peaceful co-living: "The inclusion of more peaceful voices of the past is one very tangible way to acknowledge and to legitimize peaceful ways of living in the present and for the future" (Brantmeier, 2009, p. 44). Even in teaching historical wrongdoings, we cannot forget those who went against the grain to challenge injustice. For instance, in teaching the Tulsa Race Riot of 1921, the voices of those who risked their own lives to protect Black Tulsans should not be forgotten. By questioning the dominant storylines of hegemony from multiple angles, nonviolence and peace are foregrounded to demonstrate what is possible for students.

Nonviolence as subtext refers to the hidden curriculum that subtly sends students messages that are not spoken yet equally powerful. If imposition is the main mode of education even with the good intention, if the class climate demands agreement rather than allowing different perspectives, intellectual and relational violence rather than nonviolence become the subtext. To make nonviolence a subtext is more difficult than making it an explicit curriculum because it needs pedagogical craft to infuse the energy of interconnectedness throughout the educational process that touches students and moves them out of their comfort zones.

While Brantmeier (2009) highlights peace as context through pedagogical relationships between the teacher and students, I broaden it to class dynamics that includes interactions between and among teacher, student, text, and local communities to create a class context of nonviolence. Pedagogical relationship plays a central role but must also be mediated through students' peer relationships and their relationships with difficult knowledge in a community of learners. The different class dynamics of the diversity class and the nonviolence class demonstrate this point well. Nonviolence as context means mobilizing all relationships toward a process of curbing violence and promoting compassion and social justice.

Fourth, this study also indicates the importance of not setting up violence and nonviolence as binary but to make it an ongoing process in which violence gives way to nonviolence through daily efforts. While the metaphor of a continuum as mentioned above helps to mobilize nonviolence, it seems to imply a linear movement. Centering the importance of both integrative individuality and organic relationality, nonviolence can be envisioned as an open and evolving web in which complex relationships are built to spread out compassion and constantly weave the divisions or fragmentations that violence breaks apart back to the interconnectedness. Individuals are the knots of the web, stretching out to connect with others. As a whole, the web promotes both individuals' inner peace and their connections to others—human or non-human—with healing and creative power. In teacher education, building such a web in the classroom in connection with social contexts is a big challenge.

In addition, the teacher educator's own journey of cultivating her inner peace through dwelling in creative tensionality of teaching nonviolence is an intriguing topic that calls for further research. In embodying the principles of nonviolence, the teacher educator has an opportunity for students to witness what it means to become a nonviolence educator in the midst of tensions and challenges. Dealing with controversial issues such as in social justice education or critical peace education, the teacher educator can learn peacebuilding capacities throughout the process of teaching rather than before teaching. While not necessarily always successful, her ongoing crafting of pedagogical capacities for holding on to tensions and creating a community embodies the spirit of nonviolence education. Understanding teacher educators' critical self-education will contribute to nonviolence as teacher education.

References

Allen, D. (2007). Mahatma Gandhi on violence and peace education. *Philosophy East & West, 57*(3), 290–310.
Bajaj, M. (Ed.). (2008). *Encyclopedia of peace education*. Information Age Publishing.
Bajaj, M. (2010). Conjectures on peace education and Gandhian Studies. *Journal of Peace Education, 7*(10), 47–63.
Boler, M. (1999). *Feeling power*. Routledge.
Brantmeier, E. J. (2009). A peace education primer. *Journal of Conflict Management and Development, 3*(3), 36–50.
Chubbuck, S. M., & Zembylas, M. (2011). Toward a critical pedagogy for nonviolence in urban school contexts. *Journal of Peace Education, 8*(3), 259–275.
David, D. (2009). *Mindful teaching and teaching mindfulness*. Wisdom Publications.
Derrida, J. (1992). *The other heading* (P. Brault & M. B. Naas, Trans.). Indiana University Press.
Disney, A. (Producer), & Riticker, G. (Director). (2008). *Pray the devil back to hell* [Film]. ro*co Films Educational.
Doll, M. A. (1995). *To the Lighthouse and back*. Peter Lang.
Doll, Jr., W. E. (2012). *Pragmatism, post-modernism, and complexity theory* (D. Trueit, Ed.). Routledge.
Dutta, U., Andzenge, A. K., & Walkling, K. (2016). The everyday peace project. *Journal of Peace Education, 13*(1), 79–104.
Fishman, S. (2003). Gandhi in the pre-school. *Journal of Education, 184*(2), 1–5.
Gandhi, A. (2003). *Legacy of love*. North Bay Books.
Gandhi, M. K. (2007). *Gandhi on non-violence* (T. Merton, Ed.). New Directions. (Original work published 1942)
Gemstone Peace Education Team. (2008). Peace education aimed at children everywhere in the world. In J. Lin, E. J. Brantmeier, & C. Bruhn (Eds.), *Transforming education for peace* (pp. 93–111). Information Age Publishing.
Gill, D. (2000). Giving peace a chance. *English Journal, 89*(5), 74–77.
Gunnlaugson, E. W. Sarath, C. S., & Bai, H. (Eds.). (2014). *Contemplative learning and inquiry across disciplines*. State University of New York Press.
Harris, I. (2008). History of peace of education. In M. Bajaj (Ed.), *Encyclopedia of peace education* (pp. 15–24). Information Age Publishing.
Hershock, P. (2012). *Valuing diversity*. State University of New York Press.
Jennings, P. A. (2015). *Mindfulness for teachers*. W. W. Norton.
Jhally, S. (1999). *Tough Guise* [Film]. Media Education Foundation.

Kaneda, T. (2008). Shanti, peacefulness of mind. In C. Eppert & H. Wang (Eds.), *Cross-cultural studies in curriculum* (pp. 171–192). Routledge.

Lin, J., Brantmeier, E. J., & Bruhn, C. (Eds.). (2008). *Transforming education for peace*. Information Age Publishing.

Lynd, S., & Lynd, A. (Eds.). (2006). *Nonviolence in America*. Orbis Books.

Mayes, C. (2005). *Jung and education*. Rowman & Littlefield Education.

Miller, J. (2005). *Sounds of silence breaking*. Peter Lang.

Miller, J. P. (2014). *The Contemplative practitioner* (2nd ed.). University of Toronto Press.

Muller, J. (2002). *Non-violence and education*. UNESCO.

Nagler, M. N. (2004). *The search for a nonviolent future*. Inner Ocean Publishing.

Palmer, P. J., & Zajonc, A. (2010). *The heart of higher education*. Jossey-Bass.

Pinar, W. F. (1994). *Autobiography, politics and sexuality*. Peter Lang.

Pinar, W. F. (2012). *What is curriculum theory?* (2nd ed.). Routledge.

Salomon, G., & Cairns, E. (Eds.). (2010). *Handbook on peace education*. Psychology Press.

Shagoury, R., & Power, B. (2012). *Living the questions: A guide for teacher-researchers*. Stenhouse.

Shastri, S. Y., & Shastri, Y. S. (2007). Ahimsa and the unity of all things. In D. L. Smith-Christopher (Ed.), *Subverting hatred* (pp. 57–75). Orbis Books.

Shim, J. M. (2014). Multicultural education as an emotional situation. *Journal of Curriculum Studies, 46*(1), 116–137.

Slattery, L., Butigan, K., Pelicaric, V., & Preston-Pile, K. (2005). *Engage*. Pace e Bene Press.

Smith-Christopher, D. L. (Ed.). (2007). *Subverting hatred*. Orbis Books.

Stoskopt, A., & Bermudez, A. (2017). The sounds of silence. *Journal of Peace Education, 14*(1), 92–113.

Wang, H. (2010). The temporality of *currere*, change, and teacher education. *Pedagogies: An International Journal, 5*(4), 275–285.

Wang, H. (2013). A nonviolent approach to social justice education. *Educational Studies, 49*(6), 485–503.

Wang, H. (2014a). *Nonviolence and education*. Routledge.

Wang, H. (2014b). A nonviolent perspective on internationalizing curriculum studies. In W. F. Pinar (Ed.), *The international handbook of curriculum research* (2nd ed., pp. 69–76). Routledge.

Wang, H. (2016). Unteachable moments and pedagogical relationships. *Curriculum Inquiry, 46*(5), 455–472.

Wang, H., & Olson, N. (Eds.). (2009). *A journey to unlearn and learn in multicultural education*. Peter Lang.

Weigert, K. M. (1999). Moral dimensions of peace studies. In K. M. Weigert & R. J. Crews (Eds.), *Teaching for justice* (pp. 9–21). American Association for Higher Education.

· 9 ·

CURRICULUM AS MINDFULLY LIVED IN RELATIONSHIPS (2023)[1]

Hannah Hunter-Lynch, Denise Kimblern, Danny Sexton, and Hongyu Wang

This co-authored paper grew out of a graduate class on mindfulness, teaching, and curriculum during the time when the COVID-19 pandemic swept through the United States in 2020. The class was experientially oriented with a pedagogical openness to students' own meaning-making processes. After the class, the instructor invited three students to co-author this paper based on their experiential project writings and further discussions. Thus, it is not a traditional research paper with a pre-determined goal matched with a purposefully chosen methodology, but a result of the extension of the course as an inquiry. Its purpose is not to prove how effective the teaching and learning mindful practices was, as many studies have already done that (see references below), but to demonstrate the process of experiencing mindfulness as it unfolds and to explore what it means to cultivate mindful relationships in curriculum as lived experience.

While mindfulness as an educational movement has been influential in the United States for only several decades, a significant body of literature has

---

[1] This chapter is reprinted with permission of John Wiley & Sons; permission conveyed through Copyright Clearance Center, Inc. Hunter-Lynch, H., Kimblern, D., Sexton, D., & H. Wang (2023). Curriculum as mindfully lived in relationships. *The Curriculum Journal*, 34(2), 193–207.

emerged related to the effectiveness of mindful pedagogy both at K-12 and college levels (Ergas, 2017; Lin et al., 2019; Rechtschaffen, 2014). Various empirical studies show that practicing mindfulness is beneficial for increasing students' attention, reducing anxiety in a testing climate, and improving students' well-being (Mahalingam & Rabelo, 2019; de Ruin et al., 2015). In teacher education, mindfulness has shown its effectiveness for decreasing teachers' stress and burn-out rate (Schussler et al., 2018; Taylor et al., 2021) and improving pre-service teachers' classroom practices to provide effective instructional support, emotional support, and classroom organization (Hirshberg et al., 2020). Furthermore, the benefits of mindfulness for improving teachers' resilience, self-care, emotional regulation, and relational competence, and for increasing teachers' ability to deal with internal dilemmas have also been studied (Burrows, 2015; Dorman, 2015; Kerr et al., 2017; Zimmerman, 2018). Certainly, this literature does not lead to any universal claim for the benefit of mindfulness, but it has opened up the landscape of education.

This paper does not focus on effectiveness, but on the process of students' engagement in experiential mindful relationships, although the process also shows the positive influence of practicing mindfulness. Three graduate students—practicing educators—share their writings on two companionship projects with nature and one project of interpersonal interactions bridging intergenerational distance. The relational orientation of these projects includes the possible role of difference as nature speaks in its nonverbal presence, and human relationships can be tensioned. The process and relational orientation of this paper promises to make a unique contribution to the literature.

The paper starts with the introduction of the pedagogical and inquiry contexts and moves to briefly discussing the guiding orientation of this work, curriculum as lived experience, a phenomenological hermeneutic notion elaborated by scholars such as Aoki (2005), Pinar (2015), and van Manen (1990). Second, three graduate students' separate narrations of their projects—after their editing and condensing—are included to show their process of forming mindful relationships, a process that is practice-oriented, filled with curves and frustrations, as well as revelations and potentiality for ongoing growth. Third, a conversation section discusses what we as a group learned from students' lived curriculum. It was composed after the group discussed all writings and analyzed several important themes that emerged from the process related to time, self-understanding, gender, and difference. As Pinar (2015) argues, curriculum as lived experience is a complicated conversation. In order to visibly show each individual's and the group's reflective process, an open-ended conversation is used to reveal the emergent nature of shared meaning-making. The paper ends with a brief summary discussion of these themes and the implications of this inquiry.

Contexts

A brief description of the contexts relates to both pedagogy and inquiry. The pedagogical context laid the foundation for this paper, and the process of writing this paper expanded its inquiry dimension.

Pedagogical Context

This mindfulness course was offered with the COVID-19 protocol. It included five Zoom meetings when students practiced a variety of mindfulness, weekly online discussions, and two experiential projects. Most of the students had not practiced formal mindfulness before, so it was important to build in experiential components that encouraged students to learn through their own practices, as experiential education is the best channel for such learning (Ergas, 2017; Hyland, 2016; Wang, 2019).

The class, in addition to readings (Jennings, 2015; Mason et al., 2019) and discussions, required two interrelated experiential projects: the first was individual practicing of formal mindfulness throughout the semester, including mindful breathing, mindfulness of the body and emotions, and loving-kindness meditation. The second project, the focus of this article, was a mindful interactions project and students could choose to do the project with a person or nature. The project length was two months and interaction frequency was once or twice a week. Students were required to keep a journal about all the interactions and any change that happened throughout the process. At the end, they wrote about what they had learned from the process. The second project was intertwined with the first project as practicing breathing exercises, body scan, relational meditation, and visualization enabled mindfulness in the relationships.

he instructor used the term "companionship"—rather than "object"—to refer to relationship with nature, as "interbeing" (Hanh, 2009) not only refers to human relations but also human/nature relationships. The radical differences between nature and humans speak to humans in their unique ways, and most students chose this project because of the interpersonal separation that was required during the pandemic. The instructor set up the pedagogical conditions, such as the extended time of two months, the emphasis on mindful listening to nature or another person, the reflective practice of journaling, and ongoing class discussions about the project in break-out rooms on Zoom. However, the instructor did not directly intervene in students' experiences unless students had questions, so the project was largely students' own undertaking of it, which crafted their educational experience (Doll, 2012). In this sense, the student's curriculum of mindful relationships was lived personally, rather than planned by the instructor, and was emergent, rather than predetermined. Students crafted their own experience into a curriculum of their own making.

Inquiry Context

As an inquiry—here we choose the broader term "inquiry" to move beyond the mainstream expectation of "research" as based upon quantitative data—this project includes students' individual inquiries and collective inquiry.

First, the instructor selected these three writings because she was moved by the profound life meanings they conveyed. These students not only used the formal mindfulness practices taught in the class but also went beyond to create their own relational practices. Moreover, there was a certain degree of diversity in their choices, topics, and situations. As a whole, their writings vividly demonstrate the emergent quality of lived curriculum and how mindful relationship as the focus of curriculum can unfold. It takes a learner's perspective although not intending to represent all learners' viewpoints.

Second, the three narratives are reflective constructions of their experiences with an inquiry orientation. Students started their projects not knowing where they would lead but followed emergent pathways in which the students improvised their mindfulness practices to become attuned to their companions, whether nature or another person. Relational attunement could not have been achieved without their open-minded inquiry. For the purpose of co-writing for publication with a word limit, students condensed and edited their original narratives but still kept the depictions of turns and twists during the process. They read one another's writings, including both original and condensed versions, and referred to one another's writings and ideas during their conversations.

Third, as a group we met several times on Zoom to discuss what it means to form a mindful relationship in curriculum as lived experience through attending to emergent themes from all writings. In our discussions, the instructor played the role of facilitator, but the graduate students' writings and their reflective perspectives were foregrounded, and they were free to not converge with the instructor's assumptions. We recorded our Zoom meetings to share among one another, and also created a Google folder to contain writings and a Google document for co-writing. In order to show both individual voices and the process of collective inquiry, we reconstructed a conversation from the Zoom recordings and the Google document co-writings, which we continued to revise as needed throughout the process. In writing this paper, the instructor inevitably played the role of a leader among equals in putting things together, but distinctive individual and conversational voices prevented the imposition of her ideas.

Here is a brief introduction to the participants. At the time of initiating this inquiry project, Hannah Hunter-Lynch had taught language arts in middle schools for four years and had become a Learning Coach. Denise Kimblern had taught for 16 years at high school levels and had become an Instructional Coordinator. Danny Sexton taught criminal justice and legal studies as an adjunct instructor in a community college. The instructor, Hongyu Wang, had been teaching mindfulness for a few years as a part of her commitment to Gandhian nonviolence education (Bracho & Dodson, 2020; Nagler, 2004; Wang, 2014), which centers the necessity of cultivating the integration of the body and mind within the self, promoting compassionate relationships between the self and the other, and building a community that welcomes diversity and difference. She had practiced mindful meditation for almost a decade.

Orienting Theory

A phenomenological interpretive notion of curriculum as lived experience—with the instructor's attention to the role of difference—is the theoretical orientation for this work. Aoki (2005) and Pinar (2015) both formulate curriculum as lived, questioning the drive of instrumental reason toward a predetermined outcome in curriculum planning that drains the life out of the classroom. Examining pedagogy, study, and self-other relationships as lived, Aoki (2005) points out that teaching as leading out "entails at times a letting go that allows a letting be in students' own becoming" (p. 213). Graduate students' experiential inquiry was oriented toward their own becoming. For Pinar (2015), educational experience as lived not only opens up students' emergent pathways but also contains an element of reflection "to reconstruct experience through thought and dialogue to enable understanding" (pp. 110–111) that is both intellectual and emotional. Curriculum as lived in a complicated conversation is threaded through subjectivity, temporality and social relations, and the group inquiry in this paper attempted such a conversation for reconstruction.

Mindfulness, from its origin in Buddhism, is also lived experience marked by a lived body, lived time, and lived relationality. As an embodied practice in everyday life, it is based upon Buddhist notions of impermanence, nonduality, and emptiness through interconnectedness, with a radical openness to dwelling in the present moment (Analayo, 2020; Armstrong, 2017; Ergas, 2017). Jennings' (2015) approach to mindful teachers was one of the main texts used in our class, and she defines mindfulness as "a particular state of consciousness that involves awareness and acceptance of whatever is happening in the present moment" (p. 1). For her, mindful relationships must include awareness of our own thoughts and feelings in order to "attune ourselves to another person" (p. 16) for forming compassionate relationships. With mindful attention to the unfolding of experience moment by moment (Kabat-Zinn, 1994), both mindfulness practices and relational attunement are needed for attending to others as they are in the moment.

As Terry Hyland (2016) points out, the nature of mindfulness naturally lends itself to experiential education, which allows students to reach their own insights. The experiential projects in the class were designed as non-instrumental inquiry focusing on the process of students' experiencing of relationships. The scientific reformulation of mindfulness in contemporary Western applications introduced an element of instrumentality (Hyland, 2016), but the mindful interaction project was framed as an open-ended inquiry without any particular outcome attached. Reaching new awareness and insights was seen as a possible product but not a pre-determined requirement.

What does it mean to cultivate mindful relationships in curriculum as lived experience? That became the main question in our inquiry oriented by a phenomenological interpretive study (van Manen, 1990). Three students' individual narrations already built in an element of reflection—reflecting themselves dwelling in the world—that was extended in a group inquiry through conversations. Our conversation necessarily included both self-reflection and reflection on others' experiences to seek meanings. Multiple layers of reflection are compatible both with curriculum as a complicated conversation and with mindful relationships as becoming aware of one's own body, thinking, and emotions while forming relational connections.

While our inquiry is oriented by curriculum as lived experience situated in time, place, relationality, and cultural contexts, we do not seek the essence of the phenomenon—mindful interactions—in order to leave open different possibilities. In poststructural theory, the difference of the other cannot be assimilated into the self in order to maintain a dynamic and non-controlling relationship (Wang, 2014). This was the instructor's orientation in both teaching and inquiry. However, students' respect for difference was also accompanied by their seeking of commonality. We did not seek consensus, as our interest lay in demonstrating the process and inviting others to initiate their own mindful inquiry.

Three Accounts of Experiential Curriculum

Hannah: Companionship of the Tree in Its Rootedness

A large cedar tree stood in my backyard, and I chose the tree as my companion. At the beginning, my main goal was to build a good habit of practicing mindfulness using sketching the tree as the tool. With my practices, however, the desire to gain a better understanding of myself became the center of this project, and the tree became an organic part of it. The first time I began my session, I started with sketching an image of the tree as a way to relax myself and reset for practicing formal mindfulness. At first, I categorized this "drawing time" as separate from my "mindfulness time," but quickly sketching the tree became a mindful practice of its own. It was my own version of "focused attention" as Jennings (2015) describes it, as "intentionally directing and maintaining attention on a target" (p. 19). I do not believe I would have been able to form the close connection with my tree without these focused drawings each week.

As the weeks went by my sketches shifted from basic, almost scientific drawings to something that reflected my own mental state at the time. The tree took on more detail as I noticed the life that relied on it, and eventually I moved my seat closer to it and began to include the roots and details toward the base of the trunk. Between my record of drawings and journal entries,

I noticed a sense of rootedness. I attended to how my tree companion was rooted in the ground and how that affected everything connected to it. Over time, my ponderings over my companion began to sink into my reflections of myself.

During my sketch time and mindfulness time, there were distracting thoughts. When I closed my eyes and imagined my tree breathing with me through its needles, I might hear a bird chirping from a branch or a squirrel jumping down to the fence and suddenly, my brain abandoned the tree to follow those creatures. I wrote in my journal entry about the need to "find a way to plant myself and my mind the same way my tree is planted." This sentence became my sort of mantra through the rest of the project to ground my mind.

In an effort to settle distractions, I envisioned myself side-by-side with my tree companion and imagined that as I inhaled, I was taking in the sunshine and air around me and as I exhaled, I pushed roots down into the ground. With each breath, I imagined the roots growing deeper and stronger. By visualization, I felt a kinship to this tree even though I could not communicate with it verbally. By the end of my second week, I felt stronger and more focused. I also used a shortened version of a body scan to help me re-center when distracted. Rooted in the awareness of my body and my feelings, I wrote in the journal: "I know I can go into stressful situations with teachers and imagine planting my roots in the moment, so that my emotions or the emotions of others do not take over and knock me down."

However, I did not know the stumbling blocks I was about to face. In the third week, I became ill with COVID-19 and had to self-isolate for the next two weeks. I was sick, worried about my health, and too weak to do any intentional mindfulness practices. When I felt more up to it the next week, I sat by the window in my bedroom to do a tree sketch, which reflected the disconnection I felt. The tree was farther and smaller, and I added in the fence behind it for the first time. The tree was no longer the center of attention. Previously I had added small squirrels or birds to my sketches but this week the tree stood alone, cut off from the natural landscape.

For the rest of the project time, I focused on the question I wrote down in my journal during my quarantine, "What am I mindfully rooted to?" I began to list the things my tree needed to thrive, such as sunlight, carbon dioxide, good soil, and water. Then I listed all the things I needed to thrive: "healthy food, sleep, quiet time each day, purpose in my actions, kindness to myself, flexibility...." In the next two and half weeks, I focused on these needs through my breathing practices. When I exhaled each breath, I visualized roots of my needs growing down from my breath into the ground. As I inhaled, I envisioned gaining energy from those roots. My tree could only support wildlife and provide shade to me because it built deep roots. I could only support those around me if I were rooted in a strong foundation of my needs.

I had no idea I would be able to connect with the tree in such a surprising way. Mindfulness practice stopped feeling like an assignment, and I began to realize that mindfulness is beyond guided breathing techniques and body scans. By intentionally focusing on my tree though sketching, studying, and visualization, I built a stronger connection not only with the tree but also with myself. Mindfulness has helped me to identify my own needs and practice fulfilling them. Now each time I look at the tree I ask, "What am I mindfully rooted to?"

Denise: My Back Porch as a Companion

Through a mindfulness project, I formed a meaningful relationship with my back porch, and as a result, gained more self-understanding, with more gendered awareness and a new respect for the positive role of difference and time. While I have sat on my back porch countless times, I have never taken time to be mindfully aware of it. The project gave me an opportunity to attend to my porch in a different way.

In my first journal entry, all my attention was outwardly focused:

> The wind is light. I can smell freshly cut grass as the neighbor tends his lawn, while the sound of the waterfall is mesmerizing. As I watch the ripples move out from the fall, I notice they get bigger, slower, and less pronounced. There is a hummingbird buzzing around, going back and forth between a small tree in the garden and the feeder hanging on the edge of the porch. I notice that the leaves on the Japanese Maple tree have turned almost purple in color.

I used sight, sound, and smell to pay attention to the beauty and fullness of the nature that existed on my porch, and I realized how fast I moved through my day, failing to take notice. This was the first time I intentionally slowed down, sitting for a period without distractions, except for the nature around me.

Later I became more related to what I observed and turned inward for self-reflection. I noticed how the fish in the pond nearly was stuck in the shallows chasing food pellets. I wondered if that compared to anything we faced in life. We moved at breakneck speed, made decisions on the fly based on perceptions formed by the past or predictions about the future, but failed to be present in the moment. Do we realize that we may have been stuck too? My job was fast paced and mentally and emotionally draining, especially during a pandemic. I often found myself losing focus on the present, too worried about meeting others' and my own (unrealistic) expectations As Jennings (2015) pointed out, we can be preoccupied with the past or the future to lose touch with the present.

Raised in a critical household with strict paternal expectations for a girl, I internalized gender codes that influenced my work as an instructional leader, my life as a wife, and my study as a doctoral student. Slowing down and breathing deeply helped me understand how my hypercritical mind kept taking me to those shallow, rocky edges where I became stuck in a cycle of constantly reflecting, predicting, and judging. Mindfulness became more than a practice as it revealed emotional aspects of my life to which I do not often attend. That new awareness can be seen in my next entry:

> The water in the pond is very clear. This is the last day to feed the fish as temperatures are dropping and they will begin winter hibernation. I feel relaxed and refreshed on my porch as the sounds of the waterfall just rush over me. I find myself becoming more attentive to the various parts of the porch. I am slightly calmer at work and when I am riled up, I am becoming mindful of the tension and stress. That awareness allows me to take some deep breaths, consider my thoughts, and regain a balanced attitude.

My mindful awareness was becoming more relational. My porch became a friendly companion that infuses a different orientation into my life. I was gaining an overall sense of calm and more innate attentiveness to those bodily sensations of stress or tension. Additionally, I noticed an emerging ability to be attentive to my thoughts, especially those that were hypercritical, comparing past and future actions. Being attuned to my mind helped me achieve some distance from those negative thoughts and feelings, allowing me to see those as just thoughts and feelings, not my permanent reality (Jennings, 2015). In that way, I could concentrate more on the present moment. The last journal entry showed that I had become more peaceful, less anxious, and felt freer: "I can just be."

Through this project, I learned a sense of respect for difference and its role in self-understanding. I thought it was impossible in the beginning to have a relationship with an object and projected my thoughts and feelings onto my porch. However, with more mindfulness practices, I became more aware of my porch and of the self, and the difference of nature in its own rhythm taught me how to suspend judgment and break the cycle of self-negativity. With a new way to relate to the porch, I gained a much deeper understanding of the self and became more open to others.

Danny: Mindful Interactions with My Father

The mindful interactions project helped me re-establish the bond with my father. We used to be very close and spend a lot of time together playing baseball and going to games, but somehow became more distant after I grew older. I moved back home after he was diagnosed with cancer. Since the diagnosis, he had had a difficult time dealing with stress, anxiety, and depression, but he kept his feelings inside. I told him that mindfulness is a state of being aware in the present moment, and further provided him with some literature about mindfulness and the benefits of incorporating mindfulness practices into an individual's daily life, particularly for cancer patients (Carlson & Garland, 2005; Piet et al., 2012). My father was surprised and agreed to join in my project.

As my father moved in for the project, I knew right away that there would be unique challenges and obstacles. Due to his hearing problems, he talked loudly and played the television loudly. He also went to bed early and got up early. He preferred a cold temperature, so I felt like my house was freezing. With our different schedules and life habits, I immediately started working on myself to cope with the situation. The first thing I knew I needed to do was to breathe deeply and try not to get angry. I used the breathing exercises detailed by Mason, Murphy, and Jackson (2019) to handle stress, such as the Heart Beaming exercise that instilled a sense of calmness throughout my body. I also tried to suspend my immediate reactions and introduce a mindful moment of pause before making an appropriate response.

An important aspect of mindfulness practices is developing nonjudgmental awareness to avoid "imposing our beliefs and expectations on our present moment experience" in order to be "fully aware of what is actually happening" (Jennings, 2015, p. 5). I reminded myself not to allow my frustration or annoyance to take control. After practicing mindful breathing and relaxation for 10 minutes, I politely talked with my father about the volume of the television. He apologized and said that he did not know how loud it was. After the conversation, I decided to go outside for study that afternoon. After I gently handled the need to ask my father to be less loud, I was able to respect his need to watch television while also studying on my own.

In these interactions with my father, I made efforts to practice interpersonal mindfulness in which "one is expected to be aware of one's own emotions and thoughts while at the same time compassionately understanding the other person's situation as it is" (Jennings, 2015, p. 94). I was able to get in touch with my own emotions and thoughts through practicing mindful breathing while I made efforts to emotionally connect with my father. I also wanted to contribute to relieving his pain. The following is from a journal entry:

> I have noticed today that my father is experiencing some pain.... As I sit down in the chair next to him, I turn on a baseball game on the television to take his mind off the pain. As we watch the game together, I talk to him about how much time we used to spend together when I was a kid. The conversation brings up so many good memories between us and sparks a conversation between us that we have not had in a long time. After the game is over, I ask my father to practice mindfulness of the breath with me. Then, I try to incorporate mindfulness exercises, particularly mindful listening in our time together. My father finally opens up to me about how scared he is of dying from cancer. He expresses to me how sad he has been because he cannot work anymore.

It was a turning point in our relationship when my dad opened up to express his feelings, rather than keeping so much anger, sadness, anxiety, and depression inside. My mindful listening helped me to pay attention to my father's facial expressions and tone of voice, hear what he expressed, and have compassion for him.

I savored these moments of connections when he needed our bond the most. I wrote in my last journal entry:

> Now my father practices mindful meditation every night and every morning. I have noticed he is calmer, and his outlook on life is slowly improving. Today we spend the afternoon watching the 1989 movie *"Field of Dreams"* (Robinson & Prankish, 1989). The movie always makes me cry when I watch the final scene where the son is connected to the spirit of the father on the baseball field. After the movie is over, my father and I practice a loving-kindness meditation together, and I visualize the flow of unconditional love and compassion through my body and towards my father.... Today is a beautiful day, and the one I will always remember that I spent with my father.

In short, I think bringing in the game of baseball into my mindful interactions with my father provided an important connection for us to improve our relationship, and most importantly, to communicate again. Furthermore, interpersonal mindfulness, mindful listening, and loving-kindness meditation were effective for us to reconnect. Now he sleeps better at night without interruptions, with a renewed outlook on life. I feel closer to him than ever.

A Conversation

Denise: Mindfulness gave me the gift of time as I became aware of the need to slow down and take time for myself. It was difficult initially to take the time to sit, but then I began to be comfortable just breathing and being still. I have not felt like that before. I also realized just how much time I spent projecting my worries instead of being present in the moment. Hannah, I thought your view of time was similar yet different, as you saw both positive and negative aspects to time. Danny, you seemed to receive the gift of the time spent with your father to mend your relationship.

Hannah: Similar to you, Denise, being okay with being still and being okay with being slow was something that I think mindfulness taught me. What made things different for me was that in the middle of my project I got sick with the COVID-19. Time became very slow, almost non-existent, and I could not practice mindfulness. So time very much felt abundant in a negative way. On the other hand, having two months for the project helped me to have a sense of progression and have a transformed relationship with the tree.

Danny: I share your sense of time. The extended time in this project gave me room to process my emotions and reconnect to my father, which meant so much for me. I was always busy and planning for the future, and the project taught me that all we have was today for appreciating the people we have in our lives and valuing our relationships. Also, the time of illness on my father's part might have had some impact on opening up a room for reclaiming the bond.

Hongyu: Culturally we are busy people and seldom allow ourselves to pause and take time to relate to both the self and the other meaningfully. The inner time of mindfulness and the external time of the pandemic merged with our class time, making the temporality of experience for each of us nonlinear and complicated (Wang, 2010) and providing a lived space for experiencing relationship differently. Dwelling in time and space, we become more than what we are.

Denise: Mindfulness helped me change self-criticism into a deeper sense of self and an awareness of the need for self-care (Jennings, 2015). Through the practice, I realized the emotional and mental toll caused by my hypercritical mind as I became more attuned to the self and learned to break the cycle of becoming stuck in self-negativity. It seems to me that self-understanding emerged as a shared theme among our projects. Danny, before confronting your father with the issue of noise, you spent time practicing mindfulness. Did those exercises shift your sense of the self?

Danny: Exercises helped me move away from distractions and inner frustration to become calm inside before I spoke to him. With a cultivated ability for inner work through mindfulness to attend to the "here and now," I was aware of my own feelings and kept them balanced as I began to understand my father's relationship with his own emotions. In doing so, I invited him to relate to his inner vulnerability during the time of illness. I think deeper self-understanding leads to better relationships with others. At the end of my project, my father and I practiced loving-kindness meditation, repeating the phrases "May I be happy. May I be well. May I be safe" (Baugher, 2014, pp. 240–241). Those were profoundly loving and touching moments in my life.

Hannah: Mindfulness helped my self-understanding through my growing awareness of my own needs. It helped me prioritize my needs better because many times I prioritized the needs of others over my own. My evolving relationship with the tree shifted from instrumentality to companionship (Aoki, 2005), which inspired my self-care. I was able to improvise my visualizations with the inspiration from the tree's embeddedness in the earth and developed a mindful orientation beyond formal practices. Attending to the rootedness of the tree through sketches, meditations, and visualizations helped me become more rooted in myself.

Hongyu: It seems to me that self-understanding went hand in hand with forming a mindful relationship with the other, whether it was nature or another person. Moreover, self-awareness was also coupled with self-transcendence (Huebner, 1999; Pinar, 2015) because becoming connected with nature or another person requires one to go beyond oneself or work through one's intense emotions. Interestingly, while nature presents difference in a unique way, the awareness of social difference was also evoked in relating to nature.

Denise: I internalized strict gender codes in my childhood, but mindfulness gave me a new awareness allowing for a different orientation to my self-expectation. I began to rethink my internalized thoughts and feelings around those unrealistic expectations for a female from family and society and realized they did not have to be my reality. Finding time to practice mindfulness, I learned to let go of some household tasks while being committed to the practices. This project also gave me a chance to do memory work and become oriented by "the wheel of awareness" (Jennings, 2015, p. 14) for self-care. Forming mindful relationship became a process of reorienting my gendered self. Danny, what about you?

Danny: My dad had a difficult time expressing his emotions and feelings. So did I. If I needed to talk about something, I went to my mom. His illness of cancer and my practicing mindfulness of emotions made me realize how trying to hide pain was unhealthy. This project brought me and my dad emotionally closer, as my sharing of good memories of our earlier connections invited him to share his vulnerable feelings. That had never happened before. Father-son relationships in our culture are often constructed through the normalized masculinity, which often makes men alienated from our own emotional life (Levant, 1996; Mather, 2014; Pellegrini & Sarbin, 2002).

Hongyu: Hannah, in your experience in learning to set up the priority of meeting your own needs rather than trying to meet others' needs, is there a gendered element? As Danny comments, he goes to his mom for emotional issues. Women are usually caretakers and take care of others' emotions, sometimes at the expense of attending to their own needs. This cultural script (Johnson, 2014) has often led to a lack of self-care in women's experiences. Jennings (2015) discusses the importance of self-care for teachers in cultivating mindfulness. What do you think?

Hannah: I definitely think that there was a gendered element involved in my self-discovery. Focusing on my needs was never prioritized because it felt selfish. What mindfulness practice gave me was the peace and capacity to realize that it is not selfish to take care of yourself first and then others. I think that as women we feel obligated to carry the burdens of caring for others because that is what caretakers do. However, the most effective caretakers also have to take care of themselves.

Hongyu: I am always interested in the issues of making connections across differences. Denise and Hannah, both of you mentioned that in the beginning of your companion projects you were not sure what you would get out of it but ended with a deeper sense of interconnectedness. Did the difference between humanity and nature, or between son and father, play any role in your mindful interactions?

Denise: Jennings (2015) discussed how mindfulness leads to insight as "we begin to see the subtle details that we never noticed before, thus awakening in ourselves a deeper understanding" (p. 184). For me, that awakening led to a much deeper sense of respect for the differences of nature as I became more attentive to nature and stopped projecting the self onto it. That insight also helped me discover similarities between the self and nature in ways I had not known before, such as realizing both have their own rhythm.

Danny: Similarly to Denise, I now have a deeper attentiveness to myself and the world around me. My father and I reconnected through our common interest that brought us together when I was a young boy. Spending time together around baseball had always been the one constant connector in our lives, and it brought us back together after years of distance. Throughout our mindful interactions, facing the danger of cancer together, our memory of earlier close relationships contributed to restoring our bonding. I feel in my case, rebuilding commonality is more important.

Hannah: I was very aware of the difference between me and the tree, and it motivated me to sketch its image. Comparing the beginning and the end of the project, I definitely grew more connected to the tree, and its rootedness gave me the support I needed when I suffered from illness. Initially I only used the tree as the instrument for practicing mindfulness, but soon it became a companion in my journey. I do not think the project would have had the same impact if I had chosen a pet instead, because the close relationship I already had with my pet would have gotten in the way. In the end, I felt connected to the spirit of the tree, and both mindful drawing and visualization helped me to achieve it.

Mindful Relationships Through Lived Curriculum

What does it mean to cultivate mindful relationships in curriculum as lived experience? Curriculum as mindfully lived in relationship is an emergent, multidimensional process of cultivating both deepened self-understanding and relational attunement, sustained through a lived body, lived time and space, and lived connections across difference. Here, the teaching content of mindfulness, pedagogical conditions for students' free exploration, and the learning process for establishing a mindful relationship constitute curriculum. In this curriculum, students not only learned about the formal knowledge of mindfulness but also learned through experiencing a mindful relationship over an extended period of time. Curriculum as lived includes both academic knowledge and self-knowledge, and an ever-evolving, ongoing process in which students' body, mind, and spirit are integrated to reach new knowledge, awareness, and relationality (Pinar et al., 1995). In this inquiry, students formed a new mode of relationship with the self and the world: a mindful relationship that highlighted the role of the body, a different sense of time (and space), the role of difference, and the interaction between self-understanding and relational awareness with gendered implications.

First, formal mindfulness practices through a lived body are inherently part of mindful interactions with others or attuned relationships with nature (Jennings, 2015; Wang, 2019). Three graduate students used formal practices in various ways to experience a lived body as they were growing relational attunement. For example, Hannah found rootedness as the central metaphor of her mindful companionship with the tree and went further to create her own version of mindful breathing *like* the tree. Danny used mindful breathing and listening to work through his intense emotions, and invited his father to practice mindfulness to relieve the stress of suffering from cancer. Moreover, Denise's project required a broad view of her backyard while she was paying particular attention to the fish struggling in the pond. This non-dualistic attention to both a focus and a broad, global awareness (Heitz, 2016) highlights the importance of our ability to open our inner awareness to the wholeness of experience and to discern interdependence in the whole to deal with the difficulty of the pandemic (Poindexter et al., 2021). All three students also affirmed that mindfulness is not just about formal bodily practices, but also about bringing a mindful orientation to relating to others including persons, nature, and the world.

Second, lived time (Aoki, 2005; Huebner, 1999; van Manen, 1990) in its nonlinearity and complexity is beyond the external, clock time reflected in the current emphasis on educational efficiency. The two-month length of the project and the internal time of mindfulness provided the temporal conditions for cultivating mindful relationships. The three students also had the freedom to choose their own site, which became a lived space over time, although the isolated space due to her pandemic illness was also confining for Hannah, like the added fence in her drawing showed. When pedagogical conditions were set up to allow students time and space to freely explore and grow during the process, they were more likely to dwell in difficulty and work with tensions, which was what these students were able to accomplish. Immersed relational engagement at their own pace and in their own ways led to deeper understanding and more awareness. Certainly, the pandemic further complicated this issue, as the forced slowing down of time for Hannah due to her illness was unwelcome; however, in general, the inner dwelling time of mindfulness was helpful for the three students. The temporality and the spatial dimensions of mindfulness are beneficial only when they lead to the enrichment of the experience.

Third, although the role of difference in forming mindful relationships was the instructor's interest, the three graduate students demonstrated a more intertwined relationship between commonality and differences on a continuum. The instructor believed that if educators can listen to nature, which speaks in a non-human manner, they are more likely to hear the voices of their own students who are different and to make connections with them. Both Hannah and Denise recognized the difference between themselves and nature when stepping into the unknown and acknowledged the contribution of this difference in their becoming attuned to nature at a deeper level. But Denise also spoke about the similarity between nature and humanity, as it inspired her to rethink her life, and the intergenerational distance in Danny's case was bridged through finding common ground and engaging in mindful practices together with his father.

In addition, gender emerged as a layer of experience that mindful relationships attended to, one which was not planned or expected, but which came from their lived experience and was discussed further in the group inquiry. While the social and cultural construction of gender in its restrictive impact was acknowledged by all three students, the women's reflections centered on the need for gendered self-care, while the father-son tale focused on the male-male relationship. Listening to the women's inner voices that had been pushed away by gendered norms was coupled with building male-male emotional bonding through finding room for authentic expressions. Becoming more aware of the invisible layer of the self, they went beyond their inner and outer constraints to let go of gendered mechanisms of control in order to form mindful relationships. Here self-knowledge and relational awareness were intimately connected.

Thus, cultivating mindful relationships in curriculum as a lived experience in this inquiry demonstrates a complicated, multidimensional understanding of curriculum situated in the body, the time, and relationality contextualized in culture. Furthermore, it makes several contributions to curriculum theory. First, embodiment in curriculum as a lived experience is an important dimension, often through holistic, sensory experiences and body/mind integration in educational activities, but the mindful relationship as lived adds an aspect of direct attention to bodily sensations in mindful breathing, a body scan, or mindful walking. Such a direct and specific attention heightens students' consciousness of the body, which is often neglected in formal education. Emotion involves both body and mind, and while curriculum as lived involves emotional work, mindfulness attends to the nature of specific emotions, such as anger, anxiety, or stress, as students' narrations mentioned, and they worked with these emotions through mindful breathing, drawing, and observations. Mindfulness practices, centering the body as the site for specific exercises to reduce the intensity of emotions, provide concrete channels for enriching the landscape of curriculum through a lived body.

Second, mindfulness in education is a relatively new area, and most studies, as we mentioned at the beginning of this article, focus on the effectiveness, for teachers and students, of practicing mindfulness. Such a focus can be easily subsumed into the instrumental approach to curriculum, an approach that the theory of curriculum as lived experience critiques. In this inquiry, however, the relational, emergent, and experiential orientation brings together mindfulness and curriculum as lived without reinforcing an instrumental approach. The mindful interaction project was framed as an open-ended inquiry without pre-conceived objectives, which demonstrated the non-instrumental nature of students' experiencing and becoming. The important aspects of researching lived experience, such as body, time/space, and relationality (van Manen, 1990), emerged from students' writings and the group's thematic analysis, even though the teacher educator did not ask students to pay attention to these aspects in their experiential projects. Gender emerged as an unexpected factor and appeared in all three students' writings, and students' openness to it brought a fresh lens to understand how the construction of gender was embedded in the control mechanisms, which they tried to mindfully let go.

Third, the intimate relationship between self-knowledge and relational attunement was expanded to the relationship between humanity and nature. The current mindfulness literature focuses more on individual than relational practices, and while curriculum as lived often set the natural environment as the background for interpersonal conversations, this study highlights the possibility of forming a mindful relationship with nature in experiential curriculum. Such a project is not merely suited for the pandemic situation but has general implications, as it had already been implemented in the teacher educator's teaching in the pre-pandemic era (Wang, 2018). In the current crisis of climate change, it is essential that curriculum as mindfully lived includes the relational component with nature.

This inquiry was the result of one class and the collaboration among one teacher educator and three graduate students, so it has its limitations, and a qualitative study of this topic with a bigger scope in the future can be informative. However, this inquiry does not intend to prove the effectiveness of mindfulness in curriculum, or to analyze students' writings from a researcher's viewpoint, but intends to demonstrate these students' experiential and meaning-making process, *in their own voices, on their own pathways, and through their own lenses*, of forming a mindful relationship in education. Curriculum as mindfully lived cannot be defined by a singular pathway, as it is radically open to unpredictable emergence. This chapter invites teacher educators and students to venture out on a mindful journey of curriculum as a lived experience and explore what it means for them.

References

Analayo, B. (2020). *Mindfulness in early Buddhism*. Windhorse Publications.
Aoki, T. T. (2005). *Curriculum in a new key* (W. F. Pinar & R. L. Irwin, Eds.). Lawrence Erlbaum.
Armstrong, G. (2017). *Emptiness*. Wisdom Publications.
Baugher, J. C. (2014). Contemplating uncomfortable emotions. In O. Gunnlaugson, E. Sarath, C. Scott, & H. Bai (Eds.). *Contemplative learning and inquiry across disciplines* (pp. 233–251). SUNY Press.
Bracho, C. A., & Dodson, D. (Eds.). (2020). *Teachers teaching nonviolence*. DIO Press.
Burrows, L. (2015). Inner alchemy. *Journal of Transformative Education, 13*(2), 127–139. https://doi.org/10.1177/1541344615569535
Carlson, L. E., & Garland, S. N. (2005). Impact of mindfulness-based stress reduction (MBSR) on sleep, mood, stress and fatigue symptoms in cancer outpatients. *International Journal of Behavioral Medicine, 12*(4), 278–285. https://doi.org/10.1207/s15327558ijbm1204_9
de Bruin, E. I., Meppelink, R., & Bögels, S. M. (2015). Mindfulness in higher education. *Mindfulness, 6*, 1137–1142. https://doi.org/10.1007/s12671-014-0364-5
Doll, Jr., W. E. (2012). *Pragmatism, post-modernism, and complexity theory* (D. Trueit, Ed.). Routledge.
Dorman, E. (2015). Building teachers' social-emotional competence through mindfulness practices. *Curriculum and Teaching Dialogue, 17*(1 & 2), 103–119.
Ergas, O. (2017). *Reconstructing "education" through mindful attention*. Palgrave Macmillian.
Hanh, T. N. (2009). *The heart of understanding*. Parallax Press. (Original work published 1989)
Heitz, M. H. (2016). The screening of reality. In N. Dalal, A. Intezari, & M. Heitz (Eds.), *Practical wisdom in the age of technology* (pp. 29–38). Routledge.
Hirshberg, M. J., Flook, L., Enright, R. D., & Davidson, R. J. (2020). Integrating mindfulness and connection practices into preservice teacher education improves classroom practices. *Learning and Instruction, 66*, 1–11. https://doi.org/10.1016/j.learninstruc.2019.101298
Huebner, D. E. (1999). *The lure of the transcendent* (V. Hillis Ed. W. F. Pinar collected and Intro.). Lawrence Erlbaum.
Hyland, T. (2016). The limits of mindfulness. *British Journal of Educational Studies, 64*(1), 97–117. https://doi.org/10.1080/00071005.2015.1051946

Jennings, P. A. (2015). *Mindfulness for teachers*. W. W. Norton.
Johnson, A. G. (2014). *The gender knot*. Temple University Press.
Kabat-Zinn, J. (1994). *Wherever you go, there you are*. Hyperion Press.
Kerr, L. J., Lucas, L. J., DiDomenico, G. E., Mishra, V., Stanton, B. J., Shivde, G., Pero, A. N., Runyen, M. E., & Terry, G. M. (2017). Is mindfulness training useful for pre-service teachers? An exploratory investigation. *Teaching Education, 28*(4), 349–359. https://doi.org/10.1080/10476210.2017.1296831
Levant, R. F. (1996). The new psychology of men. *Professional Psychology: Research and Practice, 27*(3), 259–265.
Lin, J., Culham, T., & Edwards, S. (Eds.). (2019). *Contemplative pedagogies for transformative teaching, learning, and being*. Information Age Publishing.
Mahalingam, R., & Rabelo, V. C. (2019). Teaching mindfulness to undergraduates. *Journal of Transformative Education, 17*(1), 51–70. https://doi.org/10.1177/1541344618771222
Mason, C., Murphy, M. M. R., & Jackson, Y. (2019). *Mindfulness practices*. Solution Tree Press.
Mather, M. (2014). Fatherly love. In J. Wyatt & T. E. Adams (Eds.), *On (writing) families* (pp. 7–11). Sense Publishers.
Nagler, M. (2004). *The search for a nonviolent future*. Inner Ocean Publishing.
Pellegrini, R. J., & Sarbin, T. R. (Eds.). (2002). *Between fathers and sons*. The Haworth Clinical Practice Press.
Piet, J., Würtzen, H., & Zachariae, R. (2012). The effect of mindfulness-based therapy on symptoms of anxiety and depression in adult cancer patients and survivors. *Journal of Consulting and Clinical Psychology, 80*(6), 1007. https:/doi.org/10.1037/a0028329
Pinar, W. F. (2015). *Educational experience as lived*. Routledge.
Pinar, W. F., Reynold W., Slattery, P., & Taubman, P. (1995). *Understanding curriculum*. Peter Lang.
Poindexter, N., Smith, L., & Wang, H. (2021). Heightened consciousness and curriculum in a time of crisis. *Prospects*. https://doi.org/10.1007/s11125-021-09542-0
Rechtschaffen, D. (2014). *The way of mindful education*. W. W. Norton.
Robinson, P. A. (Director), & Prankish, B. (Producer). (1989). *Field of dreams* [Film]. MCA Universal.
Schussler, D. L., Deweese, A., Rasheed, D., Demauro, A., Brown, J., Geenbert, M., Jennings, P. A. (2018). Stress and release. *American Journal of Education, 125*, 1–28. https://doi.org/10.1086/699808
Taylor, S. G., Roberts, A. M., & Zarret, N. (2021). A brief mindfulness-based intervention (bMBI) to reduce teacher stress and burnout. *Teaching and Teacher Education, 100*, Article 103284. https://doi.org/10.1016/j.tate.2021.103284
van Manen, M. (1990). *Researching lived experience*. State University of New York Press.
Wang, H. (2010). The temporality of *currere*, change, and teacher education. *Pedagogies: An International Journal, 5*(4), 275–285. https://doi.org/10.1080/1554480X.2010.509469
Wang, H (2014). *Nonviolence and education*. Routledge.
Wang, H. (2018). Teacher education as nonviolence. *Journal of Peace Education, 15*(2), 216–237. https://doi.org/10.1080/17400201.2018.1458294

Wang, H. (2019). From the instrumental to the existential. In J. Lin, T. Culham, & S. Edwards (Eds.), *Contemplative pedagogies for transformation in teaching, learning and being* (pp. 87–100). Information Age Publishing.

Zimmerman, A. (2018). Considering the prospect of cultivating mindfulness in teacher education. *Issues in Teacher Education, 1*, 57–72.

· 10 ·

"THINKING BACK THROUGH OUR MOTHERS": A CURRICULUM OF ORGANIC RELATIONALITY (2021)[1]

The feminist motif of "thinking back through our mothers" (Grumet, 1988, p. 187) can be traced back to Woolf's (1929/1981) search to find "a room of one's own" (p. 97). "Furnishing education with feminist theory," Grumet (1988, p. 182) told us that we need to claim the mother's heritage, not to identify with her, not to repudiate her, but to become ourselves in a middle ground. For women educators, becoming ourselves in contemporary education and society is not possible if we look only to fathers for approval. Locating women at the center of the stage and making sense of mothers' legacies, this motif is not merely about the individual mother but also about the collective history of mothers in family and cultural contexts who have worked in and against the overarching system of patriarchy. In today's world, centering women's voices and experiences that have so often been pushed to the margins also requires situating their stories in intersecting social contexts, including but not limited to race, sexuality, class, language, and nationality, or in Anzaldúa's (1999) phrase, "borderlands" that host the multiplicity and tensionality of identity.

1 This chapter is reprinted with permission of the publisher (Taylor & Francis Ltd, http://www.tandfonline.com). Wang, H. (2021). "Think back through our mothers:" Curriculum of organic relationality. *Curriculum Inquiry, 51*(3), 332–349.

Influenced by the legacies of diverse foremothers to become the teacher and curriculum scholar I am today, in this article, I think back thematically through our mothers and claim their lineages in order to interweave different aspects of organic relationality through curriculum. In contemporary U.S. education, we encounter not only the patriarchal drive for standardization, accountability, and control and the neoliberal push for profit and commodification; we also face a widespread crisis of fragmentation and division as well as the pursuit of sameness in the human psyche, social media, and society. Building meaningful, multilayered relationships is particularly difficult—and yet more urgent—in today's time. I conceptualize creative maternity in a broad sense that recognizes that women give birth not only to babies but also to new thoughts, artistic projects, and new forms of relationality (Kristeva, 1987; Martin, 2009; Wang, 2004). Creative maternity embodies these forms of relationality, as mothers have to navigate between the self and the other in multiple senses.

At the metaphorical level, the maternal is necessarily different from and contests the paternal, as psychoanalysis and Daoism make clear. Daoism claims the maternal as the origin of creativity (Wang, 2021) and in the metaphorical sense positions mothering as symbolic of integrative emergence out of the interconnectedness of life. Thus, the function of nurturing and creative mothering can also be performed by men in the contemporary family structure (Kristeva, 1987). In motherhood specifically, however, maternity does not necessarily contest the paternal structure since mothers can be implicated in the system of patriarchy. Without critical reflexivity, women educators may actively participate in the paternal drive for standardization, even if it does not serve our own interests. In thinking back through our mothers, I include both metaphorical and literal senses of maternity to explore its creative potential and limitations, but my focus is on making meaningful connections with maternal legacies as a mode of contesting patriarchy. This chapter is about making present the vibrant maternal voices in curriculum and teaching that are mostly absent, so that through this visibility, the female self is no longer a shadowy figure. Thus, this chapter explores curriculum possibilities opened up by foregrounding mothers' experiences and daughters' struggles, even though motherhood is not free from patriarchal influence.

I use the term "organic relationality" to indicate the underlying interconnectedness of life in which humans participate. It is not conflict-free but allows room for difference, tensions, and fragmentation and their dynamic interactions. The maternal body's ability to contain the alterity of the other is symbolic of such relationality, as this body gives birth to a new life yet is not in control of the baby's own pathway. In this sense, organic relationality is a particular type of relational orientation that nurtures the other while allowing the other's emergence in new directions. The ecological diversity that is beneficial for the mutual flourishing of humanity and between humanity and the planet (Hershock, 2012) also supports such an ethical position. Ecofeminism also makes the link between the dominating mechanism of humans over nature and of patriarchy over women and other people who experience gender discrimination (Li, 2013, p. 330). Drawing upon international wisdom traditions such as Daoism, Buddhism, and the African tradition of *ubuntu* that are different from Western individualism, I have argued for the essential role of dynamic interdependence in enabling organic relationality that welcomes the role of difference—including gendered difference—in its mutual contribution to a community and the web of life (Wang, 2013, 2014).

Women's lived experiences are embedded in relationships, and a mother must negotiate many relationships both in the private and the public world. For most mothers who can sustain the child's growth, these relationships embody organic relationality, not as an idealized notion but as a moment-by-moment practice that engages difference and enables emergence. In addition, I particularly refer to Indigenous[1] mothers' teachings in the United States throughout the article, because living and teaching in Oklahoma, the Native American territory, I feel compelled to bring their wisdom into this text and to highlight the unique contributions of their relational strength, even though my understanding is partial and limited. By choosing to bring not only my Chinese tradition but also Indigenous traditions to readers' attention, I also intentionally practice organic relationality that goes beyond the self to be connected to others.

In this article, the thread of thinking back through our mothers for a curriculum of organic relationality crosses different times and places and includes different racial, sexual, class, linguistic, and national contexts. I weave this thread thematically along three major lines. First, I explore the role of interconnectedness and relational dynamics as central to such a curriculum. Second, I discuss creative tensionality between mothers and daughters as generative and as having implications for reclaiming the classroom in a space of simultaneous un/attachment, un/burdening, and non/belonging. Third, I argue that nonviolent relations across differences are the site for building a curriculum community that welcomes the alterity of the other and grows compassionate relationships. While drawing upon diverse women writers and feminist curriculum scholars, I also weave in autobiographical stories about my mother, who is a retired teacher educator in China.[2] These lines of weaving for organic relationality are underscored by the necessity of deconstructing the mechanism of control and domination that supports patriarchy. In addition, while this ongoing weaving does not lead to one singular blended product, gratitude despite difficulty emerges as one path to claim the maternal legacy.

> My mother is a powerful woman, despite her petite stature. She does not fit into the Western imagination of Chinese women as a weak sex controlled by patriarchy (Mann, 2000), as she has defied authority throughout her life. To mention just one story as an example: My family, with seven members, lived in a 13-square-meter temporary public apartment for years in the 1970s. At that time, family housing in my hometown, Harbin, Heilongjiang province, was arranged publicly through employers. My mother was a professor at a teachers' college and her administrator said that the policy for new apartment allocation applied only to men as the head of the household, not to women. However, my father commuted by train to his university in order to teach and the whole family lived near my mother's college. When reasoning did not work, my mother threw her body in front of her administrator's car and demanded fair consideration, without which she would not let him drive out. She defied the paternal order, literally, with her body. We later moved into a new apartment. It happened when I was young so I do not remember it, but I have always been grateful for my mother's strength and capacity to navigate through the public world, setting an example of what a woman can accomplish in a patriarchal society.

Deeply embedded in women's lives and work, the organic relationality embraced by my "thinking back through our mothers" opens up a spirit of gratitude—the theme of this special issue—that is affirmative, critical, and transformational. As affirmative, gratitude acknowledges connections with our mothers and ancestral roots in the planet, which support women's ontological becoming in their own pathways. As critical, such gratitude does not mean that women fully identify with our mothers and their pathways, but rather we critically engage their legacies and consciously unlearn the gendered norms in their lives. As transformational, gratitude is open to a generative tensionality that gives birth to the new generation's creativity to build new modes of relationality for a better world. Thinking back through our mothers with gratitude is not about accepting their ways of knowing, being, and relating, but about affirmative, critical, and transformative engagements that open up new possibilities. In drawing upon the diverse traditions of mothers, this writing itself is an expression of my gratitude to the web of life in general that anchors a sense of belonging and to women mentors in particular who have nurtured my imagination for a curriculum of organic relationality, either from close by or from a distance. Curriculum and teaching should incorporate the maternal legacies, deconstruct social regulations, and create new modes of gendered relationships that engage productively with difference.

Shifting Relational Dynamics of Curriculum

A curriculum of organic relationality is complicated, multidimensional, and dynamic. The heart of organic relationality is the interconnectedness of all beings, in which the relational dynamics among parts are more important than the individual, separate components in an ecosystem or an educational system (Doll, 2012). This view is consistent with Indigenous (Archibald, 2008; Mankiller, 2011) and Buddhist and Daoist wisdom traditions (Nagler, 2004; Wang, 2007), and yet is largely neglected in today's U.S. curriculum. Three decades ago, Grumet (1988) argued that schooling delivered children to the patriarchal order that separated rather than connected. Three decades later, in a neoliberal age, the educational order for separation and domination through standardization and competition has hardened rather than softened.

In order to re-center curriculum through relationality, we can start by learning from Indigenous mothers' perspectives and insights, which are often absent in the school curriculum. Wilma Mankiller (2011), the first female principal chief of the Cherokee Nation in Oklahoma who served in the role from 1985 to 1994, affirmed a feminist position and acknowledged the shared relational orientation of Indigenous women from different cultures. She commented that many Indigenous women "synchronize their lives with the land and the community" and have a "more complete, whole, interconnected understanding of the world" with "a much greater degree of tolerance for the unevenness, differences, and contradictions in life" (p. 5). This orientation of interrelated understanding does not adopt dualistic "categorical thinking" (Wang, 2014, p. 92), but accepts the messiness of human life and perceives women and men to be equal, complementary, and connected.

Women played a more important role in many Indigenous communities before colonial powers imposed a patriarchal system, as women leaders from different tribal nations in Mankiller's (2011) book affirm. In the contemporary age, some Indigenous women tend to put their identity as members of tribal nations (vs. the U.S. government) ahead of their identity as women because of the pressing issues related to sovereignty as well as the limitations of Western feminism in addressing Indigenous women's struggles (Mankiller, 2011; Ramirez, 2007; Smith & Kauanui, 2008). Mankiller (2011) affirmed the Cherokee tradition of gender balance before colonization. Smith and Kauanui (2008) also asserted that "the imposition of patriarchy within Native communities is essential to establishing colonial rule, because patriarchy naturalizes social hierarchy" (p. 241). While not presenting an idealized ancient way of life, I think it is well acknowledged that Indigenous women's leadership roles became diminished through the process of colonization. The intersection between gender and race presents complicated stories that center struggles not only against patriarchy but also against racism, so a feminist curriculum project must also confront racism as well as other forms of social domination.

Ramirez (2007) argued for a "Native feminist approach" that uses "indigenous frameworks of respectful gender relations" to "*simultaneously* challenge racism and sexism" (p. 34). Contesting a White construct of feminism with its individualistic and privileged orientations—echoed by other women writers of color such as Anzaldúa (1999)—does not necessarily conflict with cultivating a Native feminist consciousness to address sexism both within and outside of tribal nations and with rethinking issues related to sovereignty and tribal self-determination in the U.S. context. Since this essay's focus is on organic relationality that supports women from different backgrounds to come together, and not on how to differentiate between feminisms such as Native and White feminisms, I do not fully discuss such differences here. It is necessary to point out that contested points such as White women's racial privilege and the notion of equal individual rights in Western liberalism are not shared experiences with Native women. However, the role of gender cannot be neglected, but should be contextualized as Native women fight against both racism and sexism. Mankiller's autobiography discusses the obstacles that she encountered in running for deputy chief of the Cherokee Nation: "I was challenged mostly because of one fact—I am female" (Mankiller & Wallis, 1993, p. 240). Indigenous women's perspectives, needs, and concerns should be foregrounded even though gendered relational dynamics are intertwined with racial, class, and linguistic issues. Fundamentally challenging patriarchy and male-dominated society is necessary to restore balance in gendered relationships.

An interrelated view of the world is also linked to interconnection within the self. Archibald (2008) pointed out that educating the body, mind, heart, and spirit of the whole person is crucial to Indigenous storytelling, and she brings this orientation into teacher education. This attention to the inner landscape goes hand in hand with the attention to the outside world. Indigenous women's ability to form connections and to negotiate across differences without factions is rooted in their connections with Mother Earth to achieve harmony and balance (Mankiller, 2011). Such attention to the person as interconnected within and the world as interrelated—also echoed in Asian philosophies (Wang, 2007)—asks educators to shift attention from the individual in isolation to the relational dynamics of curriculum, including integrating different elements within the self.

Shifting from individual achievement to integrative learning that benefits both the individual and the relational, from an emphasis on mastery and control of the world to forming meaningful relationships with the world, and from the competition model to a communal inquiry that is mutually enhancing of all participants reframes the educational landscape. In other words, it is a change from masculine knowing that centers on control to feminine knowing that centers on relationships. Here the use of "masculine" and "feminine" is Daoist, metaphorical, as a female can adopt masculine knowing and a male can adopt feminine knowing. Beyond gendered dualism, both females and males have masculinity and femininity within the self. The attention away from the individual component to relational dynamics also questions the discipline-centered modern curriculum and invites interdisciplinary and experience-based approaches to curriculum, teaching, and learning. The primary focus on the intellect in the school curriculum at the expense of other dimensions of human growth cannot engage the student on all levels of their being and "interbeing" (Hanh, 1989/2009). Feminist re-visioning of curriculum calls for the reconfiguration of curriculum structure, incorporation of embodied and relational knowing, and the non-dualistic reorientation of teaching and learning (Grumet, 1988; Hendry, 2011; Li, 2013; Miller, 2005).

Although individualism has been the mainstream of U.S. society, feminist movements have challenged its fundamental assumptions for decades. While certain articulations of feminism still uphold individual autonomy, poststructural feminisms acknowledge the crucial role of relationality in women's lives through discourses, embodiment, and social context. A relational view of the mother, as Miller (2005) argued, forms a doubled space. She discussed the doubled space her mother enacted in order to have both solitude and connections and how her mother's creative ability to dwell in two different worlds at the same time has influenced her own work and life. Claiming this fluid maternal space in which one's self-care and care for others are lovingly connected through tensions, Miller invited us to imagine a world where interconnectedness is recognized by seeing through separation and individuality is highlighted through spreading roots into the soil of deep connections. She approached women's subjectivity as always multiple, contradictory, and fluid, situated in the creative tension between freedom and interdependence, a legacy that she has learned through her mother's negotiation of individuality and relationality. Organic relationality is inclusive of relational individuality, which values interplay over categorical separation.

From a poststructural feminist view, Miller (2010) further proposed a vision for a community without consensus as "composed of 'selves' and versions of curriculum work that re-form daily and differently in response to difference and to the unknown" (p. 96). Her vision acknowledged the importance of constructing a communal space in which all can participate, but refused any universal and unified notion of the self and the collective. In Miller's view, a community is not a simple addition of individuals but something that emerges through engaging interplay. Smith's (2021) notion of curriculum as community building across differences recognizes that community should not be managed but rather created out of the messy, uncertain, and participatory space in which a teacher is able to hold tensions on a shifting, complicated, relational ground. This ability to hold tensions so that the community is not split apart by different factions is key to practicing organic relationality. Interconnectedness is, I believe, an ontological condition for humanity, and cultivating connections through differences in the movement of curriculum is a daily feminist practice of education and pedagogy.

> I used to think I was radically different from my mother until the invisible links were uncovered. My mother worked first as a rural village school teacher after her graduation from a normal school, teaching children in a mixed age classroom in the 1950s. She had a chance to attend a teacher development group in a nearby city. It was during that time that she decided to go to college. She was the only person in her family who had a salary, which was very small, and everybody was dependent on it. Giving that up to go to college was a difficult decision for her and for her mother, but her mother agreed: "Okay; it is about your future." After burning the midnight oil in order to prepare for the national college entrance exam, she not only passed the exam but was accepted by one of the best teachers' colleges. It turned out that after that year, teachers who were normal school graduates were no longer allowed to apply for college. My mother caught the last train. It was a turning point in her life: She moved from a village to the cosmopolitan city of Shanghai to study. I unknowingly followed the path of my grandmother's open-mindedness and my mother's courage and determination in my own unwillingness to stay with the given. My mother always understood my need to depart, to go to a different world, and to keep pursuing something new. Although we have opposite personalities, parts of us are quite alike.

When we acknowledge interconnectedness as fundamental for unique human becoming and the interplay between individuality and relationality, gratitude "helps us realize that we are sufficient, and that realization frees us" (Macy, 2007, p. 77). This self-affirmation is healing for women, even in the midst of difficulty. Despite centuries of collective trauma and contemporary difficulties, a group of 20 Indigenous women leaders from different Native American Nations[3] collectively affirmed that "every day is a good day" (Mankiller, 2011), expressing their thankfulness to the Earth, the natural world, human aspirations, and life in general. They are tirelessly working on rebuilding the world, connecting back to their memory of balance and harmony, and moving toward the future to heal the collective wounds. Difficulty does not diminish their gratitude since they respond in life-affirming ways. Such a spirit of gratitude is especially necessary to confront the crisis in today's educational world. In the U.S. context of standardization, competition-driven learning outcomes, and reactionary politics, it is difficult to feel gratitude and easy to feel anger and desperation. But the ability to dwell in life paves the path for moment-by-moment critical engagement with education in order to " let life work through us, enlisting all our strength, wisdom, and courage, so that life itself can continue" (Macy, 2007, p. 76).

Creative Tensionality Between Connections and Disconnections

Organic relationality includes both connections and disconnections. Intersections, parallel movements, curved routes, and empty spaces are all parts of the web of life. The doubled maternal space and the need for queering curriculum (Miller, 2005), the borderlands in which women of color make "a new culture" with their own "feminist architecture" (Anzaldúa, 1999, p. 44), and visionary feminist education against the interlocking systems of White supremacy, capitalism, and patriarchy (hooks, 2000), all point to contestation and creative tensionality in relationships. Although these feminisms have differences, they share the efforts to navigate through conflicting, contesting, and conjoined relationships while still taking a feminist stand.

The complexity of interrelatedness lies in its ability to hold the multiple—including language diversity and the importance of the mother tongue (Anzaldúa, 1999; Mankiller, 2011)—and sustain tensions in finding balance among different directions. I use the phrase "organic relationality" to describe this sustainable strength in holding differences together because we can observe it clearly from nature in mutually flourishing ecosystems. Ecofeminism also advocates forming organic relationships between humans and nature as a mode of challenging the mechanism of dualism that supports male domination and highlights "the interactive intersections of the 'natural' realm and the 'human' realm" (Li, 2013, p. 330). Therefore, here the term "organic" does not exclude human participation, but it recognizes the need for human participation to be ecological and supportive of the wellbeing of the natural and social environment. Organic relationality also necessarily embraces elements of diversity and hosts interactions among different components; without such openness and interplay, relationships can become exclusive and lose their web-weaving capacity.

Humanity is capable of sustaining tensionality, as exemplified in women's potential to host the multiple (Smith, 2021). Both tensions and connectedness lie in the relationships between mothers and daughters. The stories about their conflicts, confrontations, and reconciliations cross various cultures in many inspirational autobiographies. For example, Chernin's *In My Mother's House* (1983) narrated a daughter's negotiation with a mother who was an immigrant from Russia; Hale's *Bloodlines: Odyssey of a Native Daughter* (1988) not only depicted her struggles against racism as a member of the Coeur d'Alene tribe but also portrayed her journey of working through difficulties with her mother; and Doll's chapter "Mother Matters" in her book *To the Lighthouse and Back* (1995) demonstrated the transformation of a mutual negation to the mutual recognition of the mother-daughter relationship in the Euro-U.S. context.

While racism, homophobia, and poverty all contribute to the difficulties of a maternal space, the central role of patriarchy in limiting a mother's space and thus a daughter's room to move around is manifested in various forms in diverse cultures and is a shared theme in these autobiographies. Of course, mothers' lives, thoughts, and their guiding hands to their daughters are also imprinted in patriarchal scripts that must be questioned. Daughters, as much as they want to envision themselves as more progressive than their mothers, are also not free from new modes of gendered control (Foucault, 1978). The storyline of the struggles between daughters and mothers in the context of finding footing in an unequal society reveals the complexity of gendered relationships as well as the potential for moving through tensionality toward mutual affirmation and social transformation. I teach these autobiographies in my classes in teacher education in order to open up an uncomfortable, complicated space to unravel the impact of patriarchy and its intersections with racism, classism, or nationalism through the depths of our most intimate, interior landscapes. Students' explorations of these issues make them more mindful of the complexity of a teacher's navigation in the classroom. They also write about their relationships with their mothers, which are often full of conflicts and difficulties, and how their understandings of tensions differently lead them to more self-integration. Claiming the mother's legacy in its complexity is about finding the middle ground and negotiating the passage to become an educator who can hold tensions for herself and for her students.

The stories about mothers and daughters are also reflected in generations of feminism. Some U.S. feminists position "the third wave" of feminists as "newly revolutionary," as more youthful and superior to that of their feminist mothers (Henry, 2006, p. 149). While Henry (2006) argued that gratitude can exist even in competition, I do not believe that "thinking back through our mothers" in a competitive manner can be fruitful. Elevating the self above others reinforces the "singular," "cutting-edge," and "groundbreaking" scholarship that characterizes creativity as an act of separation from the maternal and reproduces a patriarchal storyline in which gratitude disappears in disconnection. With a critical awareness of the impact of interconnectedness on the individual, I perceive gratitude as essentially relational and approach creativity in the context of intersubjective, intertextual, and intercultural transformation.

This site of tensioned relationality is complicated, involving simultaneous un/attachment, un/burdening, and non/belonging. Women are positioned as strangers in a patriarchal society that is ruled by reason and the mechanism of domination (Kristeva, 1995; Wang, 2004); because their success is dependent upon negating their embodied selves, the sense of attachment and belonging that can be nurtured by a maternal space is often compromised by societal expectations. The marginalized position of women in society also adds burdens to motherhood that make its creative potential difficult to fulfill; these burdens can be passed on to daughters in various forms. While a woman's position is relational, the normative demand for the woman to be the one who nurtures a space for belonging is also problematic. If a woman does not feel that she belongs in the world that disrespects her voice and perspective, how can she foster a sense of belonging in the next generation? Here I do not intend to elevate motherhood as an ideal space, but want to highlight women's biological and social uniqueness in caring for the next generation, a position that is shared by the woman teacher to a certain degree. We don't always have children, but we almost always have mothers, and our choice of how to attend to the footprints of mothers—not only our own but also of diverse foremothers—in our lives influences how we attend to our students' potential for emergence and becoming.

It is a paradoxical position for a woman teacher who is expected to open the door of hospitality to her students and yet follow the patriarchal order that confines both the teacher and students to limited realms. The gendered nature of the teaching profession not only marginalizes teachers at schools and teacher educators at universities but also treats them as scapegoats for what has gone wrong in the nation, as exemplified in U.S. educational reform in the past few decades. The mechanism of patriarchy is control and domination (Johnson, 2014), and in refusing to reinforce this mechanism in the classroom, teachers have to choose the position of non-belonging in order to carve out room for students' exploration and growth. In their struggles, many women teachers have to hold out against the weight of patriarchy in order to take its heavy burden off their students. At the same time, the internalized scripts of patriarchy demand that women teachers implement and follow the neat order of schooling, and some teachers willingly comply. Transforming gendered codes requires women teachers to unlearn the patriarchal expectations in their internal landscapes. Acknowledging that society makes it more difficult for women to embrace femininity, Kristeva (1987, 2002) spoke about feminine creativity that is generated by negotiating subjectivity through a relationship with the alterity of the other. She perceived motherhood to be one mode of subjectivity with the potential for getting in touch with the lost connectedness to archaic maternity to destabilize the normalized social structure for renewal and regeneration. Motherhood is a good metaphor for generative teaching and mentoring that lovingly and painstakingly provides guidance for the students' formation of new thoughts while letting them go into the world to make their own mark (Wang, 2004). In this sense, the woman's position of non-belonging makes it possible to provide an intellectually enriching environment and nurture the sense of belonging that is necessary for the growth of the young. Her capacity to question social norms and the construction of herself implicated in these norms is critical for making new openings possible for the young to explore and seek their own paths.

Historically many Chinese women writers were able to navigate through relational complexity to create space for their own thinking and writing even under the strong grip of patriarchy (Wang, 2008). They adopted different ways of appropriating words, symbolism, and artistic expressions to redefine themselves and society. For instance, a courtesan woman writer, Rushi Liu (1618–1664) mingled with male literary figures on boats to discuss art and poetry, traveled in various landscapes, and signed her name on her works, all actions that were not socially acceptable for a woman. Unattached to Confucian codes of conduct and not belonging to the hierarchal Chinese family, she created a room of her own to give birth to new forms of poetry and artistic expression. We should attend to these foremothers' stories in order to foreground women's historical pathways of unsettling patriarchy and their creative capacity to negotiate with tensions. These stories also support Hendry's (2011) deconstruction of the dominant line in curriculum history that linearly positions us as more progressive than the older generations. In understanding how our foremothers created cracks in the system in their time, we are better positioned to explore new possibilities for now.

Reclaiming our mothers and foremothers through both connections and independence in order to recreate ourselves and our classrooms requires laboring in this state of tensioned relationality, a space of simultaneous un/attachment, un/burdening, and non/belonging. While it is a common notion that the purpose for building a community is to foster a sense of belonging, in a society profoundly influenced by (hetero)sexism, racism, classism, and other forms of social violence, belonging and attachment to a community must be simultaneously accompanied by unburdening members from the weight of domination in its various forms. Creating such an educational space means profoundly transforming curriculum, teaching, and learning. A community without consensus, as Miller (2010) envisioned, does not uphold a simplistic sense of belonging, but requires a daily practice of opening to differences.

> According to my mother, she must have passed on her anxiety to me before I was born. She was pregnant with me when the Cultural Revolution (1966–1976) in China started and she lived in uncertainty and fear on a daily basis. My mother's generation went through wars (1938–1945; 1945–1949) as children, and then the political turbulences of the new China (1949–1976) as adults, before more stability set in after they passed middle age. Mom had been the cornerstone of our family and sent four daughters to college, which was a rare achievement in her time. However, her strength as an extraordinary mother is not without its limits. I can never fully live up to her expectations of a good daughter, nor can my sisters. The unhappiness and disappointment my mother experienced have deep roots in the anger, sadness, and personal un-fulfillment of the collective psyche of Chinese women. Kristeva (1995) discussed creative "guilt-free" (p. 220) maternity as yet to come in today's patriarchal society, since it requires fulfilling the mother's own affective, intellectual, and professional aspirations while meeting the child's need for growth. In my gratitude to my

mother, there lingers an element of guilt for not reaching her expectations and not meeting her needs. Living with my mother's disappointment is a tension from which I cannot escape, not even from a distance. It calls on me to take responsibility for participating in changing the system so that a mother's fulfillment in society can be achieved.

When gratitude is based upon guilt, it is no longer generative but becomes confining. Mitchell (2012) pointed out that gratitude breaks us out of self-satisfaction, and "impels us to think about the ways our lives are related to others" (p. 19). Gratitude can also be a burden, as it "highlights the powerless of the recipient" and emphasizes "our dependence, not our independence" (p. 20). However, I believe that interdependence beyond the duality of dependence and independence is the thread of gratitude that connects. If we reveal the social root of guilt to illuminate the confining gendered structure, then the daughter's gratitude can renew intergenerational struggles to create a different kind of community. As mothers and as daughters, women teachers are the driving force to build such a school community of gratitude without guilt.

Nonviolent Relations Across Differences

Organic relationality supports and is supported by solidarity and nonviolent relations across differences. Historically, there have been exemplary women working collaboratively, even when they disagreed with each other. For instance, Jane Addams (1860–1935) and Ida B. Wells (1862–1931) collaborated for more than three decades in civil rights and women's movements, despite Wells' critique of Addams' position on the lynching of African American men (Hendry, 2011; Knight, 2005, 2010; Pinar, 2001, 2009). While their disagreement was related to the highly controversial issues of race, gender, and class, they still worked together to contribute to the founding of the N.A.A.C.P., host gatherings at Hull House that featured women of color and immigration issues, and challenge school segregation. They were able to cultivate nonviolent relations across their respective differences for the common good and community education. Hendry's (2011) historical analysis positioned Addams' and Wells' holding "difference" as "paramount" to radical democracy in their opening to "the experiences of immigrants, women, and African-Americans" (p. 150).

Citing Addams' life history and commitment to active pacifism, Pinar (2009) pointed out that nonviolence has been a feminist issue. As Harris

(2008) acknowledged, "Many leading peace educators in the early twentieth century were women" (p. 69). Before that, as Mankiller (2011) informed us, "Leadership, as in historic Cherokee communities, was exerted by the power of persuasion, not by threat of force or coercion" (p. 50), and women played that leadership role before colonization. The power of persuasion in uniting the means and the ends of nonviolent relationships is often embodied in women's relational capacity. A good example of an amazing relational capacity being used for nonviolence is a Chinese woman, Xiuling Qian—Madame Perlinghi—living in Belgium during World War II. When she was five months pregnant, she traveled to Brussels from her village to petition a Nazi general to spare the lives of many hostages. But after the war she also spoke on behalf of this Nazi general who had honored her request, asking the court where he was being tried as a war criminal to treat him with leniency (Wu, 2015).

Qian's story shows a mother who not only had compassion for all people but also had the courage to risk her life to speak and act against both the official Nazi ideology and, after the war, the popular sentiment for pursuing the death penalty for Nazi officials. She saw the humanity in a German military general and drew that out of him as she persuaded him to save enemy lives (Wu, 2015; Xu, 2021). She also invited Belgians' sympathetic understanding when she presented the evidence in court. I consider her a public educator who taught us through her capacity to form nonviolent relationships. As a woman exiled during the war, her dwelling in humanity enabled the "rehumanization" of opposite parties, "the highest kind of education" (Nagler, 2004, p. 51) through "deep persuasion that moves people below the conscious level" (p. 52).

Organic relationality also needs to be established between women and men. Advocating that "feminism is for everybody" (hooks, 2000, p. 118), hooks invites both women and men to form alliances in order to combat the White supremacist, capitalistic, patriarchal system. In her vision, "by emphasizing an ethics of mutuality and interdependency, feminist thinking offers us a way to end domination" (p. 117) and "a global ecological vision of how the planet can survive and how everyone on it can have access to peace and well-being" (p. 110). To achieve such a vision, we have to work together across differences for a pedagogy of freedom that develops critical consciousness and challenges domination. Doing so requires not only going against injustice, but also cultivating alternative visions that involve humanity and all other life on this planet.

Nonviolent solidarity across differences requires deep self-reflectivity and the ability to learn from collaborative relationships. Chambers (1994, 2008), who has lived in and worked within Indigenous communities for decades, has collaborated with Indigenous people in various curriculum-of-place projects to reclaim an educational landscape that is attentive to Indigenous voices, temporalities, contexts, and embodiments. While acknowledging her own privilege of Whiteness—realized only after she grew up—as a non-Indigenous girl living in the Indigenous communities in northern Canada, she affirmed her affinity with the Indigenous people. Later, as a teacher educator and curriculum scholar, she emphasized the importance of learning from the Indigenous experiences in teacher education. She worked with Narcisse Blood from the Kainai Nation to facilitate students' "learning from place" through seminars and field trips in Blackfoot Territory (2008, p. 114). Students used stories, songs, and performances to demonstrate what they had learned in their "wayfinding" (p. 122) to engage historical memory and renew relationships with others and the planet in enacting a curriculum of place.

Dwelling together in nonviolent relationships in Indigenous land, time, place, and wisdom is important for creating a curriculum of organic relationality, because learning from Indigenous heritages is highly marginalized in U.S. education. However, organic relationality cannot be cultivated without nonviolently engaging the Indigenous knowledge and attending to the collective trauma. I highlight Indigenous traditions in this article intentionally, because they ground us in the land, root us in Mother Earth, and confront us with the original trauma of the birth of the United States. Furthermore, as I discussed earlier, the group of Native American women's sense of gratitude for the gift of life is profoundly touching. Echoing their spirit, Macy's (2007) story of gratitude education is also educational in both explicit and tacit ways. A teacher named Freida, who works at an Indigenous school, talked about the school's morning opening, when students gather to give thanks for 20 minutes—a shortened version of the longer thanksgiving ritual. Starting with "we gather our minds as one mind," students thank the sun, the moon, the trees, et cetera, and all "the life-giving presences that bless and nourish us all" (p. 79). This daily gathering is an important lesson for students in gratitude to life.

> When my mother was 15, she left home and walked through the mountains on her bare feet from dawn until night in order to reach the normal school as a new student. Not being able to afford more than one pair of good shoes, she carried her only pair in her bag to use at school. The school nurse found the bottoms of her feet very damaged

after her arrival. Coming from a family without money, my mother has deep respect for those who are less fortunate. For all her life as a college professor, she supported those in the rural village and would stand up for poor people who were bullied on the street. How I remember those encounters! She has instilled in me a belief in equality and the necessity to support those in difficult situations, not by direct teaching, but by her embodiment and way of life. Even at an old age, when she was almost 80, she single-handedly campaigned against the corruption of officials who took land illegally from farmers in her hometown, a southern village. It took her two years (and the onset of an illness due to stress) to win the case, but her persistent efforts—with other factors—led to the local official's downfall and better compensation for farmers. The unexpected victory that she was able to accomplish against all odds, on behalf of her relatives in the village, put me in awe of her ability to persevere to achieve the impossible.

Transforming the content, process, and purpose of curriculum through an emphasis on nonviolent relationality is no easy task. First, nonviolence and peace as important messages of life are not adequately covered in our school curriculum, as Finley's (2003) question showed: "How can I teach peace when [the textbook] only covers war?" (p. 150). Her content analysis of 17 history textbooks used in U.S. schools in the 1980s and 1990s found that the textbooks' coverage of war and peace is dramatically imbalanced, with an average of 89.1 pages on war topics and 4.94 pages on peace topics. Both Boulding (2000) and Brantmeier (2009) pointed out that history books tend to privilege stories of war and battles. After examining four U.S. history textbooks, Stoskopf and Bermudez (2017) also argued that

> despite scholarship that reveals a complex network of activists who engaged in peaceful forms of protest against the institutionalized violence of slavery, text-book accounts at best either understate the role of these efforts or at worst air brush them from historical memory. (p. 92)

Doing so silences the significance of nonviolent social change. Peaceful existence and nonviolent resistance have existed throughout human history both in the United States and elsewhere in the world (Nagler, 2004), but the official U.S. school curriculum does not sufficiently portray such pathways as alternatives to the model of win/lose domination. Brantmeier (2009) reminded us that "the inclusion of more peaceful voices of the past is one very tangible way to acknowledge and to legitimize peaceful ways of living in the present for the future" (p. 44). We must address this imbalance in textbooks so that students have more access to the wisdom and insights of nonviolent relationality in the U.S. curriculum.

Second, the process of curriculum lies in dynamic interplay between and among text, teacher, student, and context. It involves pedagogical relationships of nonviolence and the teacher's intentional choices of teaching materials and pedagogical approaches to promote peace and collaboration rather than domination, students' intellectual companionship with—rather than objectification of—what they learn, and social and cultural contexts that support curriculum dynamics of nonviolent relationality (Wang, 2019). Third, we must embody the principles of nonviolent relations as we work together as educators to bridge the divide, live with tensions, and cooperate beyond conflicts for students' well-being, as is illuminated by a story about the collaboration between a Black woman teacher and a White woman teacher (Obidah & Teel, 2001). Obidah's and Teel's collaboration was complicated by difficulty and contestation related to racial and cultural differences, even to the point of breaking apart, but they were able to work through their conflicts because they shared the goal of improving children's lives in the classroom.

A Cautious Note

This cautious note at the end is to bring clarity to the central concepts of this chapter and discuss certain limits, in order to invite non-dualistic readings that attend to the complex and intertwined lines of thinking. First, "thinking back through our mothers" for a curriculum of organic relationality is not about essentializing or idealizing motherhood, nor is it about good or bad mothering. Rather, it is about the necessity of discerning and making sense of mothers' footprints in their paths under the weight of patriarchy and to share their struggles. Certainly, men can participate in such a thinking back to reclaim their relationships with their mothers, although it is not the focus of this essay. Interestingly, in Mitchell's (2012) discussion of gratitude, he mostly portrayed men's historical lineage and stories of forefathers, fathers, and sons. This essay argues for following the maternal line, precisely because it is often obscured by the dominating paternal line. Mitchell (2012) also argued for a sense of responsibility to accompany gratitude, with which I concur, and I think that educational responsibility for foregrounding mothers' experiences and women's voices in gratitude lies in transcending the one-sided storyline and re-making the intergenerational storytelling that is curriculum.

Second, organic relationality as I have defined it in this essay has a built-in opening to difference and the alterity of the other, as the web of life is dynamic and emergent through the enrichment of diversity-in-interaction. Different from specific human relationships that can be influenced by power imbalance, organic relationality as an existential condition is not a particular type of relationship that suppresses individual and collective struggles for equity because it is oriented by the mutual flourishing of all components (Wang, 2021). The general neglect of it in U.S. education and society makes highlighting its importance necessary, particularly considering the ongoing human and ecological crisis. I do not position organic relationality as the solution to all the complex educational issues we face today, but it is an essential, and often missing, element that we must attend to. Organic relationality through the mother's relational weaving should be an important part of curriculum structure, process, and practices.

Third, the relational nature of gratitude has both strength and limitations. A sense of gratitude based upon the interrelatedness of life and ecological consciousness is spiritually uplifting. In Chinese culture, gratitude is important for both cosmic and social relationships. Expressions of gratitude to nature, parents, and ancestors, not through verbal acknowledgment but through actions, are considered essential for ethics and morality. Because of the important role of the mother in the Chinese family, gratitude to the mother from the younger generation is socially expected. Gratitude education has been formally introduced into schools and universities in China recently because of the perceived self-centeredness of children who have been the only child in the family (Li, 2015). However, such a campaign can be implicated in the mechanism of social and political control, the very mechanism that organic relationality deconstructs, so advocating gratitude in itself is not necessarily gender empowering. Gratitude may constrain the individual student's free exploration and can become a tool of the state to control teachers and students.

However, I argue that gratitude that can hold tensions and complexity with a sense of responsibility has the potential for strengthening interrelatedness with others, community, and the planet in ways that erode mechanisms of control and domination. Claiming maternal legacies in gratitude despite their limitations in order to challenge patriarchy is a practice of educators' responsibility for co-creating with students a more equitable life within and outside of schools, as I have argued throughout the article. Building mutually flourishing connections in the classroom in order to foster embodied learning, creative energy, and relational growth through a curriculum of organic relationality is a feminist task for "thinking back through our mothers" to create educational conditions for nurturing students' own becoming in their seeking of a gender-balanced and ecologically aware world.

> My mother has a laughing spirit, enjoying life despite disappointment. She can find amusement and make new connections anywhere she goes. I take comfort in the fact that she does not let negativity weigh her down for long. She was a wonderful teacher educator, well beloved by her students. Her sense of humor and caring for her students were instrumental in making it possible for them to integrate knowledge. In her retirement, she was able to try new things. Even in her 80s, not knowing how to use technology initially, she managed to make a good friend with WeChat—a Chinese chat system—and discover on her own a hand-writing function that makes it easier for her to write messages. While my mother's power has its own shadow and my sisters and I each have our own unique struggles with her, I am grateful for her optimism despite her disappointments, her enthusiastic embracing of life and its imperfections, and her commitment to righting the wrongs in society. In gratitude, I try to seek my own room. If there is a guilt-free creative maternity, I want to nurture guilt-free gratitude to my mother, and all foremothers, in order to renew the mother's legacy and pass it on to my students for co-creating a more gender equitable world.

Notes

1 I use the term "Indigenous" since it is a broad term, even though I use it mainly in the context of the United States, except in the last section of the article where I also refer to the Canadian context. Other terms, such as Native, Native American, or tribal nations, are also used in the article as I follow the usage of the sources from which I cite to make the term consistent with the author's context and preference. Even in the U.S. context, authors use different terms. Since there is no uniform term that everybody accepts, I choose to respect the author's choice.

2 The autobiographical stories about my mother are woven throughout the article and are formatted as block quotes as juxtaposition. It has become accepted writing format to indicate the juxtaposition of narrative and theoretical writings in curriculum studies literature. In juxtaposition, theory and story do not have to completely correspond to each other, but mutually inform each other while allowing excesses to exist (Miller, 2005). The purpose for using autographical writings about my mother is not to offer a complete picture of her gendered life, which is not only impossible in an article but also runs the risk of objectifying her. Instead, this arrangement is for theory and life to speak back to each other to enrich discussions nonlinearly.

3 These women include: Linda Aranaydo (Muscogee Creek), Mary and Carrie Danna (Western Shoshone), Angela Gonzales (Hopi), Joy Harjo (Muscogee (Creek)/Cherokee), LaDonna Harris (Comanche), Sarah James (Nee/Tsaii Gwich'in), Debra LaFountaine (Ojibway), Rosalie Litter Thunder (Lakota), Lurline Wailana McGregor (Native Hawaiian), Beatrice Medicine (Lakota), Ella Mulford (Navajo), June Quick-to-see Smith (Salish Flathead),

Audrey Shandoah (Oneida), Joanne Shenandoah (Northern Cheyenne), Gail Small (Northern Cheyenne), Faith Smith (Ojibway), Forence Soap (Cherokee), and Octabiana Valenzuela Trujillo (Pascua Yaqui).

References

Anzaldúa, G. (1999). *Borderlands/La frontera*. Aunt Lute Books.

Archibald, J. (2008). *Indigenous storywork*. University of British Columbia Press.

Boulding, E. (2000). *Cultures of peace*. Syracuse University Press.

Brantmeier, E. J. (2009). A peace education primer. *Journal of Conflict Management and Development, 3*(3), 36–50.

Chambers, C. (1994). Looking for home. *Frontiers: A Journal of Women Studies, 15*(2), 23–50. https://doi.org/10.2307/3346760

Chambers, C. (2008). Where are we? Finding common ground in a curriculum of place. *Journal of the Canadian Association for Curriculum Studies/Le revue de l'association canadienne pour l'étude de curriculum, 6*(2), 113–128.

Chernin, K. (1983). *In my mother's house*. Harper Perennial.

Doll, M. A. (1995). *To the lighthouse and back*. Peter Lang.

Doll, Jr., W. E. (2012). *Pragmatism, post-modernism, and complexity theory* (D. Trueit, Ed.). Routledge.

Finley, L. L. (2003). How can I teach peace when the book only covers war? *The Online Journal of Peace and Conflict Resolution, 5*(1), 150–165.

Foucault, M. (1978). *The history of sexuality* (Vol. 1) (R. Hurley, Trans.). Vintage Books.

Grumet, M. (1988). *Bitter milk*. University of Massachusetts Press.

Hale, J. C. (1988). *Bloodlines: Odyssey of a Native daughter*. University of Arizona Press.

Hanh, T. N. (2009). *The heart of understanding: Commentaries on the Prajnaparamita Heart Sutra*. Parallax Press. (Original work published 1989)

Harris, I. (2008). History of peace education. In M. Bajaj (Ed.), *Encyclopedia of peace education* (pp. 15–24). Information Age Publishing.

Hendry, P. M. (2011). *Engendering curriculum history*. Routledge.

Henry, A. (2006). Enviously grateful, gratefully envious: The dynamics of generational relationships in U.S. feminism. *Women's Studies Quarterly, 34*(3/4), 140–153.

Hershock, P. D. (2012). *Valuing diversity*. State University of New York Press.

hooks, b. (2000). *Feminism is for everybody*. South End Press.

Johnson, A. G. (2014). *The gender knot* (3rd ed.). Temple University Press.

Knight, L. W. (2005). *Citizen: Jane Addams and the struggle for democracy*. W. W. Norton.

Knight, L. W. (2010). *Jane Addams: Spirit in actions*. W. W. Norton.

Kristeva, J. (1987). *Tales of love* (L. S. Roudiez, Trans.). Columbia University Press.

Kristeva, J. (1995). *New maladies of the soul* (R. Guberman, Trans.). Columbia University Press.

Kristeva, J. (2002). *Intimate revolt* (J. Herman, Trans.). Columbia University Press.

Li, H. (2013). Ecofeminism as a pedagogical project. In B. J. Thayer-Bacon, L. Stone, & K. M. Sprecher (Eds.), *Education feminism: Classic and contemporary readings* (pp. 323–341). State University of New York Press.

Li, S. (2015). Chinese parents' role modeling: Promoting gratitude. *Childhood Education, 91*(3), 190–197. https://doi.org/10.1080/00094056.2015.1047310

Macy, J. (2007). *World as lover, world as self*. Parallax Press.

Mankiller, W. (2011). *Every day is a good day: Reflections by contemporary Indigenous women*. Fulcrum Publishing.

Mankiller, W., & Wallis, M. (1993). *Mankiller: A chief and her people*. St. Martin's Press.

Mann, S. (2000). Presidential address: Myths of Asian womanhood. *The Journal of Asian Studies, 59*(4), 835–862. https://doi.org/10.2307/2659214

Martin, J. V. (2009). Currere and The Hours: Rebirth of the female self. *Journal of Curriculum Theorizing, 25*(1), 100–109.

Miller, J. (2005). *Sounds of silence breaking*. Peter Lang.

Miller, J. (2010). Response to Rubén A. Gaztambide-Fernández: Communities without consensus. In E. Malewski (Ed.), *Curriculum studies handbook* (pp. 95–100). Routledge.

Mitchell, M. T. (2012). *The politics of gratitude*. Potomac Books.

Nagler, M. (2004). *The search for a nonviolent future*. Inner Ocean.

Obidah, J. E., & Teel, K. M. (2001). *Because of the kids*. Teachers College Press.

Pinar, W. F. (2001). *The gender of racial politics and violence in America*. Peter Lang.

Pinar, W. F. (2009). *The worldliness of a cosmopolitan education*. Routledge.

Ramirez, R. (2007). Race, tribal nation, and gender. *Meridians, 7*(2), 22–40. https://doi.org/10.2979/MER.2007.7.2.22

Smith, A., & Kauanui, J. K. (2008). Native feminisms engage American studies. *American Quarterly, 60*(2), 241–249.

Smith, L. G. (2021). *Curriculum as community building*. Peter Lang.

Stoskopf, A., & Bermudez, A. (2017). The sounds of silence. *Journal of Peace Education, 14*(1), 92–113. https://doi.org/10.1080/17400201.2016.1230543

Wang, H. (2004). *The call from the stranger on a journey home: Curriculum in a third space*. Peter Lang.

Wang, H. (2007). Interconnections within and without. In P. Hershock, J. Hawkins & M. Mason (Eds.), *Changing education in a world of complex interdependence* (pp. 273–296). The University of Hong Kong Press.

Wang, H. (2008). The strength of the feminine, the lyrics of the Chinese woman's self, and the power of education. In C. Eppert & H. Wang (Eds.), *Cross-cultural studies in curriculum* (pp. 313–333). Routledge.

Wang, H. (2013). A nonviolent approach to social justice education. *Educational Studies, 49*(6), 485–503. https://doi.org/10.1080/00131946.2013.844147

Wang, H. (2014). *Nonviolence and education*. Routledge.

Wang, H. (2019). An integrative psychic life, nonviolent relations, and curriculum dynamics in teacher education. *Studies in Philosophy and Education, 38*, 377–395. https://doi.org/10.1007/s11217-019-09661-4

Wang, H. (2021). *Contemporary Daoism, organic relationality, and curriculum of integrative creativity*. Information Age Publishing.

Woolf, V. (1981). *A room of one's own*. Harcourt Brace. (Original work published 1929)

Wu, Y. (2015). Chinese "Schindler." *Journal of Literature and History, 8*, 16–20.

Xu, F. (2021). *Wang ji wo* [*Forgetting me*]. Yilin Press.

· 11 ·

FEMINIST APPROACHES TO NONVIOLENCE AND CURRICULUM THEORY

In narrating Jane Addams' life history and her cosmopolitan viewpoint, Pinar (2009) points out that nonviolence is a feminist project. Influenced by Tolstoy's notion of nonviolence, Addams nevertheless made "this idea her own" (p. 68), as she embraced active pacifism in contrast to Tolstoy's passive nonresistance. She not only played a prominent leadership role in international peace movements during wartime but also pursued everyday peace through community-based education for social, cultural, economic, and gendered equality. Jane Addams' extraordinary work embodied the unity of theory and practice, the Christian spirit of love and cooperation, and the inclusive approach of "peaceweaving" (Shields, 2017, p. 38). Her feminist philosophy of peace was enacted in her unyielding opposition to war and her advancement of peace efforts in national and international organizations as well as her transformative leadership at Hull House, which was based upon her commitment to "social change [as] dependent on cooperation and peace rather than conflict and aggression" (Hendry, 2011, p. 154).

Throughout human history, many women have not only practiced nonviolence in their daily lives but also led larger-scale nonviolent social movements (Fernandes, 2003; Hamling, 2021; McAllister, 1982; Stiehm, 2006). Interestingly, even though the intertwined thread of feminism and nonviolence has been noticed, feminist approaches to nonviolence have been sidelined by both the history of nonviolent social activism and mainstream feminist thought (Gallo-Cruz, 2018; McAllister, 1982). As Gallo-Cruz (2018) points out, women's major contributions to nonviolence movements in their own embodied manner have been neglected in social and political movements to foreground male heroes and their masculine postures and accomplishments. Pam McAllister (1982) also argues that women's commitment to a nonviolent perspective is often considered by the feminist community as reinforcing the gendered stereotypes of women as passive and thus has been dismissed as trivial.

These studies focus on feminist approaches in the United States, where hypermasculinity has been constructed since the origin of the nation (Pinar, 2001) and heteropatriarchal violence has been reinforced by the War on Terror since the 9/11 tragedy in 2001 (Burns, 2018). The gendered knot around normalizing male violence in the media, culture, and education (Deming, 1984; Johnson, 2014; Reardon, 2001) has been critically analyzed for decades. The gendered nature of nonviolence also needs critical attention in understanding the historical and contemporary achievements of women in connecting everyday practices and social movements, which are often separate in male conceptions and practices.

Selina Gallo-Cruz (2018) asserts that women's nonviolence activism started with the very first efforts of women-led abolitionist and then suffrage movements and was sustained through activism in the 1960s and into the 1980s, which also embraced nonviolent struggles for nuclear disbarment and environmental sustainability. The dual nature of feminist nonviolence— "the offering of respect and concern on the one hand and of defiance and stubborn noncooperation with injustice on the other" (McAllister, 1982, p. iii)—has been central to all this activism. At the same time, women have made unique contributions to expanding and reformulating the philosophy and process of nonviolence through gendered ways of thinking, feeling, and acting that are often not valued. Gallo-Cruz (2018) argues that the nonviolence movement and its dynamics

> will only effectively overcome gendered biases when we can follow women nonviolence activists in transcending the rigidities of gender (Flinders 2006; Reardon 1996) and when we can expand understanding of how resistance of all forms of othering translates into broad, discursive, complex, self-affirming, and transformative forms of action. (p. 288)

Positioning male leaders at the center of nonviolent activism to the exclusion of women's unique contributions is contrary to the mission of nonviolence that fundamentally challenges the dualistic controlling mechanism. Feminist challenges offer diversified channels to resist all forms of othering including gendered othering.

As educators, we must attend to "the unsung heroines of American nonviolence" (Gallo-Cruz, 2018, p. 183) and their courageous voices in our teaching to open less-traveled roads for younger generations that point us in new directions for meeting today's multilayered and entangled challenges. The normalization of aggressive and militant hero stories in the official curriculum needs to be challenged by offering other possibilities to guide the young onto pathways of nonviolence. Nonviolence is not new. It has existed for a long time in many cultures, but it has been silenced in formal schooling, and opening to its potentiality means nothing less than a radically transformative praxis, involving all aspects of education: curriculum, teaching, study, school culture, and educational systems. As nonviolence is often a grassroots movement, a curriculum and pedagogy of nonviolence start with individual teachers and students, shift relational dynamics in education, and involve the transformation of daily practice.

Just as there are different approaches to feminism, feminist approaches to nonviolence are also diverse in their interpretations and advocacy for individual and collective work. I pull out several major threads—albeit entangled rather than fully separate—from contested sites to discuss feminist curriculum theory of nonviolence, including the role of the maternal, the connected layers of the personal and the social, embodied everyday secular and spiritual practices, and nonviolent relationships to alterity.

The Role of the Maternal in Feminist Contestations

It is not surprising that the role of the maternal is a site for contestations within feminism: Some value the maternal in its embodied and different functions over the paternal while some see maternity as a site for oppression and binding women in their traditional roles. Still others go beyond the binary and articulate more complicated conceptions of maternity that transcends the patriarchal legacy and enacts new ways of relationality to create a better world for all. In women's peace movements, motherhood has frequently been evoked in nonviolent collective resistance against dictatorship or war (Gbowee, 2011; John, 2006; Nagler, 2004).

In a recent conference on a feminist ethics of nonviolence, an Italian feminist, Adriana Cavarero presented her notion of "the ethical maternal posture of inclination" (Huzar & Woodford, 2021, p. 7) in contrast to the masculine symbolic of rectitude. Two other keynote speakers—Judith Butler and Bonnie Honig—and participants presented pluralistic responses to it. Here I focus on the exchanges between Cavarero and Butler, as they indicate different perspectives.

Cavarero (2016, 2021a) offers a feminist reading of Leonardo's painting "Madonna," which shows Jesus, Mary, and Mary's mother, Anne, who are "inclined and twisted around each other" (Huzar & Woodford, 2021, p. 9). Cavarero (2016) comments that the painting disrupts symmetrical verticality, "presenting a mother who is face to face with her child; a child whose head is twisted back...[reflecting] the everyday experience of the maternal rather than the monumentality of the sacred" (p. 99). Here she not only critiques male verticality but also offers an alternative that is rooted in the everyday experience of the maternal. For Cavarero (2021a) these are two contrasting ethical orientations of "a vertical masculine subject, characterized by and for himself, and [an] inclined feminine subject, characterized by and for others" (p. 41). She further explains that this orientation is about natality as the foundational condition for human life, rather than focusing on death. For the mother, it is "an altruistic ethic" (p. 42); for the child, the constitutive vulnerability of birth and growth is foundational.

> Already indebted to the other by his coming into the world and his ongoing existence there, through his vulnerability, he belongs to a scene in which he depends on her who, inclining herself and therefore leaning outside of herself, leans over him. (Cavarero, 2021a, p. 42)

Sharing Cavarero's approach to interdependency and vulnerability as the condition of human existence, Butler (2021) nevertheless contests Cavarero's theory of maternal inclination. First, Butler argues that the inclining and upright postures are "*not* radically distinct and never fully oppositional" (p. 49; emphasis in the original). The differences between the two come from the denial of male dependency, because the upright posture comes from inclining and leaning out. Second, drawing upon psychoanalysis, she reminds us that the inclination can be destructive, in contrast to the assumption of maternal care, so we are not only obligated to "affirm interdependency but to struggle with—and work through—the aggression that emerges from the fact that we do not stand on our own and never have" (p. 60). There is maternal aggression and ambivalence within social bonds in group and international dynamics that we must attend to. Third, such a working through is not only psychic but also public, as the infrastructures and cultural conditions must be created to support the inclination of ethical relationality toward "leaning out, working through, catching the fall and being caught in time" (p. 61).

In responding to Butler's and others' critiques, Cavarero (2021b) conceded that maternity is not an exclusive imaginary of peace, as other modes such as sorority and friendship—more horizontal—can also embody the relationality of inclination. She also argues that her interest is to go beyond the "*critique-only*" tendency of the philosopher and take on "redirecting the questions of ontology, politics, and ethics toward a framework of altruism and peace capable of capturing our imagination and mobilizing our action" (p. 179). The framework of the maternal inclination directs us toward renewing everyday practice in a positive and constructive direction, rather than only critiquing the violence of patriarchy.

I do not think that motherhood is free from the tension between compassion and aggression, although the relational capacity is an essential part of maternity. Without working through different forms of difficulty with social and political support, both the nurturing and creative potential of motherhood cannot be realized. In Carl Jung's theory, the archetype of the mother carries both the positive energies of the great mother and the negative energies of the devouring mother, as any archetype has two faces (Mayes, 2005). Here the notion of the mother is symbolic rather than literal, indicating that specific motherhood needs to hold the ambivalence of conflicting directions. Under the patriarchal control in social and political reality, it is difficult for mothers to practice nonviolent relationships with their children while realizing their own potential.

In a graduate seminar on gender and curriculum I taught years ago, I assigned a semester-long writing project on the students' significant relationships. Only one among 15 female students wrote about her positive relationship with her mother, while others wrote about various difficulties and obstacles in relating to their mothers. Many were having ongoing struggles, but thinking about them from a gendered lens helped them understand how their mothers had also been shaped by family and society, which influenced their relationships with their daughters (or granddaughters). The inclination in maternal care led, in many women's lives, to ambivalence, and I argue that caring as conventionally understood as self-sacrificial and other-oriented is not necessarily nonviolent, as it may contribute to reinforcing institutional and family constraints on women's pursuit of self-fulfillment and social change.

However, motherhood can become creative without self-sacrifice (Kristeva, 1980, 1995, 1996; Wang, 2004) and provide inspiration for nonviolent relationality, depending on how it is conceptualized and practiced in different contexts and societies. As much as an "altruistic ethic" as defined by Cavarero is oriented by caring and concern for others, I doubt the degree to which altruism appeals to women's need for self-affirmation. Julia Kristeva takes another route to imagine the creativity of motherhood, one that upholds both loving interdependence and a singular invention of womanhood. Using the psychoanalytic framework of semiotic and symbolic dynamics, she argues that with the unique experiencing of the other within the self in pregnancy and the maternal balancing act of caring for the child and allowing the child to grow into a subject of her own, motherhood can become a creative act of relating to the otherness of the other through both compassion and an open relationship with alterity that unsettles and surprises. Kristeva also makes it very clear that the mother's own self-realization outside of the mother-child bond is crucial to maintaining such a balance as she guides the child toward the world:

> If maternity is to be guilt-free, this journey needs to be undertaken without masochism and without annihilating one's affective, intellectual, and professional personality, either. In this way, maternity becomes a true *creative act*, something that we have not yet been able to imagine. (1995, p. 220; emphasis in the original)

It is in the nourishment of the child and the self-fulfillment of the mother that both bond and independence can be claimed. While it is difficult to accomplish both due to existing institutional, political, cultural, and particularly gendered structures, it is a potential to be brought into existence, and there are mothers who have managed to maintain this balance. While nonviolence is not the Kristevian language, her notion of creative maternity that does not sacrifice women's own intellectual and professional pursuits but enhances their ability to destabilize the self/other relationships toward radical openness to alterity is inspirational for my definition of nonviolence, which is affirmative of both the self and the other. It is important to mention that Kristeva does not intend to essentialize maternity or support reproduction, which is often controlled by the patriarchy system. For her, maternity is also a metaphorical link to many other creative activities, of which I think education can be considered one.

Madeleine Grumet's (1988) influential work *Bitter Milk* discusses motherhood and women teachers through a complicated lens. Since women "were expected to be the medium through which the laws, rules, language, and order of the father, the principal, the employer were communicated to the child" (p. 84), the legacy of the primordial maternal relationship and its impact on students is socialized through differentiation in developing male gender identity in its denial of "its matrisexual origins" (p. 85) and female gender identity in its ambivalence. So the link between reclaiming the maternal and teaching is not a straightforward one but, as she further explains, detours through glances toward a different world, not gazing into each other's eyes: "The look trails behind the touch and the sound as a sensory link between mother and child" (p. 98). What would it be like if a fuller version of the sensory experiences were introduced into schools? Grumet invites us to refurnish the schoolhouse with creative expressions of masculinity and femininity, which resonates with me, particularly if I read masculinity and femininity from a Daoist viewpoint, as both elements exist in both men and women. It is the interaction between both elements that opens more possibilities within the self, and in educating all children to creatively play with the different combinations of these elements in their studies and in their lives, rather than educating boys for war and girls for peace (Brock-Utne, 1984), that the new potentiality of nonviolence as a feminist project lies.

The everyday practice of the maternal also goes beyond individual maternal acts. The nuclear family structure is a recent phenomenon in industrial countries, but in many cultures, both in the past and in the present, mothering can be a collective effort. Danielle Poe (2010) tells the story of an activist, Michele Naar-Obed, who participated in symbolically disarming nuclear weapons, an act which carried a prison term. She had joined a community that supported collective child-care and shared her belief so that her motherhood was "not experienced as an isolated event [in a nuclear family], but as an entry into transformed interdependence in her community" (p. 121). Leaving her young daughter under the care of her husband and the community, after her daughter had already experienced caregiving from multiple adults, she went ahead with her nonviolent action against U.S. militarism and was put into prison. In doing so, Naar-Obed's separation from her daughter was inevitable but would, later, teach her daughter the value of standing up to do something right even if it does not align with the official rules. Here the possibility of maternity becoming the site for social change was enacted not through presence but through meaningful absence.

In nonviolence activism and women's peace movements, there are numerous examples of motherhood and mother's care for children being transformed into an effective site—intersecting between the private and the public—for fighting against war, nuclear militarism, dictatorship, or injustice (Nagler, 2004; Gallo-Cruz, 2018). Chapter 5 of this book has already mentioned the Liberian women's peace movement in 2003 as a recent example, and here I discuss it again to highlight the maternal power. In the midst of heightened civil war, women organized and gathered in a public place to nonviolently protest the war and demand peace as mothers for the safety and in the interest of their children. They also worked with child soldiers after the war with disarming them and restoring them back into the community (Disney & Riticker, 2008; Gbowee, 2011).

During the protests, these women restrained themselves from directly criticizing government politics but rallied together in the campaign as mothers with a consistent message for peace. It was ignored in the beginning by the government, but the movement grew very quickly to unite both Christian and Muslim women across different social classes to fight against war. When the Women of Liberia Mass Action for Peace issued their statement for peace to the government, the movement had already became a wildfire that could not be put down. Precisely because these women evoked the maternal image, refused power struggles, and transformed relational dynamics, the movement gathered support from people from all walks of life.

A turning point came during the international peace talk in Ghana where all involved parties were negotiating for a deal and women representatives went there to make sure the talks were effective. The talks were not going anywhere, and Leymah Gbowee, a prominent leader, after much disappointment and rage at what was going on, exploded when she was threatened by a sheriff with arrest for obstructing justice:

> I was so angry, I was out of my mind. "I will make it very easy for you to arrest me. I am going to strip naked." I took off my hair tie. Beside me, Sugars [another leader] rose to her feet and began to do the same. I pulled off my *lappa*, exposing the tights I wore underneath.... I was beside myself, desperate. Every institution that I'd been taught was there to protect the people had proved evil and corrupt; everything I valued had collapsed. These negotiations had been my last hope, but they were crashing, too. But in threatening to strip, I had summoned up a traditional power. In Africa, it is a terrible curse to see a married or elderly woman deliberately bare herself. If a mother is really, really upset with a child, she might take out her breast and slap it, and he's cursed. For this group of men to see a woman naked would be almost like a death sentence. Men are born through women's vaginas, and it is as if

by exposing ourselves, we say, "We now take back the life we gave you." (Gbowee, 2011, pp. 161–162)

What a powerful summons of maternal power! After she received assurance and stopped the act of stripping, her rage was accompanied by an outpouring of tears in frustration and sadness. Gbowee explained that her action was not planned, but spontaneous. As Danielle Poe (2018) points out, "Her actions over many years had created a mindset of nonviolence such that she was able to take advantage of an opportunity using local knowledge and tradition" (p. 272). Her improvised response changed the atmosphere of the peace talks, which finally led to the ending of the war. The evocation of maternal power here is a direct challenge to the core of patriarchy: It is the mother who can give life and who also can take back the life. Here Gbowee's action was creative, responding to what the situation needed in a embodied manner through the collective body of women to reach a breakthrough.

While not every woman is a mother, everybody has a mother or significant caretaker/s who play the role of the maternal. To critique motherhood as inherently embedded in heteronormativity is too simplistic, not only because the maternal can be metaphorical for sustainable creativity in various forms (Wang, 2004, 2021), but also because historically motherhood did not always play its role within the patriarchal line and nowadays different people can play the role of mothers, not just heterosexual women. Essentialism does not work just one way.

Pinar (2001), in his analysis of U.S. violence at the intersection of gender and race with a lens of queer theory, points out that the notion of the self-made White man in its parricide tendency is implicated in the repression of both preoedipal identification with the maternal and the "longing for the father" (p. 1086), which has contributed to a violent manhood that rejects femininity and constructs masculinity at the site of the frontier. Locating homosexual repression as "intertwined with white supremacy and mob violence" (p. 1164), his project of intersecting racialized and gendered violence demonstrates the interlocking mechanism of domination on multiple sites. To reclaim the othered identification with the maternal, he suggests *currere* as "autobiographics of alterity," to "focus not only upon the production of whiteness and masculinity and their intersections and conflations, but their dissolution and re-formation" (p. 1152). While this re-formation is queered and racialized, I think that it can also be related to reformulating maternity as creative, rather than normative, and as nonviolent, rather than self-sacrificial, as discussed above.

Maternal nonviolence already exists in women's everyday existence. The unique experiences of motherhood from pregnancy to childbirth to caring relations demonstrate a great potential for thought and relationality that exceed the notion of the individual as a separate entity. The mainstream male model of rectitude and aggression denies the very ontological experience of humanity from its birth. The relational inclination of motherhood presents an alternative possibility and constructive pathways, and denying the embodied experience of maternity or the relational orientation of both men and women can only further contribute to the crisis of relationality that lies at the core of the contemporary challenges. The key task is to rearticulate women's experiences of interdependency, maternal care and vulnerability, and modes of relationality in a way that does not uphold maternal self-sacrifice as the ideal but gives birth to maternal creativity, a way which points in new directions for human relationships that are nonviolent to one another. In education, both educators' relational orientations that empty out patriarchal impositions and the infusion of sensory experience in curriculum and teaching are necessary for reclaiming creative maternity.

Connecting the Personal and the Social

I do not argue that connecting the personal and the social originates in feminist thought, as the connection between inner work and outer work is part of Buddhism, Daoism, and Confucianism as well as many other philosophical and spiritual traditions (Smith-Christopher, 2007). However, feminist perspectives highlight the unequal gendered relationships within the domain of family and home, disrupting the patriarchal separation between the private and the public that enacts various forms of violence on women and children. The feminist principle of "the personal is the political" unveils the role of power dynamics in everyday life and calls for social transformation in a deeper and more comprehensive manner. Similarly in peace studies, as Moolakkattu Stephen John (2006) points out, "While most models of peace locate[d] themselves within the macro level, feminist notions turned the conception of peace upside-down and defined peace 'from the personal, experiential level' at the micro level in terms of the lived lives of women" (p. 140).

Jane Addams (1860–1935) embodies such an integration of the personal and the social in her commitment to nonviolence as an intellectual, social, and spiritual engagement (Pinar, 2009). Losing her mother when she was two and her father when she was 20, and having a new stepmother when she was eight, Addams encountered big losses and other complications within her family (Knight, 2005). She also experienced the conflicts between her own dreams and family and societal expectations during her youth and schooling; after her father's death, she went to a women's medical college but did not find studying there satisfactory. With health issues since she was young, she did not know what to do to serve society: "Back pain and depression set in— eight years of it. Jane's twenties were unhappy and without clear direction" (Stiehm, 2006, p. 25). She was able to work through her depression in her pursuit of meaning in life as a young woman through studying at home and doing international tours where she felt connected to social settlement movements, and soon she started to set up a women's settlement house (Knight, 2005, 2010; Pinar, 2009).

Addams brought her visions of social democracy to the settlement of Hull House by bringing together those from diverse backgrounds to realize the positive role of social difference (Hendry, 2011; Stiehm, 2006), which went beyond the British model she had encountered during those tours. The inner work she had gone through the previous decade gave her rich soil for planting and growing her unique progressive outlook. As she articulates later, peace is not the absence of war, but "the unfolding of worldwide processes making for the nurture of human life" (Quoted in Knight, 2010, p. 139), which is associated with everyday lived experiences that nurture cooperation and interdependence. In so doing, Addams continued to work through the baggage passed on to her by family and society in her own complex inner life.

The interaction between the personal and the social as folded within each other, over time, made Addams embrace a dynamic view of difference and transform a sense of serving *for* (and benevolently above) others to working *with* (and learning from) others who are different, such as immigrants and the working poor. Her approach to conflicts, however, was through nonviolent ways. Pinar (2009) recounts Addams' exchanges with John Dewey: "Committed to Tolstoyan and Christian nonviolence, social Christian cooperation, and Comtean societal unity, Addams could only answer in the negative" to the question whether class antagonism was inevitable. For Addams, "opposites were never really opposites; they were elements" of emergent unity (p. 73). Her approach to opposites reminds me of Daoist *yin-yang* opposites, which are not in antagonism but in dynamic and interconvertible interactions in the unity of life. Adopting such a dynamic view is intimately related to Addams' ability to deal with her own internal dynamics.

Petra Munro Hendry (2011) argues that Addams' approach to social change through cooperation and peace clearly distinguished her from other progressives, pragmatists, and Marxists. Moreover, "her understanding of democracy was predicated on cooperation and pacifism, approaches that Addams saw as specifically linked to women's nature and values that were denied expression in a patriarchy society" (p. 154). Her advocacy for active pacifism, rejection of all forms of militarism, and her clear association of such values with women's nature made major contributions to the feminist project of nonviolence. Patricia Shields (2017) uses "peaceweaving" (pp. 38–40) as a visual metaphor for transforming a community in conflict in Addams' work. "The activity of weaving draws together" and connects strings and transforms them into a fabric; "weaving does not homogenize, rather strings of different colors and textures form a whole cloth" (p. 38). Difference is not erased but incorporated for changing violent conflicts and adding both strength and flexibility. Addams speaks of peaceweaving as important for making "lateral progress" (Quoted in Shields, 2017, p. 38) that advances the welfare of all people, particularly those in the lower layers of a hierarchal social system. This approach was also carried into her anti-war efforts and extraordinary activism for peace, even when she was shunned by the public and friends.

While exemplary, Addams also had limitations, particularly related to racial consciousness. The exchanges between her and another extraordinary feminist figure, Ada B. Wells, who almost single-handedly campaigned against lynching, reflect Addams' blind spots (Hendry, 2011; Pinar, 2001). However, she is not alone in having limitations, as Gandhi is also criticized for not practicing nonviolence at home, even though he praised women as embodied figures of nonviolence (Gallo-Cruz, 2018; Brock-Utne, 1984). We are all humans. What it does highlight is how cultivating nonviolence from both within and without is an interminable process in which no one can be all-knowing but a community of participants making efforts can change society in more peaceful directions.

For Leymah Gbowee (2014), personal healing and peacebuilding are intertwined. The rage she felt at the scene I mentioned earlier had accumulated through her life experiences (Gbowee, 2011). Growing up not having material comfort or parents in a happy marriage, she nevertheless had ambition when she graduated from high school. However, the war between a corrupt government and a rebel army destroyed her dream and shattered her world, and she fell into an abusive relationship when she was 19. By the time she was 26, she had four children, with one newly born child who slept in a cardboard box for a while and another baby who sat in her arms on a hospital floor for a week because she had no money for medical bills. With the war raging, in a life full of fear, pain, loss, and anger and lacking food and shelter, she was depressed and could not see any future, until one day, over tears and concerns about her children, she decided, "I had to stop blaming my parents, Daniel [her boyfriend], single motherhood, the war, for what I was. I had to stop hating myself, find my strength again and step forward" (p. 73). She summoned her inner strength, with her mother's support and friends' help, and began to work for a Trauma Healing program.

Her inner work of breaking the cycle of violence was enhanced by helping other women work through trauma, and she realized later that it was the beginning of her peacebuilding work. In her work, when women's stories were pushed aside, as often happened, Gbowee (2011) was able to break away from the protocol to help women find their own voices. What women wanted to share had happened long before the war started, in family and in communities. In other words, these women engaged in their own inner work "for releasing the pain that keeps them from their own strength" (p. 114), without which these women could not have become peacemakers. She also participated in the newly established Women in Peacebuilding Network in Africa, which also helped women experience self-appreciation and grow their capacity for nonviolence work. Gbowee (2014) comments on the link between personal and social healing: "I realized that there is no way you can engage this vocation of peacebuilding if you do not have that personal healing" (p. 154). The Women's peace movement itself testified to such a connection: "Using shared personal revelation to organize was completely new, and over time, it became one of the reasons our movement grew strong" (Gbowee, 2011, p. 128).

For Vietnamese peace activist Chan Khong, inner peace is the foundation for outer peace: "The responsibility of the individual is, first, to cultivate peace within the self, second, to help others cultivate peace within themselves, and, third, to cultivate peaceful social structures and peace in the natural environment" (Maparyan, 2012, p. 150). All these layers need to take place. Her daily practice of meditation and equanimity for inner peace played an important role in calming her coworkers down when dangerous situations happened. Inner and outer work are also connected in education, and *currere* as autobiographical work situated in cultural contexts in the reconceptualization of curriculum studies (Pinar, 2012) has been an exemplary example of making meaningful connections between the inner and the outer world. There are many pedagogical modes for helping students make such connections between their own lived experience and their studies at schools or colleges, not through the simplistic notion of student-centered activities, but in the sense of dynamic interplay between and among student, teacher, subject matter, and contexts (Doll, 2012). Inner work is especially pushed away in the standardization and surveillance culture imposed by today's political and economic crises displaced onto education. Listening to our mothers' and foremothers' voices, we need to affirm that the inner landscape of education also needs to grow outside of itself to change the outside world.

Nonviolence as Everyday Lived Experience: Between the Secular and the Spiritual

Peace studies tend to see nonviolence as an instrument or a tactic to the end of peace or justice. As John (2006) comments, "Even when people talk about non-violence, the emphasis is more on its strategic value reducible in terms of costs and benefits. There is more emphasis on the instrumental uses of non-violence rather than on its intrinsic worth" (p. 152). For me, the intrinsic worth of nonviolence lies in its unyielding resistance to all forms of violence while at the same time laying out a positive project of forming compassionate relationality in everyday lived experience. To practice nonviolence as an existential way of life, study, and pedagogy in curriculum as a complicated conversation can have a spiritual dimension but can also unfold as a secular experience.

Many nonviolence world leaders are religious and spiritual leaders, such as Gandhi, King, Addams, Gbowee, Thich Nhat Hanh, Mother Teresa, and Sister Chan Khong. Catholic women leader, Immaculee Illibagiza (2006), describes in her memoir, *Left to Tell: Discovering God Amidst the Rwandan Holocaust*, how her religious faith supported her to survive the horror of genocide in Rwanda and help others. In Layli Maparyan's (2012) reading, "Through her [Illibagiza's] lens, we are able to observe how terror, rage, grief, and bitterness are transformed into an unqualified love and forgiveness—even for those directly responsible for killing her family members" (p. 181). For her, the power of God's love touches the killer through her radical forgiveness, and peace in the world can be increased through prayer and direct knowing. The internal love-based transmutation of negative emotions into vibrational energy to change hearts and minds is essential for peacemaking.

Many institutionalized religions have historically played the role of restricting women's freedom and rights, but spirituality has also inspired women's peace scholarship and activism. Feminist peace educator Betty Reardon (2016) speaks about the necessity of interfaith and multi-faith engagement for peacebuilding, despite the divisiveness and exclusions of some religious organizations, since we need to reach out and to connect. She also advocates teaching about different religions in secondary schools in order to understand how they impact people's daily lives and to make meaningful connections across national and cultural differences.

Leela Fernandes (2003) argues for a nonviolent feminist approach that engages in "spiritualized social transformation of this world, one that seeks to challenge all forms of injustice, hierarchy and abuse from the most intimate daily practices in our lives to the larger structure of race, gender, class, sexuality and nation" (p. 11). There are multiple dimensions in her perspective. First, the dichotomy between material/social and spiritual realms should be set aside. Here she refers to a "lived spirituality" (p. 10) that is accessible to all in people's daily lives and goes beyond any specific religion to support social transformation, rather than hinder it. She argues that the spiritual foundation of Gandhi- and King-led nonviolent movements should be emphasized rather than neglected, as a spiritual foundation can break the cycles of retribution, conflict-based pursuit, and dualistic oppositions.

Second, Fernandes (2003) argues that the critiques of injustice in feminist movements, while powerful and impactful, need to be coupled with infusing positive forces such as compassion, love, and interconnectedness embedded in non-violence. When critiques are not backed up with illuminating different or alternative pathways, people may be left feel helpless. Spirituality, philosophy, and the practice of nonviolence offer such different pathways. She also distinguishes between activism as opposition and activism as transformational and argues that social justice that relies on strategies of retribution tends to "limit the possibilities of a deeper lasting form of transformation because they [such strategies] ultimately mirror the kinds of structures of oppression they seek to overturn" (p. 53) and cannot change "the underlying foundation of violence" (p. 65). Realizing spiritual interdependence also requires acknowledging that many third-world feminist movements do not adopt exclusive secular approaches, as many women live in faith-based societies. Third, she highlights the role of everyday praxis and that spiritualized feminism lies in engagements in many different realms of practice:

> In practice we live, indeed we enact, what seem like abstract concepts such as justice, structural oppression, social change and transformation in every moment of our lives, in every relationship, from the most mundane interactions we engage in with strangers in supermarkets to the most intimate relationships we have with loved ones to the most public interactions we have in work, school, society, the world. (p. 19)

These multiple dimensions also apply to nonviolence education as an everyday practice of holding the tensions between compassion and aggression and directing them toward mindful, inclusive, and humane relationships. When we enact nonviolent relationships with the self, the public, the structural, and the biosphere in such a comprehensive way, substantial inner and social change can be initiated and sustained. Practicing nonviolence with the stranger does require a certain sense of spirituality that goes beyond ego-consciousness. Feminist contributions to examining intimate relationships and how they can become embedded in patriarchy remind educators of the importance of critically understanding the role of pedagogical relationships in on ongoing process of emptying out imposition and sustaining mutual transformation, rather than treating nonviolence as an event, or as resolving conflicts once for all. Such a process also involves the content, process, and purpose of education infused by nonviolence to make it an organic part of formal and informal curriculum.

While Christianity has inspired women's theory and practice of nonviolence, other forms of spirituality are influential. As Layli Maparyan (2012) points out, Buddhist spirituality is based upon nonduality and interconnectedness, different from U.S. activism, which tends to be dualistic. Contemporary Buddhist communities adopt principles of nonviolence and the practice of mindfulness to engage social change not through perceiving one side as the enemy but through making efforts to stop violence on all sides and evoke the higher nature of all. In fact, advocating for a victory by one side is not perceived as *peace* activism. Sister Chan Khong's peace praxis is about "the transformation of energies, leading to the transformation of material reality, including human relationships and the human relationship with nature" (p. 163). Transforming relationships is not about elevating another party to take over the current one that is in control, but about changing the nature of a hierarchical system toward a system that is more equitable. Here the shift of relationships with nature echoes ecofeminism, which sees human controlling of nature and the gendered nature of social and political reality as sharing the same mechanism (Wang, 2021).

Feminist commitment to advancing gender equity and nonviolence does not have to be religion oriented. As Mary King points out, nonviolent action is not necessarily linked to spirituality, as "what makes a movement nonviolent is not the beliefs of the participants" (quoted in Wernitznig, 2021, p. 108), but their organized and disciplined collective action. While religious beliefs can bring people together, they can also become obstacles for connecting across different religions. When gender intersects with sexuality, institutionalized religion's constraining power can be harsher. Barbara Deming's (1984) radical lesbian feminist approach to nonviolence offers a secular pathway to combining masculine self-assertiveness with feminine sympathy to serve all people.

Deming does not believe that a religious basis is needed for understanding nonviolence as a most effective way to enact social change, one in which participants from different sides are transformed into new persons. That "we are all part of one another" (Deming, 1984, p. 167) is the basis for such effectiveness. We don't need a God in order to know that even our antagonists can reach a certain limit in justifying their violence. She argues that nonviolence is a force that balances self-assertion against injustice and humane concerns for others as persons. Self-assertiveness acts to force a new understanding of the situation and the system that opens a shift in the lens of the opponents. Arguing that "we can put *more* pressure on the antagonist for whom we show human concern" (p. 177; emphasis in the original) she shows that nonviolence has two hands, one hand resisting injustice in a forceful way and the other hand reaching out in respecting all persons.

Deming (1984) discusses sexuality in a broad sense: "If we can free ourselves of the will to dominate (or the willingness to submit), our sexuality allows us, I very much believe, to commune not only with other people but with the whole world of nature" (p. 244). Our sexuality as women "can dissolve the boundaries of our individual selves; it makes possible a deep relation with the rest of the world" (p. 245). This relational approach infuses the whole being of a woman and affirms the positive role of a woman's sexuality in experiencing social and political movements of nonviolence as reaching unity with life. Sexuality here becomes a site for getting in touch with the interconnectedness of the universe. This approach to bringing positive energy into a feminist approach is echoed by Cavarero's feminist ethics in "the articulation of forms of life that emphasize pleasure and happiness as being central to human meaning" (Huzar & Woodford, 2021, p. 20). The key for Deming here is to give up the will to dominate, and that can be achieved through understanding the damage it does as well as the pleasure of non-dominating communion beyond the self.

Here secular nonviolence through political, ethical, and embodied relationships is not religion oriented, but appeals to the positive nature of humanity to overcome individual and social violence. While I embrace a broad sense of spirituality beyond religions (Wang, 2014), I have not claimed any religious faith in my nonviolence work, although often I wonder whether I have enough inner strength to carry on, as self-doubt is a frequent guest. But I believe that sustainable strength comes from diverse sources, including my commitment as an ordinary person traveling in the world of education to a more nonviolent life. The effective introduction of nonviolence curriculum materials, conflict resolution programs, and peace circles has been part of public education. Drawing upon the Indigenous tradition, Nagler (2020) describes how a peace circle can affirm the positive qualities of offenders as a way of helping them transform their actions that damage others and the community. I think such a practice can be an effective way for transforming relational dynamics at school to subvert violence through community building and kindness to all participants. Nel Noddings (2012) also specifies how different subject matter can incorporate peace education materials, including literature, mathematics, science, physical education, and art and music at the secondary levels. Importantly, nonviolence as an orientation of education needs to be infused into different aspects of schooling including the process of education.

With many cultural and institutional factors at play, whether or not educational or social change can be enacted by nonviolence work in short term is never certain, but commitment to the work as participating in the cosmic energy and experiencing the transmutation of personhood is more important, and I believe, has long-term effects. Politics is about results, but education is existential and should not be outcome-oriented (even though we have plenty of outcome-based educational models). Whether the work is secular or spiritual or a mixture of both, the everyday practice of nonviolence in education is of paramount importance. Exploring new possibilities to create conditions for students to experience a different kind of relationship with the self and with the world, educators cannot achieve it once and for all, but are perpetually on the road with our students to develop a curriculum and pedagogy of nonviolence.

Nonviolent Relationships to Alterity: Psychic, Gendered, and Poststructural Otherness

Feminist movements have grown to attend not only to gender differences, but also to the intersections of gender with other factors such as sexuality, race, ethnicity, national origins, language, and disability (Fernandez, 2003; hook, 2000; Miller, 2005; Williams et al., 2020). The key issue is how to engage with difference in ways that challenge the mechanism of control and domination. For poststructural feminism, there are no normative criteria to set up as a universal foundation for a feminist project because, as Judith Butler (1992) argues, the identity of women cannot be essentialized or decided with certainty, which ends up being exclusive, but their identity "becomes a site of permanent openness and resignifiability" (p. 16).

Here difference is fluid and ever-changing rather than separate and categorical. Hershock (2011) uses the word *differentiation* to indicate a sense of difference as a process and movement. For Janet Miller (2005), working difference in education is an ongoing work of making strange the normalized versions of the self, the other, and the world, "refusing fixed and static categories of sameness or permanent otherness" (p. 181) and enabling individual and communal becoming that cannot be determined in advance. I would add here that we need to de-normalize various versions of violence in curriculum and education and rethink with our students about what difference and relationality mean.

Drucilla Cornell (1992) draws a distinction between ethical relations and moral regulations, and approaches morality as a system that has a repressive mechanism. Drawing upon poststructural thinkers Levinas, Derrida, and Lacan and their tensioned intellectual relationships, she explains the ethics of nonviolent relations: "By the ethical relation I mean to indicate the aspiration to a nonviolent relationship to the other, and to otherness more generally, that assumes responsibility to guard the other against the appropriation that would deny her difference and singularity" (p. 62). Sexual and gendered difference sits at the center of such a nonviolent relationship to the other, and the concern with not appropriating relations and assimilating the other is reflected in the concept of alterity, which cannot be reduced into sameness either internally or culturally. To deconstruct the legacy of colonization and patriarchy, alterity eludes the grasp of the self and cannot be mastered.

Difference exists not only externally but also internally, so the issue of alterity in the psyche is also addressed in some poststructural theories, as the unconscious cannot be assimilated into conscious thought. Sharon Todd (2003) works at the intersections between Levinas' theory and psychoanalysis to rethink social justice education. In particular, she argues for the necessity of learning *from* others in ethical encounters, not merely learning *about* others through knowledge, to enable "moments of nonviolent relationality" (p. 15). For Levinas, it is the receptiveness of the self to the Other and the "noninvestment of one's conscious ego—and one's psychical past—that allows for the preservation of the Other's alterity" (p. 11) to counteract the potential for violence. Holding the tension between the Levinasian alterity of the other and the alterity of the unconscious, Todd works on the bridges between affect and thought, highlighting the complex roles of empathy, love, guilt, and listening as well as learning from difference in social justice education and exploring pedagogical conditions for nonviolent moments and ethical possibilities.

In scholarship that draws upon psychoanalysis, there is a tendency to set individuals against society since civilization represses elements of the psyche that do not fit into societal expectations. The role of aggression, for instance, has gendered implications (society repressing it in women and promoting it in men). As I discuss in Chapters 6 and 7, there is also a psychic drive toward love, and the integrative function of the psyche in analytic psychology is toward creative harmony. In classical psychoanalysis, Freud's position on psychic aggression is not static and has shifted from time to time. But Todd (2001, 2003) considers nonviolence as possible moments but secondary to aggression, as she asserts that learning is ontologically violent, since learning is implicated in the pedagogical demand that students change themselves according to societal expectations.

As I argue in earlier chapters, I do not adopt a dualistic approach between individual becoming and societal arrangements, as the desire for belonging is part of the individual person (Nagler, 2004). If learning is ontologically violent, then learning is also ontologically nonviolent. Todd (2001) further suggests the necessity of ethical nonviolent relationships in pedagogy: it is "precisely because violence is inherent to 'learning to become' and because teachers and students are continually vulnerable to each other in the face of this violence, that the question of non-violence can even be raised" (p. 439). However, if nonviolence is not part of the human psyche in its original source, on what basis can nonviolent teaching develop? For me, only when the basis of nonviolence connects with its original possibility, rather than as a secondary counter-response to violence, can we fully speak about the ethics of nonviolence in pedagogy.

Here the difference between the choice of the term "nonviolence" or "non-violence" is not trivial, as "nonviolence" affirms itself as a positive life force rather than merely a negation of violence. Martin Luther King, Jr. uses the Christian notion of *agape* to indicate the spirituality of universal love. To a great degree, nonviolence, as I have formulated it in this book, is a form of love *without* control or domination, as there are so many controlling mechanisms in our everyday relationships of love. To say that violence is more primary than love in human life does not make sense. They can be intertwined due to our tolerance for the existence of aggression in loving relationships: from a parent to a child, from a teacher to a student, or in amorous relationships. That is why I prefer the language of nonviolence to contain and dissolve aggression to alterity within and without on an ongoing basis.

Also, facing psychic, gendered, and poststructural alterity, Judith Butler (2020) argues that socialization of gender has been decided from the beginning: "Independence and dependency have been separated, and masculine and feminine are determined" (p. 37) and "the primary and founding figure of the human" is the masculine lack of dependency. The self-made man was never a child but has always been an upright and self-sufficient adult who never relinquishes himself to caring relations (many times from women) and social and institutional support. Butler offers a profound insight into vulnerability not as a subjective state, "but rather as a feature of our shared or interdependent lives" (p. 45). Vulnerability as the existential condition for enabling human life is not an emotional, feminine, state, but is "a feature of the relationship that binds us to one another and to the larger structures and institutions upon which we depend for the continuation of life" (p. 46). Butler's critique of liberal individualism is thorough and firmly brings the male hero back to the foundation of relationality, vulnerability, and interdependency in human life. She (2021) asserts that

> our concerted action is one that can recognize and work through the aggression in and against interdependency, the ambivalence that informs and imperils all social bonds, including those that sanction our ethical conduct. The task is to find public ways of continuing to work through those forms of ambivalence. (p. 61)

This notion of working through aggression so that we can respond to interdependency in an affirmative, rather than destructive, way is consistent with Nagler's (2004) notion of transforming anger and fear to achieve nonviolent relationships with the self and the other, although Nagler holds a much more positive approach to interdependence. Buddhist peace activist Chan Khong uses mindful breathing, looking, and listening to reach more deeply beneath the surface of a dualistic view of the self and the other in order to realize interbeing. "When interbeing is realized in situ, conflicts dissolve and healing takes place spontaneously" (Maparyan, 2012, p. 152). Such a realization requires the hard work of unlearning dualism and experiencing nonduality, and working through ambivalence requires transformation. Certainly, as Butler reminds us, interdependency does not determine human responses, since hypermasculine reactions can struggle intensely against it to assert independence.

Interestingly, dwelling in psychic alterity, Butler (2020) also comments on rerouting aggression "for the purposes of affirming ideals of equality and freedom" (p. 27). Rather than transforming aggression, she draws upon psychoanalysis to argue that the repression of aggression also damages the human psyche. Psychic aggression and violence are not the same, as psychic aggression can be channeled into constructive activities of resisting violence. However, because aggression can lead to destructive activities, it needs to be channeled—i.e., changed—in the direction of constructive activities. The definition of nonviolence in thoughts, words, and actions from the *ahimsa* tradition requires changing aggression into commitment to loving relationality. Butler's term "aggressive nonviolence" (p. 27) suggests her approach to nonviolence mainly as the negation of violence, but aggression without the balancing act of compassion cannot dissolve violence. Interestingly, her recent book on nonviolence is titled "non-violence" on the book cover but "nonviolence" on the inner cover (Butler, 2020). We don't seem to have a better word in English to depict another mode of force that transcends "peace through strength," which dominates international relations (Wood, 2016, p. 24), while strength is defined by violence and aggression. But I think in education, we must find a language that educates children from the time they are young about the integrative—not destructive—power of nonviolence.

I think working *through* aggression, a psychoanalytic term, requires transforming it. Curriculum scholar, Mary Aswell Doll's (1995) metaphor of blue fire that channels the red fire of raw anger into a sustainable passion for life in her pedagogical relationships is a good example of such a working through, as discussed in Chapter 6. It is important to point out that in nonviolence studies, interconnectedness itself has the capacity to contain aggression and thus transform anger and fear when one shifts to see the bigger picture. Nonviolence is not only a response to violence, but also exists in interconnectedness prior to psychic aggression—as many international wisdom traditions demonstrate—and its potential for shifting out of the gear of anger and fear lies in life itself. To dualistically split anger into "good" anger and "bad" anger does not change the negative impact of anger on the individual well-being and the collective psyche. A group of Native American women, as I discussed in Chapter 10, rely more on gratitude for asserting their agency.

As Butler and Todd draw upon psychoanalysis and Western philosophy, I wonder to what degree such an assertion of aggression as primary is a product of social life in the Western context rather than the universal foundation of psychic life? In other words, what if the assumption of unresolvable aggression comes from Western culture as much as psychoanalysis comes from the empirical work in the specific Western social and cultural setting? The psychic and the social dimensions mutually influence each other, even though both Freud and Jung present their theories of the psyche as universal.

To form and re-form nonviolent relationships with the otherness, the alterity of the other must be attended to in such a way that allows the surprises and differences that the other may bring, but I also argue for building connections—as fluid, ever-shifting, and complicated as they can be—across differences, because without the effort to do so, we cannot work together for transformative change. Fernandes (2003) gave an example of nonviolent resistance in the Israeli-Palestinian conflict. In the Women in Black movement founded in Israel in 1988, "women dressed in black have mourned both Palestinian and Israeli victims of violence by keeping a one-hour vigil every Friday for the past fifteen years" (p. 61). In such an oppositional situation, it was women who were able to advocate for *both* the other and the self who were suffering, which demonstrates the feminist ethics of nonviolence. As Chapter 10 already discussed, women have traditionally formed alliances across difference to affirm humane relationships and promote peace.

Such alliances, however, need to be based upon self-affirmation. While Cavarero (2021) uses the term "altruistic" to describe feminist ethics and Fernandes (2003) also thinks that self-sacrifice is necessary for achieving nonviolent spiritual transformation to break the cycle of violence, I am inclined not to use the language of altruism and self-sacrifice as they collide with traditional gendered values to demand women's service to others, family, and society without respecting their work or their personhood. This demand is also reflected in the societal and cultural expectations of women teachers. I prefer to see nonviolent relationships as affirming a person's whole being, one that transcends a separate sense of the self and a dualistic opposition between the self and the other, which does not require self-sacrifice but a relational understanding of personhood. If the underlying nature of life is interconnectedness, then the well-being of the individual woman is related to the well-being of all. Gallo-Cruz (2018) also argues that one of the feminist contributions to nonviolence collective action is this shift from the self-sacrifice of male martyrs to the self-affirmation of women. Not only in public but also in domestic areas, violence against women must be addressed in nonviolence activism.

While both Gandhi and King advocate the role of redemptive suffering for social and political activism to awaken people's consciences, particularly those of oppressors, I think the gendered nature of nonviolence asks us to also contest the patriarchal expectations imposed onto women to bear sacrifice and suffering. Particularly in the context of education, what happens when we educate schoolgirls to be altruistic, to be givers rather than takers, while schoolboys are expected by society to be self-centered and to be takers rather than givers? Alterity within a woman's psyche is self-assertiveness and the affirmation of her whole being, and it is that aspect of schoolgirls that should be brought into consciousness for developing relationships that affirm female personhood. Alterity within men, as I discussed earlier, is related to the denied maternal care upon which they depend, and schoolboys should be guided toward the relational view of life and the world. Gendered differentiation through socialization, which can be deconstructed through curriculum and pedagogy, asks for a balanced dance to hold things together for different people in different ways, opening to the other and the otherness of the other.

As I conclude this chapter, it is worthwhile to note that an inclusive feminist perspective to nonviolence is not about setting up another gender dualism, but is intended to question and unsettle the system of patriarchy for the benefit of all people. It is the gendered structure of control, possession, and domination that must be challenged by women and other gendered minorities as well as men. In that sense, the Daoist notion of femininity as strong and sustainable, referring to a cosmic force not referring to women, is a language that I consider key to creating feminist curriculum compatible with nonviolence as an educational project.

References

Brock-Utne, B. (1984). The relationship of feminism to peace and peace education. *Bulletin of Peace Proposals*, 15(2), 149–153.

Burns, J. P. (2018). *Power, curriculum, and embodiment*. Palgrave Macmillian.

Butler, J. (1992). Contingent foundations: Feminism and the question of "post-modernism." In J. Butler & J. W. Scott (Eds.), *Feminists theorize the political* (pp. 3–21). Routledge.

Butler, J. (2020). *The force of non-violence*. Verso.
Butler, J. (2021). Leaning out, caught in the fall: Interdependency and ethics in Cavarero. In T. J. Huzar & C. Woodford (Eds.), *Feminist ethics of nonviolence* (pp. 46–62). Fordham University Press.
Cavarero, A. (2016). *Inclinations: A critique of rectitude* (A. Minervini & A. Sitze Trans.). Stanford University Press.
Cavarero, A. (2021a). Scenes of inclination. In T. J. Huzar & C. Woodford (Eds.), *Feminist ethics of nonviolence* (pp. 33–45). Fordham University Press.
Cavarero, A. (2021b). Coda. In T. J. Huzar & C. Woodford (Eds.), *Feminist ethics of nonviolence* (pp. 177–186). Fordham University Press.
Cornell, D. (1992). *The philosophy of the limit*. Routledge.
Deming, B. (1984). *We are all part of one another* (J. Meyerding, Ed.). New Societies Publishers.
Disney, A. (Producer), & Riticker, G. (Director). (2008). *Pray the devil back to hell* [Film]. ro*co Films Educational.
Doll, M. A. (1995). *To the lighthouse and back*. Peter Lang.
Doll, Jr., W. E. (2012). *Pragmatism, post-modernism, and complexity theory* (D. Trueit, Ed.). Routledge.
Fernandes, L. (2003). *Transforming feminist practice*. Aunt Lute Books.
Flinders, C. (2006). Nonviolence: Does gender matter? *Peace Power*, Summer, 20–21.
Gallo-Cruz, S. (2018). American mothers' nonviolence. In H. J. McCammon & L. A. Banaszak (Eds.), *Years of the Nineteenth Amendment: Appraisal of women's political activism* (pp. 273–294). Oxford University Press.
Gbowee, L. (2011). *Mighty be our powers*. Beast Books.
Gbowee, L. (2014). Nonviolence and peacemaking. *The Ecumenical Review*, 66(2), 154–156.
Grumet, M. (1988). *Bitter milk*. The University of Massachusetts Press.
Hamling, A. (Ed.). (2021). *Women and nonviolence*. Cambridge Scholars Publishing.
Hendry, P. M. (2011). *Engendering curriculum history*. Routledge.
Hershock, P. (2011). *Valuing diversity*. State University of New York Press.
hook, b. (2000). *Feminism is for everybody*. Pluto Press.
Huzar, T. J., & Woodford, C. (Eds.). (2021). *Feminist ethics of nonviolence*. Fordham University Press.
Illibagiza, I. (2006). *Left to tell*. Hay House.
John, M. S. (2006). Feminism and peace studies. *Indian Journal of Gender Studies*, 13(2), 138–162. https://doi.org/10.1177/097152150601300201
Johnson, A. G. (2014). *The gender knot*. Temple University Press.
Knight, L. W. (2005). *Citizen: Jane Addams and the struggle for democracy*. W. W. Norton.
Knight, L. W. (2010). *Jane Addams*. W. W. Norton.
Kristeva, J. (1980). *Desire in language* (L. S. Roudiez, Trans.). Columbia University Press.
Kristeva, J. (1995). *New maladies of the soul* (R. M. Guberman, Trans.). Columbia University Press.
Kristeva, J. (1996). *Julia Kristeva: Interviews* (R. M. Guberman, Ed.). Columbia University Press.
Maparyan, L. (2012). *The womanist idea*. Routledge.
Mayes, C. (2005). *Jung and education*. Rowman & Littlefield Education.

McAllister, P. (Ed.). (1982). *Reweaving the web of life: Feminism and nonviolence*. New Society Publishers.

Miller, J. (2005). *Sounds of silence breaking*. Peter Lang.

Nagler, M. N. (2004). *The search for a nonviolent future*. Inner Ocean Publishing.

Nagler, M. N. (2020). *The third harmony*. Berrett-Koehler Publishers.

Noddings, N. (2012). *Peace education*. Cambridge University Press.

Pinar, W. F. (2001). *The gender of racial politics and gender violence*. Peter Lang.

Pinar, W. F. (2009). *The worldliness of a cosmopolitan education*. Routledge.

Pinar, W. F. (2012). *What is curriculum theory?* (2nd ed.). Routledge.

Poe, D. (2010). Woman, mother, and nonviolent activism. In A. Fitz-Gibbon (Ed.), *Positive peace* (pp. 119–132). Rodopi.

Poe, D. (2018). Feminism and nonviolent activism. In A. Fiala (Ed.), *The Routledge handbook of pacifism and nonviolence* (pp. 268–280). Routledge.

Reardon, B. (1996). *Sexism and the war system*. Syracuse University Press.

Reardon, B. (2001). *Education for a culture of peace in a gender perspective*. The Teacher's Library.

Reardon, B. (2016). *A discussion with Betty Reardon, peace educator*. Berkeley Center at Georgetown University. https://berkleycenter.georgetown.edu/interviews/a-discussion-with-betty-reardon-peace-educator

Shields, P. M. (2017). *Jane Addams: Progressive pioneer of peace, philosophy, sociology, social work and public administration*. Springer.

Smith-Christopher, D. L. (2007). *Subverting hatred*. Orbis Books.

Stiehm, J. H. (Ed.). (2006). *Champions for peace: Women winners of the Nobel Peace Prize*. Rowman & Littlefield.

Todd, S. (2001). "Bringing more than I contain": Ethics, curriculum and the pedagogical demand for altered egos. *Journal of Curriculum Studies, 33*(4), 431–450. https://doi.org/10.1080/002202701300200911

Todd, S. (2003). *Learning from the other*. Routledge.

Wang, H. (2004). *The call from the stranger on a journey home: Curriculum in a third space*. Peter Lang.

Wang, H. (2014). *Nonviolence and education*. Routledge.

Wang, H. (2021). *Contemporary Daoism, organic relationality, and curriculum of integrative creativity*. Information Age Publishing.

Wernitznig, D. (2021). Past, present, and future perspectives of nonviolence and gender. In A. Hamling (Ed.), *Women and nonviolence* (pp. 96–112). Cambridge Scholars Publishing.

Williams, K. T. E., Baszile, D. T., & Guillory, N. A. (Eds.). (2020). *Black women theorizing curriculum studies in color and curves*. Routledge.

Wood, H. (2016). *Invitation to peace studies*. Oxford University Press.

· 12 ·

CURRERE OF NONVIOLENCE: STARLIGHT, A RINGING BELL, AND DREAM WORK

In this last chapter, rather than summarizing the major themes of the book, I write in the narrative language of *currere* to invite awakenings to a curriculum of nonviolence.

1

When I was a teenager, I became afraid of darkness, as I associated it with violence. Even in my adulthood, when I felt too stressed, I still did not want to see the light turned off. In 1998, during one of my crises, walking in the sand on a small shore along the campus lake at Louisiana State University during the night, all of a sudden, I felt a sense of warmth and peace as I looked at the lights coming from houses nearby: There is intimacy in the dark; there is love in the dark. I looked up into the night sky, where starlight shone through, connected to the ripple of the lake water. Starlight became my loving companion.

Little did I know at that time that 10 years later, the starlight of nonviolence would emerge from my life history to brighten my cross-cultural pathways (Wang, 2014). Starlight also accompanied my intense studies during the period of preparing for my college entrance exams in China, with the companionship of my youngest sister and two best friends, as we walked home together under the night sky in my hometown, Harbin (Wang, 2021). My latest *currere* writing brought back this endearing memory. The night sky of Oklahoma where I live now also offers amazing and clear starlight, illuminating my evening walk and contemplation. Starlight is everywhere.

Nonviolence is also everywhere, if we choose to see it. Humanity has become an endangering and endangered species, and there is a sense of unprecedented urgency, but we can choose to see not only darkness. We also can see the light in the dark, as the dark and the light are in a dynamic dance in Daoism. Throughout this book, I have tried to speak about how compassion, companionship, and love as the positive forces of nonviolence—existing throughout human history on small and big scales—can prevail over difficulty when we play with darkness and dance with the shadow.

My students did not like for me to walk in the dark. Many years ago, when they read my book on curriculum in a third space (Wang, 2004), they gave me a photo of a bridge with lamplight on it in a class presentation: "Dr. Wang, we are worried about you walking along the lake in the dark, so we'll give you some light to accompany you." We all laughed. I was moved; students put the light on for me. Boomer Lake in Stillwater was where I walked and ran to finish writing that book. Water has a spirit. And it has been my students' openness to new ways of seeing and forming nonviolent relationships that has sustained my courage and spirit in continuing to walk my path.

2

Perhaps my metaphor of starlight, although heartfelt, cannot convey the fullness of awakening, as the "eye" is privileged over the other senses and runs the risk of objectification, the very mechanism that nonviolence needs to dissolve. To see others—human and non-human—as objects, we take a vibrant life out of them. It is relationality and relationships that we must participate in. To speak of nonviolent relationality, we need to be aware that looking up at the sky must be accompanied by looking down, being rooted in the earth, in the maternal space, to stretch ourselves both up and down for connections. Starlight is different from sunshine in that it already incorporates both the maternal and paternal, in the Kristevian sense. In Chinese *qigong* practices, the visualization accompanying breathing exercises is intended to blend sunshine and moonlight and channel them into the body through the third eye.

Starlight can be sensed from within as well. I have practiced the North Star meditation—a Daoist meditation—for several years; I discovered it during the COVID-19 pandemic. I close my eyes in practice so that I can listen better and sense better, listen to the self, and listen to the world, in stillness, in a fuller sensing of the present moment, and through embodiment and imagination, to connect with the bridge of starlight. Kristeva privileges sensory experience that bridges affects and thoughts; Jung emphasizes embodied understanding and creative transcendence. Beyond sensing, *Dao De Jing* points to emptiness, the most creative and generative space, inclusive of all, vibrant with movements of *qi* and relational stillness. I have called it a zero space of nonviolence (Wang, 2010, 2014).

I sometimes use the ringing sound of a meditation bell in teaching mindfulness, inviting students to experience the difference between usual listening and mindful listening. It reminds me of the temples—with their huge bells—I visited at cultural sites in China, of university bell towers, and of church bells. The sounds of bells keep me alert and attentive to history, culture, and spirituality in fresh ways. A complicated conversation with the self, the other, and the world, which is curriculum, is full of polyphonic voices, both individual and communal, opening up alterity within and without to invite the unknown and unrecognized into emergence. While conversation is voice-oriented, it also embodies the sensory experiences of vision, orality, touch, rhythm, and communal movement. We are in the presence of one another if we remember to invite the stranger to participate in the circle. Welcoming the stranger, we do not form invisible boundaries to wall off those who are different (Quinn, 2010). Instead, the aporia of hospitality (Derrida, 2000; Smith, 2021) presses on us to open our doors and extend our hands, not knowing where it may lead.

Mindful listening can discern sounds and voices that are often hidden, but such attentive listening is important for enacting a pedagogy of nonviolence. Through relating to students and their inner worlds by attentive listening, we can bring the potentiality of students into existence by their own experiential openness and meaning-making process. Mindful listening simultaneously attends to both the self and the other in interactions, and further enables pedagogical responses based upon relational attunement (Pinar, 2019; Wang, 2021) not only to the human world but also to the natural world. In today's climate, ecological sustainability should become an essential aspect of curriculum and teaching. Students' mindful relationships projects (see Chapter 9) tell us that nature speaks in a different voice, and we must listen to reach new awareness.

The dream world also speaks. For more than a decade, participating in a Jungian dream group to descend into the subconscious has helped me build bridges between affects and thoughts. Not that I can actually *know* what dreams mean, but the ongoing effort of descending has brought surprising discoveries. There are many ways of integrating the subconscious and the conscious, such as aesthetic activities, hands-on experiences, dream work, meditations, and intellectual work, but the key is to reach insights through experiences and to formulate thoughts through creative activities.

Dream *work* is work in its double sense of accessing the wisdom of dreams during sleep and of releasing the social imagination for a better-shared world in the future. Without working through the unrecognized, we cannot dream forward. The work of integrating the individual subconscious and the cultural unconscious also informs social justice education and ecojustice endeavors (Cunningham, 2021; Taylor, 2009). Cunningham (2021) argues that the complexity of racism needs to be unraveled at the site of archetypal energy. Making friends with the shadow, we become fuller and acquire more capacity to practice noncooperation with and defiance against injustice while forming compassionate relationships with others.

3

The last step of *currere* is to synthesize the temporality, place, subjectivity, and culture in the present moment to transform, to mobilize, and to renew (Pinar, 1994). My present moment is tearful. At the time of this writing, my father passed away, unexpectedly, two months ago in China. With visa complications, I could not travel home to see him before he died. His sudden death shocked me. I wrote about unteachable moments and unrecognized loss in Chapter 6. This time, it is my unrecognized desire to connect with him, shadowed by my mother's power and her claim on her children's love, that comes back in full force, creating a sense of heaviness in my body, mind, and spirit. Although I live in my normal routine, teaching, reading, writing, and talking to others, the world feels different now.

While I have experienced the impact of international relations on my individual life for many years, this time is the most intense, when the antagonism between the United States and China creates extra roadblocks. It has been disheartening to hear enemy talk on both sides. The simple truth is that international cooperation and collaboration, not dualistic opposition, is more important than ever in today's world. To merely calculate one's own interest and mobilize nationalistic and ethnocentric defenses cannot lead to one's own benefit. The notion of the international has never been an abstract concept for me, as it is embodied in the everyday educational world in our relationships with "the stranger" in multiple senses. Without withdrawing shadow projections to re-imagine nonviolent relations in the international realm, we *all* remain vulnerable.

More than a year ago, I had a dream. My father cooked something special for me and he told me happily that since the electricity was off, he was able to steam something nice. I shared this dream with my Jungian dream group members, and I wondered aloud why he needed the electricity to be off to do that. How could I have known that the electricity of his life would be turned off and that his death would teach me nourishing lessons? At the time of waking up from the dream, I realized that I needed to do something different during the next visit. But alas, no next time! Why do we wait until we lose someone to understand our desire to be more loving with them?

Of course, my father had his responsibilities as a parent, just as my unteachable moment (see Chapter 6) was also about a student who refused to learn. But the change in any relationship needs initiation from one participant who is willing to work from within as the basis for shifting the terrain. Is it not an irony that I have spoken about nonviolence for over a decade but did not hear my inner voice for reconciliation with my dad? I cannot tell now where my mourning will lead me, but I would like to imagine that the heartache I am suffering now can be transfigured into creating more pathways of nonviolence in my everyday life and teaching, into holding tensions and seeking room for upholding love over resistance to love.

Both Kristeva (1996) and Butler (2020) speak about the significance of loss and vulnerability for making connections and creating a shared life with compassion. When we are born, and when we are dying, we are utterly vulnerable in different ways, needing loving support from others. In "cries and whispers" (Pinar, 1992), we need to make sense of loss and death in the midst of life. Friends and colleagues have shared with me how they made sense of losing their parents, and each has a different metaphor to describe the process. What if we not only attend to the discourses of privilege but also share our meaning-making of loss for building more connections across difference in social justice education (Thomas, 2017)? In a global time of crises and disasters, is it possible that working through loss in a communal body could awaken us to the integrative power of nonviolence?

Currere is about seeking the unrecognized aspects of one's inner life and making connections with "the lost language" (Pinar, 1994, p. 253) to recreate meanings. I recovered my lost language of nonviolence (Wang, 2014), and now I speak of difficult love, in mourning, in an interminable process of becoming, and in facing the difficulties of our time as an educator. Without nonviolence, love can become enmeshed in a controlling mechanism. Without love, the integrative power of nonviolence cannot be enabled. Despite the difficulty, educators are the midwives to a world renewed daily, and we must embrace nonviolence education before it is too late, in this world, on this planet. "Colonizing" another planet, as a U.S. TV news reporter unabashedly announced as the future of humanity, is not an option.

4

Often there are not healthy outlets for working through difficult emotions, leaving one stuck on the site subconsciously. At the same time, the positive force of nonviolence through connectedness is often hidden, especially in a highly competitive and individualistic culture. So I want to also speak of joy. My mentor, William Doll—who passed away more than five years ago—was a master teacher who genuinely enjoyed students and playing with ideas and relations (Wang, 2016). His sense of playfulness softened institutional constraints for students, and he refused to see anybody through the lens of any category but worked on bringing out the best potential in everyone.

There is joy in playing with limits, with the self, with tensions, and even with the very notion of nonviolence. Laughter, humor, and play are transcendent, as they lift up people's spirits to aspire beyond the boundaries of self and institutions. As Ugena Whitlock (2012) points out, nonviolence leaders are often quite humorous and joyful. When one can see through divides and broken relationships, one can play. There is joy in nonviolence work: making serendipitous connections (Wang, 2014), transforming hostility into mutual understanding, knowing the world anew through companionship, integrating body and mind to release a creative flow, filling the heart with love to leave no space for hatred (Nagler, 2020), and being a part of nonviolent resistance and protests against injustice.

Isabel Nuñez (2021) speaks of joy in the vocation of daily teaching, reading, and working for educational justice in a difficult time. One of the joys I have been fortunate to experience is to witness students' integrative work in multiple dimensions, with or without my company. They are the ones who labor to achieve their own awakenings, and I have learned to create pedagogical conditions for such labor. I am often moved by their courage and compassion in the midst of difficulty, loss, and trauma. Although the message of nonviolence does not reach everyone, and sometimes reaches only a few, those occasions when students achieve revelations about their lives and their work through reading, discussions, and engagement in experiential projects have brought me immense joy, revealing how worthwhile nonviolence work is in teacher education.

Once in a while a student can read my work and predict the next step in my scholarship just as I move in that direction. The almost simultaneous steps of pedagogical relationships can happen on the part of both the teacher and students when nonviolent relationality is introduced into teaching. The formation of my teaching approaches has been profoundly influenced by my own mentors who connected intellectual work and life in meaningful ways (Wang, 2023), not only through books, but through the laughter and joy from sharing food, drinks, and ideas in gatherings and parties. Curriculum is deeply intergenerational and multi-generational, and that is why nonviolence is necessarily an educational work and how nonviolence can have long-term impact, one person a time.

Quoting Thich Nhat Hanh who urges that even one peaceful person can make a huge difference in a dangerous world and that every one of us can be that person, Molly Quinn (2014) discusses the peace work of "studying the goodness and humanity still present amid the horrors of human history" and experiencing "joy and beauty even amid suffering and tragedy" in pedagogy (p. 66). Cultivating personhood at the intersection between the inner and outer work is the foundation for nonviolence education. Enabling students to reach new understanding, new awareness, and new relationships in their own sense-making and joy-making process is the work of creative maternity and loving paternity in dynamic interactions through nonviolent relations.

5

Although I don't deny that there is a destructive tendency in the psyche and in society, I refuse to see aggression as the primary psychic and social force and compassion as secondary and reparative. During those breakdown moments in my cross-cultural life history, the return of the subconscious did include the elements of anger and aggression, but it revealed a much stronger desire for reconciliation, connections, and love, the desire to be inclusive of all, not doing harm in the human and non-human world. While recognizing that repressing difficult emotions is not the route to go, I insist that working *through* those difficult emotions requires the support of love and gratitude for individual and social change. Routing aggression out without transforming it into sustainable energy runs the risk of releasing a destructive force; rather, aggression needs to be "consciously experienced, contained, and challenged through nonviolent interventions" (Cunningham, 2021, p. 96).

In my memory, moments of feeling free happened when I felt deeply connected to others or nature (Wang, 2022). The best teaching experiences have occurred with a sense of flow when everything clicked, and the relational dynamics of the class were productive, creative, and humorous. It is in relationship that freedom and creativity are made possible. There have also been moments of despair and anger for me in seeing how human cruelty can unfold on small and big scales, and how certain human lives are objectified as ungrievable (Butler, 2020). There is a danger that nonviolence will become pure light, not recognizing that aggression exists in the human psyche and needs to be channeled and harnessed into constructive energy. That's why I use the metaphor of starlight, which integrates the dark and the light, and sunshine and moonlight. The key is integration, and integration requires recognition, transformation, and the transcendence of aggression.

A group of Native American women (see Chapter 10) affirmed their gratitude to life and Earth, despite individual and collective trauma, to connect the past with the future in repositioning their present everyday practices. Restoring eco-relationality itself is a decolonizing process that fundamentally deconstructs the colonial mentality of possession, control, and domination. It is worthwhile to mention that the normalization of violence is sometimes justified by reading violence into nature: If nature can be violent, why cannot human beings be? As Nagler (2004) points out, violence is a human phenomenon with the intentionality to harm. Violence is not nature's problem.

Violence against violence in word, thought, and action, "peace" through military strength, and passive acceptance of current school reforms for commercialization and standardization only reinforce the cycle of violence as "an eternal struggle for power," while only nonviolent interruptions of such a cycle can bring conflicts back to the interconnected source of life (Cunningham, 2021, p. 75). Although the modern age of technology, science, and media seems to provide speedy, visible connections, the deeper need for affiliation, fellowships, and reconciliation has been subsumed into the cultural subconscious in our society under the guise of toughness. Instead of worrying about repressing the aggressive psychic tendency, why do not we worry more about repressing our desires for love and nonviolence? It is my faith as an educator, without relying on God, that nonviolence is the way out in meeting today's interlocking challenges.

Nonviolence is spiritual with or without a religion (Nuñez, 2021; Quinn, 2014; Wang, 2014; Smith-Christopher, 2007); it upholds the human capacity for converting aggression, anger, and fear into compassion, courage, and passion for creating a mutually flourishing life in an ongoing process. Nonviolence is a calling for me and keeps ringing in my heart, despite my re-occurring self-doubts in following this path. When I teach students mindfulness, I tell students that I teach it not because I am good at it, but because I am not good at it. Nonviolence includes both inherent and acquired capacities, and continually practicing it faithfully is necessary for holding tensions. I convince myself that I will go as far as I can go as an ordinary soul, and along the way, invite my students and colleagues to co-travel.

I approach my nonviolence work as self-affirmative, rather than self-sacrificial, as it fulfills my longing for love, affiliation, and integration, and my aspiration to convert anger, fear, and resentment into a sustainable passion for meaning in life. Giving up a part of one's own self-interest for the shared collective interest is not the same as the self-sacrifice demanded by patriarchy, as the relational nature of humanity is fulfilled in serving the higher and bigger good. Cunningham (2021) points out that "the constellation of the archetypal experience of nonviolence emerges between the self and the other long before the conscious intent of nonviolence" (p. 48). Nonviolence is archetypal.

Holding the tensions between aggression and compassion, we work for the positive force of nonviolence to prevail in the day-to-day practice of education. It is a difficult but also a playful labor, with love, patience, and perseverance. Occasionally I debate with myself about whether love or compassion is primary, or whether aggression is an equal partner in human nature. But I am clear that interconnectedness is the condition for specific, various forms of relational responses, including violence as overcompensation for vulnerability. Human nature is not fixed but can be shaped through education and evolves over time, and we have the capacity to hold tensions to bridge divides and transform our own nature and attune ourselves to the cosmic dance toward nonviolence as mutual flourishing that we create in a class and in a community.

There is so much more to say, but words do not mean much if we don't experience it. Enacting nonviolence in the everyday practice of teaching, education, and studies in lived experience is the path that each one of us needs to walk, one step a time, alone and together. This book is an invitation, not a demand. So let the ringing sound of a bell linger in our ears, let the starlight guide our stumbling steps, let the vibrant pulse of life through the dream world breathe cosmic energy into our walking. We as educators are on a journey of embracing the integrative power of nonviolence and accompanying our students in paving sustainable pathways in curriculum and pedagogy practiced here and now, leading to the shared flourishing future that can still exist on this planet......

References

Butler, J. (2020). *The force of non-violence*. Verso.
Cunningham, R. M. (2021). *Archetypal nonviolence*. Routledge.
Derrida, J. (2000). *Of hospitality* (R. Bowlby, Trans.). Stanford University Press.
Kristeva, J. (1996). *Julia Kristeva: Interviews* (R. M. Guberman, Ed.). Columbia University Press.
Nagler, M. (2004). *The search for a nonviolent future*. Inner Ocean Publishing.
Nagler, M. (2020). *The third harmony*. Berrett-Koehier Publishers.
Nuñez, I. (2021). Joy as sustenance. In I. Nuñez & G. Jason (Eds.), *Hope and joy in education* (pp. 3–9). Teachers College Press.
Pinar, W. F. (1992). Cries and whispers. In W. F. Pinar & W. M. Reynolds (Eds.), *Understanding curriculum as phenomenological and deconstructed text* (pp. 92–101). Teachers College Press.
Pinar, W. F. (1994). *Autobiography, politics and sexuality*. Peter Lang.
Pinar, W. F. (2019). *Moving images of eternity*. University of Ottawa Press.
Quinn, M. (2010). "No room in the inn"? The question of hospitality in the post(partum)-labors of curriculum studies. In E. Malewski (Ed.), *Curriculum studies handbook* (pp. 101–177). Routledge.
Quinn, M. (2014). *Peace and pedagogy*. Peter Lang.
Smith, L. (2021). *Curriculum as community building*. Peter Lang.
Smith-Christopher, D. (2007). *Subverting hatred*. Orbis Books.
Taylor, J. (2009). *The wisdom of your dreams*. Jeremy P. Tarcher/Penguin.
Thomas, S. (2017). *Grief and the curriculum of cosmopolitanism* [Doctoral dissertation, University of British Columbia]. UBC Theses and Dissertations Open Collection. https://open.library.ubc.ca/soa/cIRcle/collections/ubctheses/24/items/1.0348886
Wang, H. (2004). *The call from the stranger on a journey home: Curriculum in a third space*. Peter Lang.
Wang, H. (2010). A zero space of nonviolence. *Journal of Curriculum Theorizing*, 26(1), 1–8.
Wang, H. (2014). *Nonviolence and education*. Routledge.

Wang, H. (2016). *From the parade child to the king of chaos*. Peter Lang.
Wang, H. (2021). *Contemporary Daoism, organic relationality, and curriculum of integrative creativity*. Information Age Publishing.
Wang, H. (2022). Freedom, interconnectedness, and curriculum attunement. *Journal of Curriculum Theorizing, 37*(3), 1–16.
Wang, H. (2023). Transcendent integration in the everyday practice of curriculum. In M. Quinn, P. Munro Hendry, J. Bach, & R. Mitchell (Eds.), *Curriculum histories in place, in person, in practice* (pp. 94–101). Routledge.
Whitlock, R. U. (2012). "All we are saying...": The case for peace in curriculum theory. *The Journal of Curriculum Theorizing, 28*(1), 227–230.

INDEX

activism 14, 18, 157, 165, 230, 231, 240, 243
  nonviolence 82, 84, 158, 236, 252
  as opposition 243
  peace 93, 244
  political 14, 87, 252
  social 18, 41, 165, 230
  as transformational 243
acupuncture 12, 52
Addams, J. 1, 32, 35, 39, 44, 85, 87, 92–93, 136, 218, 229, 238–240, 242
aesthetics 14, 17, 77, 91, 121, 135, 145, 151, 258
aggression 16, 32, 48, 53–57, 76, 84, 89
  psychic 16, 83, 115, 116, 248, 250
  repression of 248, 250, 263
  working through 249, 250
ahimsa 10, 12, 13, 82, 90, 132, 146, 154, 158, 250
alterity 231, 234, 237, 247–252
  of the other 160, 173, 207, 216, 222, 248
  of the unconscious 248, 250

altruism 233, 234, 251
Analayo, B. 188
Analects, the 66–68, 73, 75
analytic psychology 9, 15, 22, 130, 142, 248
anima 138, 150
animus 138
Anzaldúa, G. 205, 210
Aoki, T. T. 3, 21, 45, 57, 87, 118, 151, 184, 187, 196, 199
aporia 7, 18, 257
archetype 132, 134, 136, 137
  of mother 233
Archibald, J. 209, 210
assimilation 17, 42, 132, 161, 172
attention 10, 52, 66, 88, 126, 141, 165, 170, 184, 187, 200, 207, 211, 230
  focused 189, 190
  mindful 188, 191, 194
  non-dualistic 199
attunement 12, 21, 35, 199, 200
  relational 186, 198, 199, 201, 257
autobiography 7, 169, 210

Bai, H. 5, 51, 83
Bajaj, M. 1, 88, 158, 164
Bar-On, D. 97, 98, 99
becoming 19, 67, 71, 146, 151, 188, 196, 201, 208, 213, 224, 247, 248, 260
  subjective 15, 146, 152
belonging 117, 160, 165, 207, 208, 215–217, 248
beyond the intellect 143–146
binary 12, 116, 168, 176, 179, 231
Black Lives Matter 5
body 2, 12, 20, 23, 40, 47
  and mind 11, 21, 40, 91, 96, 115, 117, 121, 187, 260
  collective 95, 237, 259
  individual 95, 99
  lived 188, 198, 199, 201
body scan 185, 190, 191, 200
Boler, M. 51, 166
Bolliger, L. 121
border-crossing 35, 97
borderlands 205, 213
Bracho, C. A. 187
Brantmeier, E. J. 62, 74, 88, 149, 178, 179, 221
Britzman, D. P. 42
Brock-Utne, B. 235, 240
Buddhism 10, 11, 54, 58, 82, 87, 133, 145, 168, 188, 207, 238
Burns, J. P. 6, 230
Butler, J. 6, 230, 232, 247, 249–251, 259, 262

Cairns, E. 62, 88, 158
calling 37, 39, 150, 263
  collective 5–9
  personal 2–5
caring 18, 19, 70, 140, 178, 197, 215, 238
  maternal 232, 234
categorical thinking 3, 7, 17, 119, 125, 126, 209, 237
Cavarero, A. 232–234, 245, 251
censorship 5
Chambers, C. 220

Chang, C. Y. 70
chaos and complexity theory 70, 94
Cherokee Nation 209, 210
Christianity 164, 244
class struggles 2
classism 7, 15, 31, 39, 49, 58, 84, 139, 215, 217
Cohen, A. 5, 51, 83, 130
colonization 3, 10, 30, 46, 81, 84, 210, 219, 247
commonality 8, 17, 20, 133, 141, 142, 160, 161, 171, 172, 189, 198, 200
companionship 152, 163, 172, 173, 178, 184, 185, 196, 256, 260
  cosmic 14
  intellectual 222
  mindful 199
  nonviolent 151, 189–193
  pedagogical 118, 123, 147
compassion 4, 11, 13, 36, 84, 150, 158, 167, 179, 194, 219, 234, 243, 256, 259, 261
  and aggression 16, 48, 76, 116, 159
  Daoist 71, 76
community 6, 14, 29, 34, 47, 52, 67, 118, 124, 131, 140, 152, 159, 174, 212, 218
  beloved 137
  concepts of 36, 47
  compassionate 5, 31, 35, 40, 97, 149
  without consensus 212, 217
  engagement 56, 135
  feminist 230
  global 21, 48
  Indigenous
  loving 93, 131
  polyvalent 35
community-based education 6, 92, 93, 229
conflict resolution education 89
conflicts 10, 22, 34, 56, 88, 158, 164, 229
  cultural 66
  ethnic 98, 99
  international 1, 20
  peace out of 72–75
Confucianism 2, 22, 61–78
Confucius 64–69, 73, 75

connections across differences 20, 21, 50, 142, 172, 198, 259
conscience 13, 252
consciousness 11, 51, 91, 100, 132, 138, 188, 210, 240
  critical 41, 43, 107, 219
  ecological 223
  ego 132, 244
  moral 67, 68
controlling mechanism 3, 131, 231, 249, 260
conversation 9, 11, 16, 109, 185, 242
  intergenerational 36
  transformative 174
conversion 43, 55, 115, 139, 142, 143
  of difficult emotions 139, 143, 144, 150
  pedagogy 122
cooperation 49, 147, 152, 229, 239, 240
Cornell, D. 247
cosmic energy 12, 246, 264
cosmopolitan education 229
COVID-19 pandemic 6, 257
creativity 5, 23, 36, 43, 70, 89, 208, 216
  maternal 206, 215, 238
  sustainable 237
critical race theory 6
critical theory 8, 22, 42–45, 58
Cultural Revolution, China (1966–1976) 2, 3, 217
culturally responsive pedagogy 41
Cunningham, R. M. 13, 258, 262, 263
currere 15, 23, 121, 145, 169, 237, 241
  of nonviolence 255–265
  teaching 56, 145, 150, 168–169
curriculum 1, 5, 7–9, 11, 13, 29, 41, 81, 93–100, 142, 145, 148–153, 178, 183–195, 209–213, 231, 241, 242, 246, 247, 252, 256, 261
  as community building 212
  as a complicated conversation 9, 11, 14, 30, 185, 188, 189, 242, 257
  discipline-centered 145
  dynamics 22, 23, 129–131, 133, 142, 148–152, 222

feminist 208, 210, 231, 252
formal and informal 62, 244
hidden 178
history 8, 217
  as lived experience 2, 130, 183–185, 187–189, 198–202
  materials 149, 152, 246
  of nonviolence 255
  official 2, 4, 99, 149, 231
  of organic relationality 205, 207, 209, 220, 222
  of place 220
  postmodern 16
  process of 222
  queering 213
  school 87, 92, 209, 211, 221
  theory 3, 229, 231
  vision 4, 23, 29–37

dance 33, 91, 252, 256, 263
Dao 63, 64, 69, 71, 76
Dao De Jing/Tao Te Ching 24, 30, 53, 63–74, 76, 257
Daoism/Taoism 2, 12, 22, 24, 49, 53, 58, 61–78, 85, 86, 206, 207, 238, 256
De 63, 64
de Bary, W. 68
deconstruction 18, 19, 217
de Dijn, A. 3
dehumanization 34, 35
deliberation 1
Deloria, J., V. 9
Deming, B. 19, 230, 245, 246
democracy 1, 3, 4, 18, 32, 39, 45, 53, 84, 87, 90, 157, 218
  liberal 3, 4
  social 239–240
depression 193, 194, 239
desire 3, 29, 43, 49, 116, 258, 259, 262
  for new knowledge 123
Derrida, J. 18, 160, 172, 247, 257
Dewey, J. 239
Dialectics 71, 111
Dialogue 17, 100, 109, 188

Difference 6, 23, 40, 47, 53–56, 72–75, 88, 93–97, 99, 119, 123–126, 138, 142, 151, 152, 160, 165, 171–173, 187, 189, 196–200, 206–209, 218–222, 239, 247–252
  approaches to 17–18, 20, 42, 53, 72–75, 85, 134, 161, 175, 177–178, 184
  commonality and 8, 17, 133, 141, 160, 171, 189, 200
  concepts of 36, 47
  engagement with 8, 17, 29
  gendered 47, 96, 178, 207, 247
  psychic 17, 141
  radical 42, 185
  social 17, 41, 58, 142, 178, 185, 196, 239
differing for 36, 47, 55, 58, 96, 97
differing from 36, 47, 96
difficult emotions 49, 51, 52, 58, 110, 114, 116, 117, 122, 123, 139, 140, 144, 146, 150, 151, 167, 172
difficult knowledge 31, 40, 42, 43, 49, 58, 106, 108, 112, 114, 117, 118, 120, 122, 124, 125, 140, 157
  resistance to 42, 42, 108
difficulty 15, 31, 44, 48, 105, 142, 148, 169, 199, 208, 222, 233, 256, 261
  relational 120
  staying with 119–122, 123, 124
discourse 7, 8, 15, 18, 42, 43, 95, 96, 211, 259
dissonance 51, 55, 57, 106
diversity 7, 18, 41, 47, 96, 125, 133, 161, 213, 223
  cultural 7, 41, 175
  ecological 207
division 5, 9, 21, 23, 134, 144, 146, 179, 206
Doll, M. A. 108–110, 140, 141, 144, 168, 214, 250
Doll, Jr., W. E. 16, 17, 94, 125, 152, 176, 186, 209, 242, 260
domination 3, 12, 16, 17, 21, 30, 31, 41, 49, 53, 83, 97, 135, 209, 214, 219, 221, 249
dream work 121, 138, 139, 140, 258

dualism 30, 40, 41, 58, 83, 89, 95, 134, 144, 160, 177, 250, 252
  between active and passive 84
  mechanism of 214
  modern 47, 133
  psychic 84
  social 84
  between teacher educators and students 41, 43, 122
  of "us" versus "them" 34, 97

Easwaran, E. 13, 49, 147
ecofeminism 207, 214, 244
eco-relationality 10, 262
educating the whole person 210
Ellsworth, E. 43, 118, 119, 121, 125
embodiment 63, 77, 89, 99, 175, 200, 211, 221, 257
emergence 24, 171, 202, 206, 207, 216
emotional work 12, 56, 98, 110, 166, 167, 178
emptiness 11, 71, 188, 257
enlightenment 33, 51, 71, 113, 118, 147
Eppert, C. 30
equality 7, 41, 45, 82, 87, 132, 158, 221, 229, 250
equity 1, 6, 39, 223, 245
Ergas, O. 184, 185, 188
essentialism 17, 237
ethics 29–37, 219, 223, 233, 245, 247
  of love 14
  of mutuality 219
  of nonviolence 29, 35, 232, 248, 251
existentialism 145
experiences 19, 23, 54, 145, 148, 150, 152, 168, 177, 178, 186, 189, 197, 205, 207, 218, 238, 258
  aesthetic 121, 134
  educational 15, 121, 145, 186, 188
  everyday 232, 239
  life 169, 240
  sensory 33, 117, 126, 140, 238, 200, 235, 257
  whole-being 52, 56

experiential learning 183–203

feminism 15, 210, 211, 219, 229, 231
  and education 229–250
  generations of 215
  lesbian 245
  Indigenous 210
  poststructural 247
  spiritualized 19, 243
  third world 243
Fernandes, L. 19, 229, 251
Fiala, A. 10
flow 15, 36, 54, 111, 124, 125, 126, 137, 170
  creative 260
forgiveness 18, 32, 44, 48, 52, 55, 169, 242
Foucault, M. 17, 42
Fowler, L. 106, 119, 120, 125
free association 143, 145, 169
freedom 3, 14, 45, 66, 71, 72, 74, 89, 97, 147, 174, 212, 219, 243, 262
Freire, P. 41
Freud, S. 16, 132, 134, 251
Fung, Y. L. 63, 65

Gallo-Cruz, S. 18, 19, 230, 231, 236, 240, 252
Galtung, J. 81, 88
Gandhi, A. 86, 167
Gandhi, M. K. 1, 9, 13, 19, 20, 30, 46, 49, 86, 87, 92, 93, 131, 134, 136, 147, 158, 159, 160, 166, 167, 187, 240, 242, 243, 252
Garrison, J. 106, 123
Gay, G. 41
Gaztambide-Fernández, R. 121
Gbowee, L. 1, 85, 87, 94, 232, 237, 240, 241
Gender 5, 7, 23, 41, 95, 125, 140, 161–163, 166, 178, 184, 200, 224, 230, 235, 243, 245, 247–252
  and expressing anger 109–110
  awareness 190

  balance 210, 223
  biases 192, 196, 230
  image of teacher 140
  norm 20, 48, 141, 200, 208
  oppression 93, 207, 231
Gitz-Johansen, T. 149
globalization 100
Gough, N. 95
gratitude 208, 213–217, 220, 222–224, 251, 262
  education 223
  limitations of 223
  without guilt 218, 224
Great Learning, the 63–63, 67
Greco-Roman tradition 3
grief 143, 242
Grumet, M. 19, 121, 205, 209, 211, 235
Guillory, N. 124
guilt 31, 49, 51, 116, 150, 166, 172, 218, 248
  guilt-free 51, 217, 224, 234

Hamling, A. 229
Hanh, T. N. 186, 211, 242, 261
harmony 10, 54, 64, 70, 72–75, 88, 213
  creative 12, 248
  in difference 22, 62, 72, 73, 74
  as dynamic 73
  ecological 54
  social 68
Harris, I. 85, 86, 88, 164, 178
healing 11, 32, 40, 52, 144, 169, 213, 250
  organic 12
  personal 240, 241
  social 241
Heitz, M. H. 199
Hendry, P. M. 32, 211, 217, 218, 229, 239, 240
Hershock, P. 8, 18, 36, 45, 47, 94, 96, 131, 133, 158, 161, 164, 178, 207, 247
heteronormativity 237
hierarchy 13, 30, 31, 210
Hinduism 10, 13, 82

history 4, 6, 7, 12, 18, 46, 56, 65–67, 77, 82, 87, 114, 150, 161, 178, 205, 221, 229, 256, 261
  of nonviolence, 1, 4, 6, 9, 12, 30, 82, 90, 157, 221, 256
holding tensions 18, 21, 23, 259, 263
holism 72
homophobia 31, 39, 84, 139, 214
hooks, b. 213, 219
hospitality 18, 152, 257, 264
Howard, G. 10, 13, 51, 116
Huebner, D. 119, 196, 199
Hull House 32, 85, 92, 93, 218, 229, 239
human rights education 89
Hyland, T. 185, 188
hypermasculinity 6, 31, 230

identification 34, 35, 97, 237
  preoedipal 237
identity 7, 8, 17, 31, 34, 43, 52, 94, 97, 109, 113, 126, 140, 166, 205, 209, 235
  building 54, 55
  collective 42
  critiques of 9, 125
  gender 42, 235, 247
  modern notion of 17
  politics 7, 8, 31, 47, 54, 91, 96
  racial 7
  social 41, 95, 96
ideology 3, 11, 90, 112, 113, 219
Illibagiza, I. 242
imagination 9, 16, 30, 48, 106, 143, 173, 208, 209, 257
  active 143
  social 134, 135, 258
  spiritual 48
impermanence 11, 188
improvisation 21, 107
in-between space 94
  liberal 249
independence 13, 16, 30, 36, 74, 115, 123, 217, 218, 234
  through interdependence 36, 249
Indigenous mothers' teaching 10, 209

Indigenous peacemaking, 83
individual, the 29, 36, 45, 47, 62, 66, 68, 96, 117, 129, 132, 133–135, 138, 150, 159, 161, 169, 177, 179, 205, 209, 211, 241, 248, 251, 252, 258
  rights 1, 11, 45, 210
  a separate sense of 3, 44, 91, 238
individualism 1, 6, 33, 133, 164, 176, 207, 211, 249
individuality 16, 29, 44, 50, 63, 72, 115, 132, 134, 151, 179
  and relationality 212, 213
individuation 132, 133
injustice 5, 7, 12, 14, 32, 43, 46, 49, 58, 62, 87, 147, 172, 178, 219, 230, 236, 245, 258, 261
inner work 2, 11, 15, 48, 49, 53, 58, 107, 140, 160, 167, 170, 196, 239, 242
  and outer work 2, 21, 144, 238, 241
inquiry 142, 183, 185–189, 198, 200–202
  collective 186, 187
  curriculum 15, 95
  experiential 188
  individual
  mindful 189
insights 18, 22, 54, 55, 107, 108, 119, 209, 258, 120, 122, 147, 151, 161, 167, 188
instrumentality 188, 196
integral education 91
integration 14, 22, 34, 48, 52, 56, 129, 130, 131, 142–143, 146–148, 158, 159, 160, 177, 215, 262
  of body and mind 2, 56, 187, 200
  of community 152
  of the conscious and the unconscious
  of the personal and the social 231, 238–242
  of psyche 15, 138, 139, 145, 148, 149, 152
  of self and other 2, 56, 187
intentionality 262
interbeing 185, 211, 250
interconnectedness 1, 5, 9, 11, 12, 16, 22, 47, 51, 53, 54, 83, 86, 91, 115, 116117,

126, 131–134, 135–138, 142, 151, 159, 163, 164, 171, 173, 179, 188, 197, 206, 207, 209, 212, 215, 243, 245, 250, 251, 263
interdependence/interdependency 115, 133, 199, 207, 212, 219, 232, 238, 249, 250
  between self and society 68
  of difference 40, 50, 53
internal sagehood and external kingship 64
interplay 53, 88, 144, 177, 212, 214, 222, 242
  between individuality and relationality 213
  of opposites 62, 88
  between the personal and the global 99
  between the semiotic and the symbolic 121
  between the singular and the general 34
International Association for the Advancement of Curriculum Studies (IAACS) 82
internationalization of curriculum studies 22, 35, 82, 94
intimacy 106, 111–117, 119, 126, 256
intuition 106, 135
Islam 10, 86

Jackson, M. 10, 193
Jainism 10, 82, 86
Jennings, P. A. 150, 171, 185, 188, 189, 192, 193, 194, 195, 197, 199
Johnson, A. G. 84, 197, 216, 230
journey 1, 40, 49, 57, 87, 118, 124, 136, 150, 170, 179, 198, 234, 264
  autobiographical 1
  cross-cultural 3
  intellectual 1
  pedagogical 1
  transcendent 151
  transformative 151
joy 95, 124, 260–261
Jung, C. 129–138, 140–141, 143–144, 146, 148, 150, 251, 257

Jupp, J. 43, 122
juxtaposition 52, 99, 145

Kabat-Zinn, J. 90, 160, 188
Kaneda, T. 90, 91, 160
King, Jr., M. L. 1, 5, 9, 13, 14, 19, 30, 44, 51, 92, 93, 132, 136, 147, 150, 158, 159, 242, 243, 245, 249, 252
Kliebard, H. M. 8
Knight, L. W. 85, 87, 92, 218, 239
knowing 50–51, 55, 73, 135, 208, 240, 242, 260
  embodied 135
  feminine 211
  relational 211
Kohl, H. 43
Krishnamurti, J. 91
Kristeva, J. 15, 16, 33, 34, 38, 105, 106, 110–115, 117–125, 160, 206, 215, 216, 217, 234, 257, 259
Kumar, A. 91

Lacan, J. 247
Ladson-Billings, G. 41
  for expressing emotions 111
  language 10, 15, 33, 93, 115, 125, 163, 172, 177, 234, 247, 249, 250, 252, 255, 260
  lost 260
leadership 13, 18, 40, 53, 62, 75, 77, 165, 219, 229
learning about 46, 110, 248
learning from 43, 46, 51, 110, 171, 176, 209, 220, 239, 248
le Grange, L. 11, 12
letting go 11
Levinas, E. 160, 247, 248
Lin, J. 62, 74, 88
listening 166, 194, 199, 200, 248, 250
  attentive 257
  deep 152
  mindful 170, 175, 186
Liu, Rushi 217
Loewen, J. 30, 53

loss 17, 68, 72, 105, 109–113, 120–123, 150, 166, 169, 239, 241, 258, 259
love 10, 48, 62, 68, 82, 115–116, 136, 194, 229, 242, 243, 244, 248, 255, 256, 261–263
  agape, 14, 136, 144
  difficult 260
loving third 15, 114–115, 117, 120, 126
Loy, D., 76
Lynd, A. 12, 30, 39, 59, 82, 85, 157
Lynd, S. 12, 30, 39, 59, 82, 85, 157

Macy, J. 213
Mandela, N. 48, 87
Mankiller, W. 203, 209, 210, 211, 213, 219
Maparyan, L. 241, 244, 250
marginalization, 41
Martin, J. V. 206
Martin Luther King, Jr's Center for Nonviolent Social Change, 92
Martusewicz, R. A., 41, 51
masculine rectitude 232, 238
mass shootings 5, 6, 130
maternal inclination 232, 233, 238
maternal legacies 23, 208
maternity 18, 19, 85, 86, 206, 216, 217, 224, 231, 233, 238
  as communal notion 235
  creative 234, 237, 238, 261
  metaphorical meanings of 234
  power of 165, 236, 237
Mayes, C. 130, 131, 135, 137, 139, 150, 160, 233
McAllister, P. 229, 230
media 165, 206, 262
  social 206
meditation 56, 91, 144, 160, 170, 185, 187, 241, 257
  loving-kindness 194, 196
Mencius 66, 68, 69, 73, 75, 76
Metta Center for Nonviolence 92
Miller, J. 99, 110, 121, 166, 170, 177, 211, 212, 213, 217, 247

militarism 235, 236, 240
mindful interactions 144, 152, 188, 189, 193, 194, 197, 198, 199, 201
mindfulness 11, 23, 150, 160, 168, 170, 183–202, 244, 257, 263
  of breathing 170, 185, 193, 194, 199–201, 250
  of body 185
  of emotion 170, 197
  interpersonal 194
  practices 160, 199, 201
modernization 2, 22
morality 33, 63, 134
  Confucian 63
Muller, J. 89, 90, 159
multiculturalism 8, 157
mutual flourishing 2, 35, 36, 133, 207, 223, 263

Nagler, M. N. 5, 10, 16, 20, 30, 31, 32, 34, 35, 46, 82, 84, 115, 116, 131, 132, 134, 137, 139, 158, 159, 160, 162, 163, 167, 170, 187, 209, 219, 221, 232, 236, 246, 249, 260, 262
narratives 83, 145, 186, 98, 99
natality 232
nations 3, 4, 20, 34, 64, 93, 173, 209, 210, 235
  without nationalism 30, 34, 97
nationalism 34, 35, 77, 89, 91, 215
nature and humanity 173, 200
neoliberalism 3, 100
network effects 124
Ng-A-Fook, N. 10
Noddings, N. 246
non-belonging 216
non-competition 71
noncooperation 147, 230, 258
nonduality 1, 8, 10, 33
  of body and mind 1, 40
  of commonality and difference
  of self and other 1, 40
  of subject and object 47, 96

INDEX

nonviolence 1–22, 29–36, 39–58, 81–100, 105–126, 129–152, 157–180, 187, 218, 219, 221, 222, 229–252, 255–265
  and non-violence 10, 16, 135, 158, 159, 249, 250
  as continuum with violence 23, 116, 176, 179
  as a positive force 5, 31, 83, 84, 158, 164, 243, 256, 260, 263
  as a radical concept 175
  as a vision 29–36
  as a way of life 9, 13, 14, 30, 177
  as holding tensions 18, 21, 23, 259
  double gestures of 116
  gendered nature of 19, 230, 252
  integrative power of 143–146, 259, 260, 264
  work 23, 44, 117, 138, 148, 149, 178, 241, 246, 260, 261, 263
nonviolence curriculum 21, 246
nonviolence education 21, 22, 23, 29, 40, 46, 82, 87, 88–93, 95, 99, 100, 126, 148, 157, 159, 177, 178, 180, 187, 244, 261
nonviolence studies 9, 20–21, 30, 110, 116, 131, 143, 149, 159, 160, 162, 250
  limits of 20
nonviolent communication 56
nonviolent governing 30, 46, 84
nonviolent relations 16, 19, 21, 22, 34, 36, 40, 49, 50, 96, 129–155, 171, 219, 220, 231, 233, 256, 259, 261
  with difference 129, 160, 177, 247–252
  between local, national, and international 3, 94–100
  with others 33, 144, 151, 160, 168, 177, 220, 251, 256
  with the self 22, 33, 47, 130, 141, 144, 233, 244, 256
  with the world 2, 33, 244
  nonviolent social change 9, 13, 14, 55, 161, 265
normalization 5, 17, 36, 231, 262
  of aggression 231

  of violence 5, 262
no-self 11, 54, 55
Nuñez, I. 260, 263

objectification 41, 43, 222, 256
  pedagogical 43
Oliver, K. 114, 115, 117
oppression 12, 18, 30, 31, 41, 86, 89, 93, 136, 231, 243, 244
othering 230, 231

pacifism 32, 218, 240
pain 2, 32, 48, 52, 53, 87, 98, 113, 120, 123, 146, 150, 166, 169, 171, 194, 197, 241
Palmer, P. 174
paternity 112, 261
patriarchy 19, 84, 166, 205–210, 213–217, 222, 237, 240, 247, 252
  internalized 196, 216
peace 10, 12, 13, 32, 40, 44, 61–78, 84, 85–87, 91, 97, 99, 158–159
  as process 74
  as text, subtext, and context 178
  definition of 74, 93, 164
  ecological 20
  inner 13, 20, 31, 48–49, 58, 62, 66, 69, 72, 73, 75–77, 86, 91 160, 170, 179, 241
  movement 62, 85, 87, 88, 94, 135, 162, 165, 178, 231, 236, 241
  through strength 32, 250
  Tolstoyan 139, 239
  world 3, 4, 13, 62, 69, 72, 77
peace education 20–21, 61–78, 88, 98, 161, 171, 177, 179, 246
  critical 159, 177, 179
  definition of 88–89
  limits of 171
  materials 246
Peace Research in the Middle East 98
peace studies 1, 4, 61, 88, 158, 169, 238, 242
peacebuilding 10, 62, 98, 176, 179, 240, 241, 243

peacemaking 10, 20, 62, 83, 242
peaceweaving 229, 240
pedagogical authority 46, 109, 126, 141
pedagogical dynamics 107
pedagogical gap 109, 126, 175
pedagogical relationships 77, 85, 89, 105–126, 147, 149, 151, 152, 161, 169, 173, 177, 179, 244, 250, 261
  of nonviolence 118–127, 149, 152, 222
pedagogical thoughtfulness 57, 151
pedagogy of nonviolence 8, 18, 23, 40, 46, 50–58
Penn, William 30, 85
personal cultivation 4, 8, 14, 54, 61–72, 91, 99, 100, 158
  moral 69
personhood 8, 9, 22, 29, 61–75, 77, 87, 131, 246, 251
  authentic 64, 71
Phelan, A., 140
philosophy 16, 52, 66, 72, 77, 96, 129, 131, 132, 137, 158, 159, 230, 243, 251
  Asian 77, 211
  Western 90, 251
Piirto, J. 91
Pinar, W. F. 3, 6, 7, 15, 30, 48, 56, 94, 96, 116, 121, 130, 145, 160, 166, 167, 168, 169, 177, 184, 187, 196, 218, 230, 237, 238, 239, 240, 257, 258, 259, 260
Pitt, A. 108, 109, 119
playfulness 9, 17, 74, 152, 260
playing with 125, 260
Poe, D. 86, 235
Poindexter, N. 6, 199
polyphony 21, 257
post-conflict education 20
poststructural theory 18, 22, 40, 42, 43, 160, 169, 189
poverty 75, 214
  power relationships 42, 54
  power struggles 7, 8, 48, 54, 94, 95, 133, 165, 236
practices 30, 31, 43, 56, 70, 73, 85, 89, 91, 122, 144, 148, 183, 185, 189, 190

caring 18, 19
  of education 2, 9, 131, 212, 263
  everyday 23, 131, 233, 235, 244, 246, 264
  feminist 19, 212
  of nonviolence 4, 13, 93, 167, 243, 246
Pray the Devil Back to Hell, 135, 162
praxis 1, 143, 144, 231
presence 15, 54, 120, 175, 184, 235, 257
present moment, the 100, 188, 192, 193, 257, 258
privilege 20, 43, 210, 220, 259
projection 15, 22, 116, 138, 139, 140, 259
psyche 2, 7, 15, 16, 22, 33, 111, 116, 129, 131, 132, 138, 142, 143, 145, 148, 169, 206, 248, 250, 252, 261, 262
  collective 217, 251
psychoanalysis 9, 15, 16, 22, 33, 83, 115, 116, 130, 132, 160, 168, 206, 232, 248, 250, 251

qi 12, 52, 257
Qian, Xiuling 219
qigong 256
queer theory 8, 237
questioning 4, 15, 17, 22, 57, 111, 112, 113, 114, 115, 118, 119, 123, 124, 125, 126, 147, 148, 151, 178, 187
  communal 124
  ongoing 112, 114, 118
  social 118
quietude 71, 73, 76
Quinn, M. 257, 261, 263

racism 6, 7, 15, 31, 39, 49, 58, 84, 107, 121, 125, 139, 150, 210, 214, 215, 217, 258
rationality 1, 18
Reardon, B. 230, 243
reconciliation 10, 11, 32, 35, 44, 62, 135, 259, 262, 263
reflection 56, 109, 110, 135, 142, 150, 152, 188, 190, 191, 200
  archetypal 150, 151
  teacher 139

rehumanization 32, 35, 219
relational dynamics 5, 8, 11, 18, 23, 31, 41, 43, 47–49, 50, 53, 55, 56, 58, 75, 83, 90, 122–124, 134, 145, 149, 158, 161, 164, 165, 168, 173–175, 177, 207
  nonviolent 46, 48, 56, 75, 82, 133
  of community 6, 40
  of curriculum 129, 209–213, 231, 246, 262
relationships 105–126, 129–152, 183–202, 204–224
  authentic 18, 110, 145
  compassionate 6, 11, 21, 115, 116, 129, 131, 138–140, 148, 158, 160, 176, 187, 188, 258
  ethical 17, 22, 134
  father-son 193–195
  gendered 209, 210, 214, 238
  human/nature 70–72, 91, 94, 106, 173, 184, 196, 199, 201, 244
  intergenerational 135, 184, 200, 218, 222, 261
  international 1, 3, 5, 34, 133, 158, 250, 258
  loving 130, 158, 249, 250
  mindful 22, 183, 184, 186, 188, 189, 198, 199, 200, 257
  mother-daughter 214
  self-other 33, 40, 44, 47, 67, 69, 96, 121
  self-self 29
  teaching-learning 105
religions 19, 91, 136, 164, 243, 245, 246
Ren 67, 68–69, 70, 75, 76
renewal 15, 112, 114, 119, 123–126, 148, 216
reparation 16, 115, 135, 161
repression 33, 97, 116, 121, 139, 141, 237
  of aggression 250
  homosexual 237
resistance 6, 16, 18, 19, 40, 42, 51, 107, 113, 122, 136, 147, 251, 259
  collective 109, 167, 232
  nonviolent 19, 93, 136, 161, 165, 221, 251, 260

  against official knowledge 43
responsibility 17, 18, 31, 32, 35, 64, 116, 123, 146, 150, 172, 222, 247
  pedagogical 35, 118, 123, 148
  social 116, 150
retribution 35, 243
revolt 22, 105–127
  intimate 22, 105, 110–118, 120, 123, 124–127
  oedipal 111–117, 126
rootedness 11, 189, 190, 196, 198, 199
Rosenberg, M. B. 56, 57
Rowland, S. 151, 158

Salomon, G. 62, 88, 158
satyagraha 13
  school culture 231
  school security 6
self 7, 17, 19, 29, 33, 93, 107, 142, 148, 162, 169, 171, 187, 190, 193, 196, 197, 198, 199, 200, 201, 210, 211, 213, 215, 220, 223, 234, 241, 245, 249
  affirmation 19, 213, 234, 252
  authentic 64
  care, 184, 195, 196, 197, 200, 211
  creation 17, 42
  cultivation 61–64, 67–69, 73
  difference 7
  education 4, 149, 151, 152, 169, 177, 180
  forgetting 64, 72
  interest 7, 36, 94, 263
  organization 70
  questioning 118, 126
  realization 68, 71, 234
  sacrifice 234, 251, 252, 263
  understanding 118, 138, 168 184, 191, 192, 196, 198, 199
self-so-ness 69, 70
semiotic/symbolic dynamics 15, 33, 111, 112, 115 119, 125
  definition of 111
separation 35, 135, 178, 186, 209, 212, 215, 235, 238

sexism 15, 31, 39, 49, 51, 58, 84, 125, 139, 210, 217
sexuality 7, 97, 140, 205, 243, 245, 247
shadow 15, 20, 22, 33, 137–142, 150, 224, 256, 258
  awareness 131, 140
  definition of 137–138
  integration 1, 151, 138, 139, 167
  projection 14, 22, 139
  realizing 140–142
  withdrawal 138, 259
shame 31, 34, 49, 51, 52, 69, 116, 150, 172
Shapiro, S. B. 95
Sharp, G. 84
Shastri, S. Y., 10, 11, 82, 83, 132, 158
Shim, J. M. 116, 120, 121, 123, 130, 139, 160
silence 81, 91, 108
Slattery, P. 43, 122, 167
Sleeter, C. E. 41
Smith, D. G. 100
Smith, L. 214, 257
Smith-Christopher, D. 10, 12, 46, 77, 82, 83, 164, 238, 263
social change 9, 11, 15, 19, 42, 62, 86, 123, 229, 244, 245, 246, 262
  nonviolent, 9, 13–14, 46, 55, 92, 161, 221, 234, 235, 240
social justice 1, 7, 8, 11, 22, 45, 96, 106, 114, 122, 138, 144, 157, 158, 165, 179, 243
  concepts of 45
  education 7, 8, 22, 39–58, 106, 113, 116, 117, 122, 171, 179, 248, 258
  literature 8, 40, 51
  pedagogy 22, 119, 124
  restorative 11, 144
  retributive 44
solidarity 6, 45, 218, 220
spirituality 4, 11, 164, 143, 244, 246, 249, 257
  lived 143
  of interconnectedness 136–137

Sri Aurobindo 91
Sri Sri R. Shankar 91
standardization 36, 89, 206, 209, 213, 242, 262
starlight 255, 256, 257, 262, 264
  of nonviolence 35, 255
stillness 73, 91, 257
storytelling 170, 210, 222
stranger, the 15, 36, 97, 119, 224, 257, 259
  to ourselves 30, 33, 97
  welcoming 15, 33, 124, 257
Strong-Wilson, T. 146
study 3, 4, 10, 56, 165, 231, 242
subjectivity 7, 15, 106, 109, 111, 112, 113, 114, 115, 121, 145, 149, 216, 258
  student 106, 109, 113
  teacher 106, 140
  women's 212
suffering 14, 19, 33, 95, 140, 199, 251, 259, 261
  redemptive, 14, 19, 252
surveillance 6, 12
  culture 242
sustainability 12, 230, 257
  ecological 257
  environmental 230
  of femininity 12
Swanson, D. M. 11, 137
symbol 53, 73, 115, 132, 136, 142, 146

Tagore, R. 91
Taiji 53, 56, 73
Tarc, A. M. 113
Taubman, P. 14, 37, 110, 130, 145
Taylor, J. 121, 138, 139, 258
teachable moment 105–108
teacher research 22, 159, 161
  teaching and learning 41, 105, 106, 109, 124, 125, 151, 152, 158, 177, 183, 211, 217
  teaching content 77, 89
  teaching process 157, 179
temporality 147, 176, 188, 195, 258
  as experienced 195

tensions 2, 5, 6, 7, 18, 21, 40, 94, 98, 116, 125, 148, 159, 179, 199, 206, 213, 214, 215, 217, 222, 223, 259, 260
  between aggression and compassion 244, 263
  between connections and disconnections 213
  creative 21, 179, 207, 212
  holding 18, 23, 134, 142, 212, 259, 263
  between the particular and the universal 21
third way 44
Todd, S. 16, 41, 45, 51, 116, 119, 123, 135, 248, 251
tranquility in turbulence 22, 62, 72–75
transcendence 33, 147, 196, 257, 262
transcendent function, the 131, 136, 137
transformation 3, 8, 23, 31, 53, 76, 77, 91, 112, 115, 119, 125, 132, 147, 150, 164, 171, 215, 231, 244, 250
  cultural 41, 152, 215
  curriculum 89
  of difficult emotions 15, 167
  individual 8, 16, 68, 72, 87, 100, 126
  of personality 143
  of relationships 94
  social 16, 66, 68, 72, 87, 126, 130, 131, 214, 238, 243
  spiritual 251
transgression 112, 118
transnational space, 94, 95
trauma 12, 32, 44, 139, 146, 240, 241, 261, 262
  collective 213, 220, 262
  historical 7, 51, 146, 150, 171
  national 3
  personal 3
Truth and Reconciliation Commission, South Africa 11, 32, 35, 44, 135
Tu, W. M. 68
Tulsa Race Massacre of 1921 7, 150
Tulsa Race Riot of 1921 7, 24, 51, 52, 55, 109, 113, 163, 171, 178
Tutu, D. 1, 11, 35, 52, 83, 132, 136

ubuntu, 10, 11, 12, 32, 33, 40, 44, 47, 52, 55, 58, 83, 132, 136, 137, 207
unconscious, the 15, 33, 36, 118, 120, 129, 132, 133, 136, 143, 144, 146, 148, 248
  collective 15, 16, 129, 132, 134, 136, 138, 144
  cultural 15, 16, 258
  personal 2, 138
understanding 17, 50, 55, 57, 71, 107, 108, 109, 114, 118, 119, 122, 130, 136, 138, 140, 145, 149, 157, 163, 167, 168, 184, 188, 196, 199, 207, 209, 215, 219
  delayed 108, 109
  embodied 257
  experiential 15, 16, 49, 143, 144, 147, 151
  imaginal 100
United Nations' International Decade for a Culture of Peace and Non-violence 89
unity 13, 20, 62, 69, 75, 82, 88, 90, 91, 94, 131, 134, 144, 158, 163, 164, 229, 239, 245
  heart 94, 131, 134, 144, 164
  of means and end 146, 147, 173
  spiritual 136
  of thought and action 161
Universal Declaration of Human Rights 90
unlearning 31, 55, 70, 87, 124, 158, 166, 176, 250
  meditative 56
unteachable moments 105–106, 110, 112, 118, 119–126, 258
  definition of 106
  and teachable moments 107

van Manen, M. 184, 199, 201
violence 2, 3, 10, 13, 19, 29, 31, 34, 39, 43, 57, 68, 82, 83, 84, 87, 88, 90, 91, 93, 96, 98, 110, 115, 129, 130, 135, 148, 158, 161, 165, 176, 179, 217, 221, 233, 237, 238, 241, 243, 244, 245, 246, 247, 248, 249, 250, 251, 255, 263
  concept of 83
  culture of 6, 90, 165

cycle of 19, 83, 90, 241, 251, 262
gendered nature of 19
heteropatriarchal 230
intergenerational 36
internal 14
logic of 6, 175
male 230
means of 130
physical 14, 83
prevention 92
roots of 130
school 130, 158
social 30, 39, 41, 43, 48, 49, 51, 58, 83, 118, 122, 131, 139, 148, 214, 217, 220, 246
structural 83, 175
against women 19, 252
virtue 63, 64, 67, 68, 70
Confucian 63, 64
Daoist 63
visualization 145, 185, 190, 191, 198
voices 4, 19, 124, 125, 149, 178, 187, 231, 241, 257
inner 200
maternal 206, 242
of nonviolence 169, 178
women's 166, 205, 200, 222
vulnerability 33, 54, 196, 232, 238, 259, 263

Wells, I. B. 218, 240
White supremacy 31, 213, 237
Whitlock, R. U. 260
Williams, K. T. E. 247
win-or-lose mentality 47, 49, 54
wisdom 54, 58, 70, 72, 105, 161, 207, 213, 220, 221, 250, 258

wisdom traditions 9, 22, 40, 82, 207, 209, 250
Indigenous, 2, 9, 12
international 10, 30, 40, 207, 250
Women in Black Movement 251
Women in Peacebuilding Network in Africa 241
women teachers 110, 216, 218, 235, 251
Women's International League for Peace and Freedom 85
Women of Liberia Mass Action for Peace 236
Wood, H. 3, 250
Woolf, V. 205
working from within 14, 15, 116, 119
working through 33, 49, 52, 87, 96, 109, 110, 112, 116, 117, 120, 122, 123, 138, 149, 167, 172, 214, 233, 249, 258
difficulty 21, 31, 260, 262
loss 109, 110, 259
psychic 116, 117, 160
public 116
wuwei 10, 12, 30, 75, 76
concept of 76

Ye, L. 100
yin and *yang* 12, 53, 54, 73, 74
yoga 56, 91

Zajonc, A. 174
Zembylas, M. 159, 165, 175
zero space 4, 257
Zhuangzi 30, 66, 70, 71, 74, 76
Zinn, H. 12, 13, 82, 84

COMPLICATED CONVERSATION

A BOOK SERIES OF CURRICULUM STUDIES

Reframing the curricular challenge educators face after a decade of school deform, the books published in Peter Lang's Complicated Conversation Series testify to the ethical demands of our time, our place, our profession. What does it mean for us to teach now, in an era structured by political polarization, economic destabilization, and the prospect of climate catastrophe? Each of the books in the Complicated Conversation Series provides provocative paths, theoretical and practical, to a very different future. In this resounding series of scholarly and pedagogical interventions into the nightmare that is the present, we hear once again the sound of silence breaking, supporting us to rearticulate our pedagogical convictions in this time of terrorism, reframing curriculum as committed to the complicated conversation that is intercultural communication, self-understanding, and global justice.

The series editor is

> Dr. William F. Pinar
> Department of Curriculum Studies
> 2125 Main Mall
> Faculty of Education
> University of British Columbia
> Vancouver, British Columbia V6T 1Z4
> CANADA

To order other books in this series, please contact our Customer Service Department:

> peterlang@presswarehouse.com (within the U.S.)
> orders@peterlang.com (outside the U.S.)

Or browse online by series:

> www.peterlang.com

www.ingramcontent.com/pod-product-compliance
Ingram Content Group UK Ltd.
Pitfield, Milton Keynes, MK11 3LW, UK
UKHW022238230426
12048UKWH00018BA/1331